SOTHEBY'S
ART AT AUCTION 1988–89

SOTHEBY'S
ART AT AUCTION 1988–89

SOTHEBY'S PUBLICATIONS

First published for Sotheby's Publications by
Philip Wilson Publishers Ltd,
26 Litchfield Street, London WC2H 9NJ
and
Sotheby's Publications,
Harper & Row, Publishers, Inc.,
10 East 53rd Street, New York, NY 10022

ISBN 0 85667 365 X
ISSN 0084–6783
Library of Congress Catalog Card Number 88–060430

Editor: Sally Liddell
Assistant Editors: Liz Brooks; Julie Targett (London);
          Lynn Stowell Pearson (New York)

Design: Andrew Shoolbred and Liz Jobling
Printed in England by Jolly & Barber Ltd, Rugby, Warwickshire,
and bound by Hunter and Foulis Ltd, Edinburgh

Note
Prices given throughout this book include the buyer's premium applicable in the saleroom concerned.
These prices are shown in the currency in which they were realized. The sterling and dollar equivalent
figures, shown in brackets, are based on the rates of exchange on the day of sale.

Sotheby's galleries at Bond Street, Bloomfield Place and Conduit Street are indicated by the designation
'London'.

Frontispiece
A Qajar oil painting of a lady, early in the reign of Fath 'Ali Shah,
circa 1798–1805, 65½in by 35in (166.4cm by 88.9cm)
New York $60,500 (£38,535). 23.VI.89
From the collection of Zare Basmajian

Contents illustration
Synaxarium or *Book of the Saints of the Ethiopian Church*, in Ge'ez,
illustrated manuscript on vellum, Gondar, Ethiopia, dated *1700* (AD 1709),
13¾in by 10⅝in (35cm by 27cm)
London £14,300 ($23,738). 20.VI.89

Contents

እዳም፡ ወሐዋ ፃ ፟ ፤ ዘከሰሙ፡ ተእርፉ
እየ እስ በሊ ሆሙ፡ በያ ክሬ፡ ከዴ ሊ ፦

Claude Monet
ALICE HOSCHEDE AU JARDIN
Signed and dated *81*, 31$\frac{7}{8}$in by 25$\frac{5}{8}$in (81cm by 65cm)
New York $8,800,000 (£5,269,461). 9.V.89
From the collection of Mr C. Douglas Dillon

Preface

A. Alfred Taubman
Chairman, Sotheby's Holdings, Inc.

The 1988–89 season was the most successful in Sotheby's history. Our worldwide sales, reaching a new milestone in the history of fine art auctioning, exceeded $2 billion. These exceptional results demonstrate the sustained strength of the art market at many levels and Sotheby's continuing ability to attract the finest works to the market.

Remarkable private collections gave the year a special character. Highlights included Chinese art from the collection of Paul and Helen Bernat; ornithological masterworks and medieval manuscripts from the libraries of H. Bradley Martin and Major J.R. Abbey; and paintings from the collections of Walter P. Chrysler, Jr, Jaime Ortiz-Patiño, and Mr and Mrs Victor W. Ganz. Equally, the ongoing dispersal of British Rail Pension Fund holdings brought masterworks of French furniture, Chinese ceramics, tribal art and Impressionist paintings back to the market after more than a decade.

As the market continues to expand internationally, Sotheby's remains committed to providing the highest standard of service to our clients. During the year, we opened offices in Budapest – the first auction office in an Eastern Bloc nation – and we held our first auction in Vienna. Recognizing the major role of Japanese collections, we conducted an inaugural sale of prints in Tokyo in October 1989. To meet international demand, the programs of Sotheby's Financial Services are now available throughout the world. In addition, we are completing a major renovation of and addition to our Bond Street auction and office facilities in London. The first of two additional new auction rooms to accommodate our ever-expanding business will open in the spring of 1990.

In this period of growth and change, we are extremely fortunate to have the commitment and contributions of exceptionally talented people in our offices around the world. We are particularly gratified that Mr Giovanni Agnelli, Mrs Charles H. Price, II, and The Hon. Sir Angus Ogilvy have recently joined our supportive and creative Advisory Board. On behalf of the Board of Directors, I extend congratulations and appreciation to the senior management of Sotheby's for the achievements of 1988–89; Michael L. Ainslie, President and Chief Executive Officer, Sotheby's Holdings, Inc.; for the UK, Europe and Asia, The Rt Hon. the Earl of Gowrie, Chairman, and his colleagues Julian Thompson, Deputy Chairman, Asia, Simon de Pury, Deputy Chairman, Europe, and Timothy D. Llewellyn, Managing Director; for North America, John L. Marion, Chairman, and Diana D. Brooks, President; and for Financial Services, Mitchell Zuckerman, President.

Pablo Picasso
LE GARÇON BLEU
Gouache on board laid down
on panel, signed, 1905,
39⅜in by 22½in (100cm by 57cm)
London £3,960,000 ($7,167,600).
4.IV.89
From the collection of the
British Rail Pension Fund

Introduction

Jasper Johns's *False Start* being sold at auction in New York.

1988–89 may well be remembered as the season of contemporary art, a year in which pivotal works by the major artists of the Post-War period appeared on the market and were eagerly received by collectors in the Far East and Europe as well as the United States. Foremost among them was Jasper Johns's *False Start*, which brought $17.1 million, the highest price ever paid for the work of a living artist. The tremendous growth in this field reflected the immense fascination of modern collectors for the art of their own day and confirmed the saleroom as the principal venue for the sale of contemporary art.

It was especially fitting that this remarkable year included works from the collections of Mr and Mrs Victor W. Ganz, the late Karl Ströher, and the late Edwin Janss, Jr, each of whom had been an early and enthusiastic supporter of contemporary artists. Mr Ströher, who focused on American Pop Art, is generally credited with introducing those artists to a broader European audience. The Janss collection included works by contemporary British painters who now have a wider international audience; Francis Bacon's masterpiece *Study of a Portrait of Van Gogh II* and an early Hockney, *A Grand Procession of Dignitaries in the Semi Egyptian Style*, were the major highlights.

Sales in London confirmed the current enthusiasm for British and European artists, Lucian Freud and Lucio Fontana among them, and revealed an emerging interest in contemporary Japanese art.

The Ganz collection was particularly intriguing in linking the work of Johns, Rauschenberg, Stella and others to that of Picasso. The six paintings from the collection spanned five decades of Picasso's career, a range extended by a number of other major works offered during the year. This array did full justice to the artist

Exhibition of the ornithological library of H. Bradley Martin in London.

Ivan Sergeevich Turgenev
The autograph manuscript of *Fathers and Sons*, 180 pages, in Russian, signed and dated
I.S. Turgenev. Finished at Spasskoye on Sunday 30 July at 25 minutes to one, 1861
Sold by private treaty through Sotheby's to the Cultural Foundation of the USSR.

Lord Gowrie, Chairman of Sotheby's, presenting Mrs Raisa Gorbachov with a portrait of Tsar Peter III by Alexander Rokotov, as a gesture of thanks for the co-operation that Sotheby's received in Moscow leading up to their sale there last July. Lord Gowrie also presented the manuscript of Turgenev's *Fathers and Sons*, one of the masterpieces of Russian literature.

A *famile-rose* bowl, mark
and period of Kangxi,
diameter 8in (20.3cm)
Hong Kong
HK$10,450,000
(£818,324:$1,344,916).
16.V.89
From the collection of the
British Rail Pension Fund

Exhibition of the Paul and
Helen Bernat collection
of Chinese ceramics in
Hong Kong.

whose towering genius dominated the first three-quarters of this century. The
supreme self-confidence of the early self-portrait *Yo Picasso*, the intricacy of the *Cage
d'Oiseaux*, the monumental classicism of *Head of a Woman*, and the vital, sensuous late
works, such as *Femme Assise*, all testified to Picasso's irrepressible creativity.

Throughout the year, the market remained buoyant, with exceptional results in a
number of collecting areas, due, in large measure, to the appearance of works of art
of extraordinary quality and rarity. More than a dozen masterworks of American
art were offered in the spring, including Frederic E. Church's *At Home by the Lake*, a
quintessential Hudson River landscape, which brought $8,250,000, a new high for
the field.

The tremendous rise in prices for antiquities was a recognition that ancient
artefacts are not simply symbols of remote cultures, but works of art that challenge
modern sensibilities. The Cycladic head sold in December, in New York, with its
smooth, mysterious planes, easily ranks with the masterpieces of twentieth-century
sculpture. It was remarkable to have seen a complete Cycladic figure in such good
condition in the saleroom in New York in the same season. From the collection of the
late Madame Marion Schuster, a part of which was sold in London this summer,
came a group of highly important pieces, recognised for their quality and rarity.

Medieval craftsmanship was represented in London with an outstanding group of
enamels from several sources. It was again unusual to have such a fine selection on
the market at one time, and interesting to have seen these pieces exhibited side by
side. Particularly exciting was the twelfth-century Mosan plaque depicting the
Sacrifice of Cain and Abel, the first of such quality to emerge since the late 1970s.

There is, perhaps, no more personal expression of genius than a literary manuscript,
where not only the finished work, but the stages leading to it can be retraced. In
London, the original manuscript for Kafka's *The Trial*, written at white heat in the
summer of 1914, was bought by the Deutsches Literaturarchiv. Another great work
of literature, Turgenev's *Fathers and Sons*, returned to its country of origin when the
Soviet government bought the manuscript by private treaty this spring.

Collectors were the keynote of this season's auctions: collectors who nurtured artists, who pushed back the boundaries of scholarship, who changed the course of fashion. In London, the season opened with the Elton John Collection – the souvenirs of a profession, as well as the pursuit of leisure hours. Elton's seven-league Doc Marten boots, from the film *Tommy* jostled with sunglasses, sequinned stage suits and more conventionally collectable objects – Bugatti furniture (although Elton was a pioneer collector), Cartier jewellery, Chiparus bronzes.

Jacques Doucet (1853–1929), the great Paris couturier and collector of eighteenth-century paintings and furniture, dramatically changed the course of his collecting which resulted in the execution of daring new designs by Pierre Legrain and Eileen Gray. Without the early patronage of Doucet, much of the Modernist furniture sold in New York in the spring would never have been made. Part of the same sale was another masterpiece of patronage and creativity combined, the Philip Johnson townhouse, designed for Mrs John D. Rockefeller, 3rd.

Other distinguished collections included that of Jaime Ortiz-Patiño – a select group of Impressionist paintings, among them Gauguin's *Mata Mua* and Cézanne's *Pichet et fruits sur un table*, bought to complement the legacy of a superb Renoir, *Jeune Fille au Chapeau garni de Fleurs des Champs*. The Chrysler Collection was vast and dazzlingly eclectic, encompassing Géricault and Ingres as well as works by Tiffany.

Furniture from the collection installed in the Philip Johnson townhouse including the cubist armchair and canapé, *circa* 1920, by Pierre Legrain, and Legrain's lacquer birdcage, also *circa* 1920, made for Jacques Doucet.

Elton John photographed among objects from his Art Deco collection auctioned in London in September 1988.

Stage costumes and rock 'n' roll memorabilia from the Elton John Collection (Photographs by Terry O'Neill).

Among several outstanding book and manuscript collections was the eleventh and final part of the collection formed by Major J.R. Abbey. He began collecting private press books and book bindings in 1929 and bought his first medieval manuscript in 1934. Sotheby's has been selling the collection since the late 1960s. The final part of the sale took place this summer, eleven years since the previous Abbey sale. It contained such treasures as the Clarence Hours, illuminated *circa* 1421 for the Duchess of Clarence, and the Monypenny Breviary, a Bourges manuscript made for a Scottish diplomat. The last Abbey sale marked the conclusion of a great age of English collectors of medieval manuscripts.

The highly specialized Chinese book and map collection of Philip Robinson provided a unique archive of Western contacts with China, which began with the Jesuit missions. A passion for books likewise filled the life of H. Bradley Martin, a meticulous and highly knowledgeable collector whose library is considered one of the finest in private hands. His ornithological collection, which ranked with the foremost institutional holdings, was dispersed in June to intense competition that testified to the quality and rarity of the books and manuscripts he had assembled.

Of an entirely different character was the collection formed by the British Rail Pension Fund. The collection was started in 1974, as an alternative investment when both stock and property markets were low. Covering all major areas of art collecting, the returns from the sales have been encouraging. The most spectacular gains were made by the Fund's twenty-five Impressionist and modern paintings, sold for £35.2 million in London this spring. Not simply investments, paintings such as Renoir's *La Promenade* and Picasso's *Le Garçon Bleu* had been on loan to various British galleries.

In November, the French furniture from the British Rail Pension Fund collection was sold in London. Each piece, chosen as a superb quality, representative example of its type, not surprisingly attracted fierce competition among the bidders. An ormolu-mounted console table made for Marie-Antoinette's *cabinet-intérieur* at Versailles fetched a record for a piece of French furniture. Exceptional objects bought by British Rail in other fields, especially Tribal art, fetched high prices almost without exception because of the quality and good condition of the pieces. Eager collectors in Hong Kong bought objects of excellent quality and provenance, this time in the field of Chinese art, the second most successful area of the collection.

The Chinese art market is truly international with national preferences for special areas – early ceramics are favoured by Western buyers, whereas nineteenth-century jades are bought by collectors in the Far East. This was true of the collections formed by Paul and Helen Bernat (sold in Hong Kong) and Frederick and Antoinette Van Slyke (sold in New York). The Bernats collected works by the Qing imperial work-shops. They bought early and with discrimination, as is evident in the exceptionally fine yellow-ground imperial bowl decorated with four exquisite pink monochrome landscapes, the highlight of their collection.

Collecting is never a static process. Whether for enjoyment, study, or sharing, the cycle keeps art alive, constantly forcing its reassessment or revision and always charting shifts in taste. The auction rooms provide the opportunity to view well-documented works of art as well as exciting new discoveries, works which have often been hidden, or presumed lost, for decades as well as some of the most celebrated contemporary works.

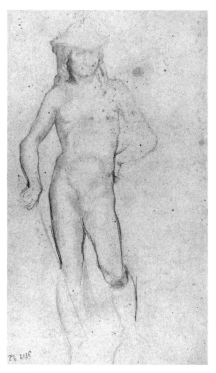

Fig. 1
STUDY OF DONATELLO'S DAVID
Pencil, *circa* 1858

Fig. 2
PETIT RAT A LA BARRE
Black chalk on pink paper

Fig. 3
THE DANCER JULES PERROT
Black chalk and charcoal, 1875

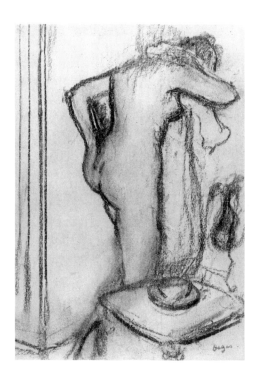

Far left
Fig. 4
FEMME A SA TOILETTE
Charcoal, *circa* 1890

Left
Fig. 5
NU AU BRAS LEVE
Charcoal, *circa* 1897

These drawings by Edgar Degas (Figs 1–7) were bequeathed to the Fitzwilliam Museum, Cambridge, by Andrew Gow through the NACF in 1978.

Art for the Nation

Richard Cork

A view of the National Art-Collections Fund loan exhibition 'Monet to Freud', held to launch the Modern Art Fund.

The loan exhibition 'Monet to Freud', held at Sotheby's in January 1989, provided a rare opportunity to see collected together the great wealth of works of art dating from the 1850s to the present day which has been acquired for the nation with the assistance of the National Art-Collections Fund.

The wall devoted to Degas drawings, bequeathed to the Fitzwilliam Museum, Cambridge by Andrew Gow, compelled special attention. It started with a pencil copy of Donatello's *David*, one of many studies made by the young Degas during a visit to Italy in the late 1850s (Fig.1). Alive to the internal modelling of the lithe bronze torso, the drawing asserts a crisper and more summarising authority lower down the body. Degas's pencil stresses the contours of hip and thigh with a sharp, almost stringent line. He breaks away from the soft, passive approach evident in David's head and claims the right to a simplification which searches for the figure's essential rhythms. Despite his admiration for the *quattrocento*, Degas is already quickening his work with an analytical rigour and economy which would come to characterize his draughtsmanship.

The other eight Degas drawings in the exhibition revealed the artist's development in all its richness and complexity. We find him defining the intricacy of the Duchessa Morbilli's shawl and dress with an Ingres-like exactitude around 1865 (Fig.7). But in a contemporaneous sheet, he moves away from this sumptuously upholstered world

 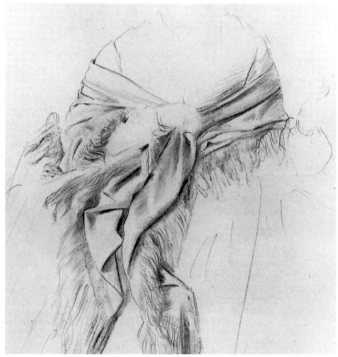

and goes outdoors, covering the entire page with quick, alert studies of a pony grazing in a field. Once again he delights in juxtaposing the most skeletal of pencilled outlines with a superbly finished drawing of the animal. Degas the draughtsman seems capable of anything, and he reveals here a Leonardesque passion for catching the horse's movements from a multiplicity of viewpoints.

However empirical he could be on such an occasion, Degas always retained the most profound respect for the lessons to be learned from the past. He retained a great deal of sympathy with Ingres's belief that 'everything has been done, everything has been discovered. Our task is not invention, but continuity.' Another drawing from the Gow bequest offers a marvellously judicious assessment, in black chalk, charcoal and stump, of Antonio Moro's portrait of Elisabeth de Valois. He leaned on the knowledge gained from these exercises even when portraying the features of people he knew intimately. A profile study of his sister Thérèse, whose face he painted many times over, takes on a chaste antique *gravitas* (Fig.6). Thérèse's plump, large-nosed humanity is seen through eyes profoundly conscious of classical and Renaissance precedents.

As Degas matured, however, his debt to tradition became less overt. The caught moment is paramount in his exquisite study of a little apprentice dancer practising at the bar (Fig.2). Her attention, as well as the artist's, is focused on the leg's swivelling movement from the hip. But while the action of this *ronds de jambe* exercise is rendered with absolute precision, Degas does not neglect the other, more lyrical aspects of the scene – the rush of loose hair flowing back from the girl's head, or the light, playful frills of the tutu above her bony limbs.

Above, left
Fig. 6
HEAD OF THERESE DEGAS
Pencil

Right
Fig. 7
DRAPERY FOR THE
DUCHESSA MORBILLI
Pencil and black chalk,
circa 1865–66

The spontaneity is, nevertheless, deceptive. For Degas returned to the same motif again and again, obsessed by the inexhaustibility of the figures he scrutinised. The distinguished dancer and choreographer Jules Perrot, represented here in a painterly chalk study heightened with white on pink paper (Fig.3), appeared in several pictures presiding over his classes at the Opéra. He knew, as well as Degas, how often even the simplest movement could be profitably analysed and refined.

This attitude reaches its culmination in the protracted series of nude studies which preoccupied Degas during his later years. The Gow Collection includes two vigorous examples of these frank, direct exercises, where charcoal is deployed with a new breadth and forceful assurance (Figs 4 and 5). Both drawings have a roughness which reveals how far Degas had travelled since the restraint of his early Italian period. The motion of the human body is now seen as abrupt, unselfconscious and at times quite ungainly, and although lessons imbibed from the past still lie behind these images, the overwhelming impression is of a raw, candid encounter between the ageing artist and the bodies he defines with such avidity.

Gow's Degas drawings, displayed for many years in his rooms at Trinity College, provide an ideal example of how one collector's passion can ultimately become a national asset. As a long-standing member of the National Art-Collections Fund, he was in an excellent position to know how a discriminating gift or bequest can transform a museum's holdings. His own collection, assembled over a thirty-year period before accelerating prices obliged him to stop in the mid 1960s, also contained Degas bronzes along with other French paintings and drawings from that period. They made a vital contribution to the Fitzwilliam's representation of a great moment in European art, and Gow's generosity places him among the NACF's most outstanding benefactors.

This admirable tradition continues today, with donations embracing the present century as well as the past. The connoisseurs who established the NACF in 1903 focused, quite understandably, on paintings long-hallowed by history. But as the Fund matured, its involvement with twentieth-century art grew. Now, aided by a recent initiative to strengthen this side of its activities, an increasing number of members are eager to assist in the acquisition of contemporary art. The policy makes absolute sense, at a time when escalating prices have placed so many modern works beyond the reach of museum purchase funds. This exhibition was held to launch the new Modern Arts Fund which is seeking an endorsement of £3 million; £165,000 has been raised to date. One of the most gratifying recent gifts was made by an anonymous collector whose enthusiasm for contemporary painting began after the Second World War. Moving into a penthouse flat in a Kensington block designed by Maxwell Fry, he found the austere interior 'rather bare.' Pictures alleviated the starkness, and he formed a habit of buying several English paintings each year.

Among these early acquisitions was John Piper's *Redland Park Congregational Church, Bristol* (Fig.8), one of a sustained sequence of images which explored buildings devastated by German bombs. The ruins were still smoking when Piper, an Official War Artist, inspected them in November 1940. Exposed to the sky, and disfigured by the charred remains of its wooden roof, the interior presents a mournful spectacle. But even as dissolution is emphasized in the loose, broken brushmarks, another mood asserts itself as well. For the rose window near the centre of the picture remains miraculously in position – a survival which Piper, with his love of stained glass, would have

cherished. He picks out the tracery of the window in pink, thereby transforming the flare of the fire into a manifestation of the building's will to outlast its assailants.

The most remarkable painting in this collection, which has been bequeathed to Pallant House, Chichester, is the Severini *Danseuse No. 5* (Fig.9). Painted in Paris during the most harrowing period of the Great War, when the French army was suffering intolerable losses not far from the capital, this effervescent image refuses to be affected by the conflict. It is less frantic than Severini's pre-war paintings of the same night-club performers, and the sobriety of black has penetrated several areas of the explosive dress. The painting marks a transitional moment in Severini's development, when he moved away from Futurist dynamism towards a calmer, classicising Cubist idiom. But the old sense of *élan* still animates the composition, most notably in the wild, upflung yellow leg. It thrusts past a confetti-like assortment of coloured lights, glinting among the deep purple shadows as they affirm the pleasure principle in defiance of the carnage of the Front.

Since public collections in this country have failed to acquire significant examples of Futurist painting, this boisterous canvas is especially welcome. The Sotheby's exhibition also contained another Severini from the same period, a train painting acquired by the Tate in 1968 with the aid of £5,000 from an NACF member. It seemed pallid and oddly perfunctory in comparison with *Danseuse No. 5*, however, and I can only hope that the Fund will in time be able to rectify some of the most lamentable gaps in our national representation of twentieth-century art.

Above, left
Fig. 8
John Piper
REDLAND PARK
CONGREGATIONAL CHURCH,
BRISTOL
1940, 23⅛in by 19⅛in
(58.7cm by 48.7cm)
Bequeathed to the Fund by
a private collector.

Right
Fig. 9
Gino Severini
DANSEUSE NO. 5
Signed, circa 1915–16,
36in by 28¼in
(91.2cm by 71.8cm)
Bequeathed to the Fund by
a private collector.

No one should underestimate the size of the problems involved in such a task. The time has long passed since the members of the NACF were able to visit a London gallery and purchase, for £135, a major work by one of Britain's most impressive modern artists. The painting in question was Paul Nash's *Pillar and Moon*, exhibited at Tooth's in 1942 soon after he brought this long-gestated picture to completion (Fig.10). It is a complex and haunting image, which juxtaposes a long diagonal avenue of trees with the stone wall and pillar dominating the foreground. Although a gentle meditation on the contrast between natural growth and man-made structures seems to be established here, the ruined condition of the pillar suggests that it will in time be overtaken by the wild grass already climbing its base. Moreover, a mesmeric correspondence is set up between the blanched sphere at the pillar's apex and the equally cold moon. Its white light gives the entire scene an unearthly pallor, unveiling the strangeness inherent in the English countryside as if for the very first time.

This potent ability, to transform our understanding of even the most quotidian scene, is just as much the preserve of the finest modern artists as it was in the past. While continuing to assist the acquisition of painting and sculpture from previous centuries, the Fund is fully justified in helping the nation to secure some of the most memorable images created during our own era.

Fig. 10
Paul Nash
PILLAR AND MOON
Signed, *circa* 1932–42,
20in by 30in
(50.8 by 76.2cm)
Purchased by the
NACF for the Tate
Gallery in 1942.

Heritage sales

Timothy Sammons

Peter Tillemans
THE ARTIST'S STUDIO
Signed, *circa* 1716
Negotiated by Sotheby's in
lieu of tax; to be on
permanent view at the
Norwich Castle Museum.

Opposite
Sir William Beechey
PORTRAIT OF THE CHILDREN
OF THE 1ST LORD
PORCHESTER
55in by 44½in
(139.7cm by 113cm)
Negotiated by Sotheby's in
lieu of tax; to remain *in situ*
at Highclere Castle.

Sotheby's have continued this year to advise owners of works of art on the suitability of negotiated sales to the nation in the right circumstances, and many clients have availed themselves of these arrangements, when advantageous. Increasingly, since the changes in the rates of capital taxes, it has been important to look at each situation afresh. A selection of this year's Heritage sales is set out below.

Early in the season, at the end of 1988, a collection of letters by Augustus John was sold to The National Library of Wales and a collection of poetry from the Archives of the Poetry Book Society was sold in the same month to The British Library. In March 1989, The British Library also bought the Coke Family Archive, which consisted predominantly of the papers of Thomas Coke (1674–1727), who was Lord Chamberlain to the Royal Household.

A flintlock silver-mounted sporting gun by Simpson of York, *circa* 1738
Sold by private treaty through Sotheby's to the Royal Armouries, HM Tower of London.

The National Trust for Scotland benefited from the sale to them of two works of art by Charles Rennie Mackintosh (1868–1928), the Scottish architect and designer, leader of the Glasgow School of Art Nouveau. One was an armchair and the other a watercolour, *Pyrénées Orientales – Collioure, Summer Palace of the Queens of Aragon.* Both will be kept at The Hill House, Helensburgh, near Glasgow, where they have been for many years and for which the armchair was specially made. The Hill House itself was designed by Mackintosh for the publisher Walter Blackie and it is Blackie's descendants who offered these items to Scotland.

Early in 1989 a superb eighteenth-century flintlock silver-mounted sporting gun by William Simpson of York, dated around 1738, was acquired by The Royal Armouries at The Tower of London for £235,000. It is considered to be one of the finest known of its type and is the only known surviving piece by Simpson.

As part of the arrangements on the estate of the late 6th Earl of Carnarvon, Sotheby's, on behalf of the executors, negotiated the acceptance in lieu of tax of a superb portrait by Sir William Beechey, RA of the children of the 1st Lord Porchester. The picture has hung at Highclere Castle for many years and will remain *in situ* now that the castle is open to the public.

Ipswich Museum has acquired a sketch by John Constable in lieu of tax and another picture *The Artist's Studio* by Peter Tillemans is now permanently on view at the Norwich Castle Museum. This latter picture has special connections with that part of the world, coming from the collection of Dr Cox Macro, who was Tillemans' most prominent patron and who lived outside Bury St Edmunds. The collection has remained in the family since that time.

The main advantages of a Heritage sale are that the owner incurs only 75% or so of his tax liabilities, and the institution or the Treasury benefits by acquiring the work of art at a reduced special price. This procedure is most likely to be of use to an owner of a work of art with a substantial capital gains tax liability, or on which there is a latent charge from a previous exemption from tax.

A Heritage sale is either a sale by Private Treaty to one of the bodies listed in the Inheritance Tax Act 1984 (this includes such institutions as The British Museum, The National Gallery and museums and galleries run by local authorities), or a surrender of a work of art to the government in lieu of tax.

Charles Rennie Mackintosh
PYRENEES ORIENTALES – COLLIOURE, SUMMER PALACE OF THE QUEENS OF ARAGON
Watercolour, *circa* 1924–26
Sold by private treaty through Sotheby's to the National Trust for Scotland; to be on permanent
view at The Hill House, Helensburgh, near Glasgow.

Hill House itself ranks as Mackintosh's most important achievement after the Glasgow
School of Art. His client, the publisher Walter Blackie allowed Mackintosh the fullest
expression of his ideas on the integration of architecture, decoration and furniture. In
1904 the house was completed on a hill in the small Scottish town of Helensburgh. It
was in sharp contrast to the new houses nearby, incorporating witty and irreverent
Tudor, Gothic and Classical pastiche details.
   Pyrénées Orientales – Summer Palace of the Queens of Aragon, was painted *circa* 1924–26,
during Mackintosh's early years in France where he went in 1923. Deeply depressed by
the treatment his major projects were receiving and suffering from lack of funds,
he abandoned architecture and design and went to France to begin a new career as
a painter. This picture was included in the 'Mackintosh Memorial Exhibition' in
Glasgow in 1933, where it was purchased by Mrs Walter Blackie. Sadly, Mackintosh
died in 1928 before he was able to exhibit publicly the superb watercolours he had
painted in France. He was sixty years old and the contents of his Chelsea Studio were
valued at only £88.16s.2d.

Fig. 1
Théodore Géricault
LANDSCAPE WITH AQUADUCT (EVENING)
98½in by 86½in (250.2cm by 219.7cm)
New York $2,420,000 (£1,541,401). 1.VI.89
From the collection of Walter P. Chrysler, Jr

The collection of Walter P. Chrysler, Jr

Scott Schaefer

At the end of the spring sale season, Walter Chrysler's sixty-five year collecting career came to a close. With the auctions of the old master and nineteenth-century paintings on 1st June, and his works of art later in the same month, the final disposition through gift, trade, bequest and sale of some 15,000 objects was completed. Although the final history of Mr Chrysler's collection has yet to be written, there is no question that he was one of the most prescient and driving forces in the art world. His interests encompassed many fields, including old master and nineteenth-century academic paintings, decorative works of art, and modern and contemporary art. The Chrysler Museum in Norfolk, Virginia, to which he gave more than 11,000 works of art, will stand as a monument to his multifarious interests and to his tremendous generosity.

Walter Chrysler was a most extraordinary collector. By his own recollection, he bought his first work of art, a watercolour by Renoir, in 1923 at the age of fourteen. The first comprehensive exhibition of his collection which opened in January 1941, at the Virginia Museum of Fine Arts in Richmond, contained 341 paintings, sculptures, and drawings. Included were works by Cézanne, Gauguin, Renoir, Degas and Manet, but more important and more startling was Mr Chrysler's contemporary art. By the age of 32, he owned thirteen Arps, fifteen Braques, five de Chiricos, ten Gris, thirty-one Legers, twenty-two Matisses, ten Mirós, and eighty-nine Picassos!

Within ten years, however, Mr Chrysler began to disperse his contemporary paintings as he pursued collecting interests of a different sort. He turned to earlier pictures, generally large, narrative Baroque paintings and nineteenth-century Salon works. By 1956, when Mr Chrysler's 'new' collection went on tour, there were only a few of the contemporary pictures seen in 1941. Instead, he sent Flemish, French, English, Italian, and Spanish paintings from the sixteenth to the nineteenth centuries, major works by Rosa, Rubens, Largillière, Romney, and Géricault. This move towards collecting more expensive old master paintings must certainly have been precipitated by the sale in 1953 of the Chrysler Building in New York. Moreover, given his collecting proclivities, the possibility of putting together a comprehensive collection of Western painting and sculpture 'avoiding the compromise of collective taste of museum boards,' as Alfred Frankfurter had put it in reviewing the 1941 exhibition, must have gradually occurred to him. Given this shift in interest and taste, Walter Chrysler must also have been thinking in terms of creating a more public forum for his not-so-private collection. This vision was ultimately achieved in Norfolk, where the Museum of Arts and Sciences was renamed in his honour in 1971.

According to Mr Chrysler's will, the works of art still remaining in his possession, almost 130 paintings, and 500 sculptures and decorative works of art, passed to his

nephew, who consigned them to Sotheby's. It was the most significant group of old master and nineteenth-century paintings offered in New York in a generation, and the quality of Tiffany lamps (see p. 422) alone generated equal excitement among collectors of decorative arts. Overall, the sales totalled $21.5 million with works going to private collectors, dealers and institutions.

In the course of the preparations, some tantalizing facts emerged about one of the most important works, Géricault's *Landscape with Aquaduct* (Fig.1). The painting has long been grouped with two others of the same dimensions, *Landscape with Fishermen* (Neue Pinakothek, Munich; Fig.2) and *Landscape with Roman Tomb* (Musée du Petit Palais, Paris; Fig.3) the latter also had once been owned by Mr Chrysler. Because of their scale and specific but retardative subject matter, it seemed likely that these three panels had been commissioned by a patron of Géricault's, probably as a part of a decorative ensemble. The dealers who sold Mr Chrysler his pictures believed the patron was a M. Marceau in Villers-Cotterêts (possibly a Jean-Henri Marceau who died there in June 1840) just outside Paris. As the Munich panel can be traced back to the Ary Scheffer sale of March 1859 (lot 28), it seems certain that the series of pictures had been dismantled and at least partially dispersed by that time.

About a month before Sotheby's sale, Nat Leeb, a European dealer and restorer, disclosed that he had once owned all the Géricault landscapes and produced other information and documents which related to their history. First of all, and most importantly, according to Leeb, there were four paintings. Only three had been

Above, left
Fig. 2
Théodore Géricault
LANDSCAPE WITH
FISHERMEN (MORNING)
1818, 98½in by 86½in
(250.2cm by 219.7cm)
(Reproduced courtesy of
the Neue Pinakothek,
Munich).

Right
Fig. 3
Théodore Géricault
LANDSCAPE WITH ROMAN
TOMB (MIDDAY)
1818, 98½in by 86½in
(250.2cm by 219.7cm)
(Reproduced courtesy of
the Musée du Petit Palais,
Paris).

known, although some assumed the possibility of a fourth. If one accepts that the paintings are a kind of homage to Géricault's teacher Carle Vernet, who often painted suites of the four times of day, then the missing canvas should be night. The Chrysler painting, now at the Metropolitan Museum of Art in New York, represents evening; that in Paris, noon, and in Munich, morning. As restorer of the pictures, Leeb made 'cartoons' of the paintings in his charge, and that of the lost picture does indeed depict a night scene. It should be called *Landscape with Shipwrecked Figures*. According to Leeb's notes, all four paintings were at the Chateau de Jeurre of the comte de Saint-Léon by 1937. From 1937 to 1949, they were stored in a warehouse in Paris where the *Landscape with Shipwrecked Figures* was badly damaged during the war. This picture was then consigned to Ladislas Bein, who sold it to a collector in Rio de Janiero. The three undamaged panels were sold to Alexandre Uchlaki, Philippe Brame, and Cesar de Hauke. At some point during this period, the pictures were offered to the Louvre, but they were rejected as 'simples décorations sans intérêt'. The Munich picture was acquired by Huntington Hartford at a Galerie Charpentier sale in 1959 (lot 52); he later sold it to Wildenstein, who in turn sold it to Munich in 1979. Although the damaged shipwreck landscape remains untraced, there is now a basic provenance for the four paintings during the last fifty years.

But what of their earlier history and possible commission? In 1879, Charles Clément, Géricault's biographer, recorded only two of the decorations, one of which, *Landscape with Fishermen*, he had seen himself. The other picture apparently remained in Géricault's studio at least during the time he was painting *The Raft of Medusa*, which was completed for the 1819 salon. It is known that Géricault bought three large canvases on 10th July, 4th August and 18th August 1818 and therefore assumed that he painted the pictures during that period, virtually the same time he was working on transferring the drawings of *The Raft* onto an even larger canvas. Of all Géricault's paintings, only *The Raft of Medusa*, *The Chasseur* and *The Cuirassier* are larger than the landscapes.

M. Leeb further reported that the family of the comte de Saint-Léon believed that the group had been previously owned by the duchesse de Montebello. She apparently sold two in 1850, and the others were sold separately, sometime before World War I, in Paris. A transcription of a letter dated 21st June 1850 to her cousin, presumably written at the time of the first sale, was also proffered by M. Leeb. In it the duchesse explains that the four large panels are unframed: 'Mon mari a fait peindre les quatre paysages aux dimensions des murs du salon, ils étaient encastrés dans les moulures.'

The fact that there were four paintings is no real surprise, nor is the fact that the fourth depicts a night scene or even that the subject is a shipwreck. After all, Géricault had been immersed in his *Medusa* sketches and drawings. If the paintings were part of a decorative scheme, they would not have been framed; they would simply have been incorporated into the *boiserie* of the room. But the identity of de Montebello and whether there was a relationship with M. Marceau of Villers-Cotterêts (if indeed he had been involved in the commission at all) remains a mystery. So, too, do the whereabouts of the panels from their completion to the sale of the *Landscape with Fishermen* in 1859. Hopefully, these serendipitous and seemingly scattered discoveries will be sufficiently intriguing to persuade others to take these bits of information and better weave them into the fabric of Géricault scholarship.

Overleaf (p. 30)
Jean-Auguste-Dominique Ingres
RAPHAEL AND THE FORNARINA
Oil on canvas laid down on panel,
27⅛in by 21¼in (68.9cm by 54cm)
New York $1,430,000
(£910,828). 1.VI.89
From the collection of Walter P. Chrysler, Jr

Overleaf (p. 31)
Bernardo Bellotto
ARCHITECTURAL CAPRICCIO WITH A SELF-PORTRAIT IN THE COSTUME OF A VENETIAN NOBLEMAN
60½in by 44¼in (153.7cm by 112.4cm)
New York $1,870,000
(£1,191,083). 1.VI.98
From the collection of Walter P. Chrysler, Jr

Agnolo Gaddi
THE MADONNA AND
CHILD IN GLORY
ATTENDED BY
MUSIC-MAKING
ANGELS, WITH
SAINTS ANTHONY
ABBOT(?), JOHN
THE BAPTIST,
CATHERINE AND
LUCY
Oil, tempera and
gold ground on
panel, 23¼in by
15¾in (59cm by
40cm)
London £660,000
($1,115,400).
5.VII.89

Opposite
Ferrando Yáñez
THE SALVATOR
MUNDI BETWEEN
SAINTS PETER AND
JOHN
Oil on panel,
inscribed
S. PEDRO and
S. IVAN, 29½in by
24⅜in (75cm by
62cm)
London £506,000
($855,140).
5.VII.89

Opposite
**Tiziano Vecellio,
called Titian**
THE PENITENT MAGDALEN
Oil on panel, 43½in by 31in
(110.5cm by 78.5cm)
New York $2,640,000
(£1,650,000). 2.VI.89

Bernardo Cavallino
LOT AND HIS DAUGHTERS
Each canvas 16in by 14¾in (40.5cm by 37.5cm)
New York $1,925,000 (£1,081,461). 12.I.89

Bernardo Cavallino
THE DRUNKENNESS OF NOAH

Mattia Preti, called Il Cavaliere Calabrese
SAMUEL ANOINTING DAVID
83½in by 120¼in (212cm by 305.4cm)
New York $1,155,000 (£648,876). 12.I.89

Opposite
Bartolomé Esteban Murillo
THE VIRGIN OF THE
SWADDLING CLOTHES
Oil on panel, 53½in by
40⅛in (136cm by 102cm)
London £1,705,000
($2,881,450). 5.VII.89

Giovanni Battista Tiepolo
THE MADONNA OF THE
ROSARY WITH ANGELS
Signed ^{S}*BATTA
TIEPOLVS F.* and dated
1735, 92⅞in by 60in
(236cm by 152.5cm)
London £1,265,000
($2,137,850). 5.VII.89
Formerly in the collection
of Sir Joseph Robinson, Bt

Two paintings by Carlo Dolci: a discovery and a rediscovery

Charles McCorquodale

The scarcity of major autograph paintings by Carlo Dolci made the appearance at auction this year of not one, but two such works doubly unusual. The so-called *St Joseph with the Infant Jesus* (Fig. 2) has been known ever since the perceptive and peripatetic German art historian Waagen described it in Earl Cowper's collection at Panshanger in 1854, while the *Adoration of the Magi* (Fig. 1) was discovered in the New York salerooms where it sold for a world record price for a Dolci painting. The wide difference in prices paid for the two pictures reflects perhaps the continuing incomprehension of Dolci's more 'pious' images, considering the exceptional quality of the *Joseph* picture. Both paintings are outstanding examples of the artist's style, and each attests in its own way to his claim to being one of the finest painters of the Italian Baroque period.

Of the two, a great deal more information is immediately available on the *Adoration*, which has a flawless provenance to match its scintillating appearance. It is an art historian's delight: in his most obliging manner Dolci not only inscribed the back of the canvas with his name and his age when he painted the picture but also with his patron's identity: *Al Sig^{re} Tommaso genero^{tti},/ di mia età il trentesima/ terzo/ Io carlo dolci/ Fiorentino* – and the date, *ANO/SALVTIS/MDCIL* – 1649. Dolci was at the peak of his abilities in that year, painting the masterpiece of his first maturity, *Christ in the House of the Pharisee* (Corsham Court, Methuen Collection).

Dolci was happy to make other versions of both the Corsham picture (now unfortunately lost) and the *Adoration*; the appearance of the present *Adoration* seems to complete all the recorded variants from the artist's own hand. The composition relates to a group of Dolci *Adorations*, both of the shepherds and of the Magi. The three others depicting the Magi are in Glasgow; the Exeter Collection at Burghley House and in the Marlborough Collection at Blenheim Palace. Two versions are mentioned by the artist's biographer, Baldinucci, in his exhaustive study of contemporary Florentine painting, the *Notizie dei professori del disegno*, the first painted for Prince Leopoldo de' Medici, the second for a certain Tommaso 'Genitori'. As Dolci had to entrust the canvas to his patron, it seems more likely that he would have spelt Generotti's name correctly, and in corroboration of this, there is no other mention of 'Genitori' except in connection with this painting. The composition's success is suggested not only by the many versions but also by Baldinucci's story that Dolci, having asked only twenty-five *scudi* from Prince Leopoldo was in fact rewarded with forty.

Of the four, the present version is undeniably the finest in every way, representing the perfection of form and content to which the others clearly aspire. Dolci, in this

Fig. 1
Carlo Dolci
THE ADORATION OF THE
MAGI
Signed on the reverse
within a cartouche *Al Sig^{re}
Tommaso genero^{tti},/ di mia età
il trentesima/ terzo/ Io carlo
dolci/ Fiorentino*, dated
ANO/SALVTIS/MDCIL,
seal of the Galleria Mozzi,
Florence,
46in by 36¼in
(116.8cm by 92cm)
New York
$1,760,000 (£1,100,000).
2.VI.89

Above
A detail from *The Adoration of the Magi*, showing the Virgin's face, a central focus to the composition.

Left
A detail from *The Adoration of the Magi*, showing the third king turning away to take the silver urn from his servant.

version alone, achieved an aristocratic elegance through the greatly increased emphasis on luxury textiles and precious metalwork and jewellery – and, more subtly, by depicting the Virgin and St Joseph as more mature, idealized figures than in previous versions. We know both from Baldinucci and from the paintings themselves that Dolci repeatedly used the same models, often his wife and children; his many deeply touching drawings of children, and of his beautiful wife, often relate directly to his paintings. Dolci married Térésa Bucherelli four years after painting this *Adoration*, yet it seems almost certain that she already appears here as the Virgin. The features are only slightly idealized from those in the drawings of Térésa in the Institut Néerlandais in Paris and the Louvre, and are identical with those of the magnificent Virgin fragment from Dolci's now tragically dismembered Montevarchi altarpiece of 1656, whose whereabouts are unknown. Dolci loved to include portrait likenesses in his subject paintings, and himself makes a guest, if not star appearance in this picture, as the bearded onlooker against the background arch, looking for all the world like one of Hilliard's melancholy young men.

Certain critics of the last century have regarded Dolci's art as the product of a simple mind and religious mania, coupled with a breathtaking technique, but this opinion is becoming increasingly untenable in the face of more evidence of the artist's sophisticated knowledge and use of earlier painting, much respected by his contemporaries. The *Martyrdom of St Andrew* (Birmingham City Museum and Art Gallery) includes tiny figures in homage to paintings by other masters, among them Titian's *Youth with a fur collar*. Similar figures appear in the background of the *Adoration*, now awaiting identification. Gradually the jigsaw puzzle of his sources is being fitted together; the *St Andrew* dates from 1643, six years prior to the *Adoration*, and in both Dolci borrowed freely from earlier prototypes, by Matteo Rosselli, Lorenzo Lippi, and, in this case, from Santi di Tito, Cigoli and possibly Sigismondo Coccapani. There is no doubt that, with the exception of Cigoli's great *Adoration of the Magi* of 1605 (National Trust, Stourhead House), Dolci's is the most resolved and exquisite of all the variants.

What are the ingredients which make this painting so completely enchanting and which outweigh those religious elements which so often present an impediment to the wider appreciation of Dolci's work? Undeniably, Dolci's technique is seen here at its most seductively flawless. Correggio (whom Dolci also copied for the Medici) lies behind the *sfumato* allure of the Virgin's face, creating a gently radiant central focus for the composition, totally without sentimentality but filled with expressive piety (see detail opposite). Every gesture and facial expression is as meticulously observed as the decorative detail: as in St Joseph's delicate but nonetheless Baroque gesture, which implies control rather than simple surprise or adoration of the infant Christ. The child's gesture is of confident benediction, while His face captures astonishingly the wonderment of a tiny child being offered a strange, glittering toy. With fine theatrical sense, a momentary distraction is provided by the genre-like vignette of the third king turning away to take the silver urn from his servant (see detail opposite), while beyond, the painter himself provides further subtle incident by not watching the main protagonists and appearing lost in contemplation. Every detail is imbued with an exquisite, fragile tangibility, from the breathtakingly beautiful costume of the black king to the older bearded companion's gold-embroidered,

Fig. 2
Carlo Dolci
SAINT JOSEPH AND THE
INFANT JESUS
(OR THE INFANT CHRIST
REQUESTING THE CROSS
FROM ST JOHN THE BAPTIST)
57½in by 46½in
(146.1cm by 118.1cm)
New York
$121,000 (£77,070).
1.VI.89
From the collection of
Walter P. Chrysler, Jr

jewel-bedecked mantle and the gold and silver crowns and containers. Their sumptuousness (as usual in Dolci) provokes reflection on the transience of material things rather than on their immense value. The model for the crowned king at the right appears in other Dolci paintings, including the Methuen picture mentioned above, where he plays the part of Christ, and, surprisingly, in the so called *St Joseph* picture now to be discussed, where his is the elder figure.

Who is he in that painting? Traditionally described as St Joseph (highly unlikely even from a superficial reading since the saint was already old at Christ's birth and He is clearly at least four or five years old here), it is virtually certain that the picture's subject must be *The Infant Christ requesting the cross from St John the Baptist*. Close examination of this idea too reveals weaknesses, since according to legend, John was himself only about seven when he retired to the desert, although pictorial convention normally shows him as a youth in this phase of his life. St Bonaventura states that the Holy Family met St John on their return from Egypt, and it is not unusual for the latter to press into the Christchild's hand his symbol, the reed cross; here Christ begs for the instrument of his own future Passion.

If the *Adoration* is a more superficially pleasing image from every point of view, the *St John* is arguably the finer work of art. While the *Adoration* is like the sudden opening of a jewel cabinet, where the eye moves quickly and restlessly from one tempting treasure to another, here Dolci achieved a grandeur of composition, based on the favourite Florentine High Renaissance pyramidal form. Dr Waagen, in his *Treasures of Art in Great Britain* published in 1854, wrote perceptively, 'This picture . . . is distinguished from others of the master by the agreeable composition and truth of feeling. The careful execution is combined with great clearness and warmth of colouring.' If the *Adoration* is a rich mixture of Flemish with Florentine, the *St John* is quintessentially a Florentine masterpiece. Although the faces are inspired by Correggio, the clear drawing, lucid disposition of limbs and drapery, and the finely attuned relationship between form and iconographical content revive the best principles of Raphael, Andrea del Sarto, Fra Bartolomeo and the early Cinquecento. Waagen's attention to its colouring was not misplaced, for this reveals Dolci as capable of tonal and colouristic harmonies found in none of his Florentine contemporaries. His use of warm reds and golds offset by St John's violet-grey tunic show an understanding of colour which might appear to be absent from the *Adoration* were not the latter's intentions very different. This painting reveals the unexpected wealth of Dolci's visual sources, blending elements from Correggio with neo-High Renaissance style and a knowledge of Caravaggio, and ultimately borrowing the pose from Michelangelo's *Doni Tondo*. There is even a hint of Guido Reni, a painter whose influence in Florence at this time was probably greater than has been accepted.

As the study of Italian Baroque painting now moves from the pioneer period of the 1920s to the 1970s, Dolci's art is reaching a wider and much more appreciative audience outside Italy. One of these pictures hung for many years at Panshanger among the long-acknowledged masters of European art. If Britain were fortunate enough to secure these paintings for public collections, official recognition would then be given to an artist whose importance is now widely accepted.

Hendrik van Minderhout
A MEDITERRANEAN HARBOUR SCENE
$65\frac{1}{8}$in by $94\frac{1}{4}$in
(163cm by 239.5cm)
London £385,000
($700,700). 19.IV.89

Jan Steen
FIGURES IN AN INTERIOR WITH A MAN AND WOMAN SEATED AT TABLE PLAYING CARDS
Oil on panel, signed,
$18\frac{1}{2}$in by 24in
(47cm by 61cm)
New York
$2,970,000
(£1,856,250).
2.VI.89

Matthias Stomer
CHRIST DISPUTING WITH THE DOCTORS
53½in by 71¼in (136cm by 181cm)
London £660,000 ($1,115,400). 5.VII.89

This subject, which is taken from the gospel of St Luke II, v.42–52, was extremely popular among the artists in the Roman circle of Manfredi who was Caravaggio's earliest and most imaginative follower, with a refreshing capacity for secularizing religious subject matter. Manfredi's prototype, in the Uffizi, which dates from around 1615, certainly influenced Stomer who is first recorded in Rome *circa* 1630–32. In this painting he has adopted Manfredi's horizontal format and the staccato rhythm of his design, based on the juxtaposition of standing and seated figures closely grouped in an enclosed space against a neutral background. An earlier version by Stomer in Munich, with full-length figures in a vertical format, shows the influence of further pictures of the subject by other close followers of Manfredi, such as Baburen from whom he took the powerful posture of the doctor with his chin in his hand. The picture stands apart from all the influential Caravaggesque versions that preceded it on account of Stomer's masterly use of brilliant local colours to focus attention on the diminutive but commanding figure of Christ.

Opposite
Frans Hals
PORTRAIT OF A GENTLEMAN
Inscribed *ÆTAT SVÆ*
52/A.N^O 1639,
45¼in by 35¼in
(115cm by 89.5cm)
London £748,000
($1,458,600). 7.XII.88
Formerly in the collection
of Sir Joseph Robinson, Bt

Francisco de Goya y Lucientes
PORTRAIT OF GENERAL ANTONIO VALDES
31¼in by 40¾in (79.5cm by 103.5cm)
Madrid Ptas 54,451,200 (£277,105:$470,218). 25.IV.89

Hubert Robert
ITALIAN LANDSCAPE WITH THE ARTIST AND HIS WIFE
Signed and dated *1779*, 97⅝in by 148¾in (248cm by 378cm)
Monte Carlo FF6,660,000 (£634,286:$1,110,000). 2.XII.88

In this large imaginary landscape, inspired by Tivoli, the artist seems either to have
represented himself as a tourist contemplating the site, or he has represented Bergeret de
Grandcourt accompanied by Fragonard and his wife on their voyage in Italy around
1773–74. Bergeret de Grandcourt commissioned this painting for his castle in Nègrepelisse,
near Montauban, France.

Opposite
François Boucher
A LANDSCAPE WITH A RUSTIC BRIDGE
Oil on panel, signed and dated *176.*, 30in by 23¼in (76cm by 59cm)
London £616,000 ($1,041,040). 5.VII.89
Formerly in the collection of Sir Joseph Robinson, Bt

If Boucher was the pre-eminent French landscape painter of the day, his vision of nature was
wholly artificial, inspired by a preoccupation with virtuoso brushwork and pleasing colour
and a desire to subordinate the natural world to his own artistic vision. Diderot observed,
after commenting on Boucher's landscape style in the Salon of 1761, 'He is made to turn the
heads of two types of people – society figures and artists ...'.

Old master drawings

Right
Giovanni Francesco Barbieri, called Il Guercino
CHRIST CROWNED WITH THORNS
Red chalk, 7½in by 7⅜in (19.3cm by 18.7cm)
New York $82,500 (£46,348). 13.I.89

Below
Paris Bordone, attributed to
FALLEN WARRIOR
Black chalk heightened with touches of white on grey paper,
bears old attribution *Giorgione*, 8in by 12in (20.3cm by 30.7cm)
London £148,500 ($247,995). 3.VII.89
From the collection of the late Theodore Allen Heinrich

Portrait of a Young Man wearing a Plumed Hat and Holding a Sword, by Agnolo di Cosimo Allori, called Il Bronzino, *circa* 1550–55 (Nelson-Atkins Museum, Kansas City).

Agnolo di Cosimo Allori, called Il Bronzino
HEAD OF A YOUNG MAN
Black chalk, 5⅜in by 4in (13.7cm by 10.3cm)
London £121,000 ($202,070). 3.VII.89

This previously unpublished drawing is probably a study for Bronzino's *Portrait of a Young Man wearing a Plumed Hat and Holding a Sword*, *circa* 1550–55 (see above). It was an exciting discovery; as one of an inherited group of mostly Victorian drawings it was consigned to the Victorian paintings department with a tentative attribution to Holman Hunt. Bronzino's skilful and refined portraits of the Medici family and Florentine nobility are among his most famous works, but very few have survived to illustrate his working methods. The present study is unique in its high degree of finish, and in its examination of the head alone. It must have been drawn from life, but shows a very classical approach which is particularly focused on the curling hair and on the dignified expression of the sitter.

Fig. 1
Francesco de' Rossi, called Il Salviati
THE RESURRECTION
Pen and brown ink and wash heightened with white on blue paper, 7in by 6⅞in (17.7cm by 17.4cm)
London £25,300 ($42,251). 3.VII.89
From the Clifford Collection

Fig. 2
Francesco Primaticcio
BACCHUS IN A NICHE
Pen and brown ink and wash heightened with
white, 13⅝in by 5in (34.5cm by 12.5cm)
London £38,500 ($64,295). 3.VII.89
From the Clifford Collection

Fig. 3
Pellegrino Tibaldi
TWO DEVILS, AFTER MICHELANGELO
Pen and brown ink and wash over red chalk, inscribed *manni* and numbered *45*,
5½in by 7⅜in (14cm by 18.9cm)
London £17,050 ($28,474). 3.VII.89
From the Clifford Collection

Tim Clifford has held curatorial positions at the Victoria and Albert
Museum and the British Museum, was Director of Manchester City Art
Galleries and is currently Director of the National Galleries of Scotland.
He began collecting while still a schoolboy, but his taste was formed
under the aegis of some of the foremost collectors and connoisseurs of that
time. With only modest means available, he was encouraged to look to the
neglected area of Florentine and Roman Mannerism where the highest
quality drawings could still be acquired for relatively little.

Clifford ceased collecting drawings in 1975 and since then a few of the
most important sheets have been dispersed, some finding their way into
the great national collections. What remained for the recent sale was a
remarkable group of 'discoveries', several of which have now been
identified as studies for documented paintings and frescos. It was first
proposed that *The Resurrection* (Fig. 1) be attributed to Salviati in 1967,
when it was pointed out that this is a study for his fresco above the altar of
the Markgrafen (or Brandenburg) Chapel in S.Maria dell'Anima, Rome.
Salviati worked on the decoration between 1541 and 1543, when he left
Rome, and completed it after his return between 1549 and 1550. The
Bacchus in a niche (Fig. 2), together with its companion showing a female
figure with a lion (Kupferstichkabinett, Berlin) may have been studies for
decorations in the hall above the Porte Dorée at Fontainebleau, possibly
representing scenes from the Trojan War. The *Two Devils* (Fig. 3) is a
study after figures in Michelangelo's *Last Judgement* in the Sistine Chapel.
Vasari records that Tibaldi made copies after Michelangelo in Rome.

Pieter Jansz. Saenredam
THE INTERIOR OF THE SINT BAVOKERK, HAARLEM
Pen and brown and grey ink, wash and watercolour over black and red chalk, indented on the *recto* and
blackened on the *verso* for transfer to panel, inscribed and dated *dit aldus geteyckent in November/int Jaer
1634. is en gesigt inde/grootte kerck binnen Haerlem./eende is even dus groot geschildert./Dit volleijndt ofte= /ghedaen
met schilderen/Den 15.ᵉ october 1635.* ('This so drawn in November in the year 1634 is a view in the Great
Church in Haarlem and is just as large painted' and 'This finished or done with painting the 15th of
October 1635'), 14¾in by 15⅜in (37.5cm by 39.1cm)
Amsterdam DFl 2,127,500 (£597,612:$1,079,949). 14.XI.88

Opposite
Frans Crabbe van Espleghem
ESTHER BEFORE AHASUERUS
Pen and black ink with touches of grey wash, inscribed in brown ink *Aisuerris/Hester.*,
10¼in by 7⅝in (26.1cm by 19.4cm)
Amsterdam DFl 379,500 (£106,601:$192,640). 14.XI.88

British paintings and watercolours

Arthur Devis
PORTRAIT OF SIR THOMAS
CAVE, BT. AND HIS FAMILY
IN THE GROUNDS OF
STANFORD HALL,
LEICESTERSHIRE
Signed and dated *1749*,
40in by 49in
(101.5cm by 124.5cm)
London £247,500
($470,250). 16.XI.88
From the collection of the
British Rail Pension Fund

The past year at auction has witnessed some of the best examples of British portraiture to come on to the market for many years. The growing demand for fine and decorative early portraits from the sixteenth and seventeenth centuries was clearly demonstrated by the interest shown in John de Critz's pair of marriage portraits of Richard, 1st Lord Lovelace and his young wife Margaret and the rare depiction of Queen Henrietta Maria painted in the 1630s for Charles I by Cornelius Johnson and Gerard Houckgeest (all shown on p.64).

British portraiture reached its height in the eighteenth century and the season saw fine examples from major artists, notably the celebrated portrait of Mrs Drummond, painted in 1779 by Thomas Gainsborough. The portrait was commissioned by the sitter's father together with companion portraits of her sisters and of George Drummond, now in the Ashmolean Museum, Oxford.

The approachable charm of Arthur Devis's portraits is increasingly in demand, and his portraits of the Cave family in their garden at Stanford Hall, and of Mr and Mrs Dashwood (also shown on p.64) show the artist at his best. British portraits of quality are no longer purely of local interest and are finding buyers throughout the world.

Opposite
**Thomas Gainsborough,
RA**
PORTRAIT OF MRS
DRUMMOND
49⅝in by 39⅜in
(126cm by 100cm)
London £1,650,000
($3,135,000). 16.XI.88
Formerly in the collection
of Sir Joseph Robinson, Bt

Fig. 1
Sir Anthony van Dyck
PORTRAIT OF PHILIP HERBERT, 4TH EARL OF PEMBROKE AND 1ST EARL OF MONTGOMERY
$52\frac{1}{2}$in by $42\frac{1}{2}$in (133. 5cm by 108cm)
London £462,000 ($877,800). 16.XI.88
From the collection of James R. Herbert Boone

The Boone Collection

James Miller

Mr and Mrs James R. Herbert Boone,
circa 1930, in a photograph by
Dorothy Wilding.

It was in their shared British ancestry that James R. Herbert Boone and his wife
Muriel Wurtz Dundas Boone found the starting point for a life-time of collecting.
After their marriage, they spent much of the 1930s in London and Rome; at this
time they acquired much of the English and Continental furniture and decorative
works of art which were to transform the family home, Oak Hill, Baltimore into an
ancestral home in the English style. The house was hung with family portraits, both
inherited and acquired. The library reflected the Boones' wide-ranging interests in
literature, history and art, including, for example, several sets of Gould's Birds,
bound in green morocco.

The greater part of the contents of the house was sold in September 1988 in New
York and the catalogue testifies to the wide range of the Boones' interests: from the
natural history drawings, originally owned by the great seventeenth-century Roman
patron Cassiano del Pozzo, which had later belonged to George III, to a massive
pair of sidetables supported by interlocking dolphins which had originally come
from Bulstrode near Gerrard's Cross, the seat of the Dukes of Portland in the
eighteenth century.

The Boones' collection of ancestral portraits was sold in London in November
1988. One of the finest pieces to come to light was a remarkable Van Dyck portrait
of Philip Herbert, 4th Earl of Pembroke, an important work which had all but disappeared from critical attention (Fig. 1). Numerous studio pieces and copies of Van
Dyck's work exist, but this portrait was unquestionably from the master's own hand.

Fig. 2
David Martin
PORTRAIT OF HENRY DUNDAS,
1ST VISCOUNT MELVILLE
A pair, each 49⅝in by 39in (126cm by 99cm)
London £29,700 ($56,430). 16.XI.88
From the collection of James R. Herbert Boone

Fig. 3
David Martin
PORTRAIT OF ELIZABETH RENNIE,
VISCOUNTESS MELVILLE

The delicacy of painting, especially in the face, and the marvellous deft way he had of describing fabrics are qualities unique to his work and make him one of the greatest portrait painters. Standing back from the picture, you are immediately struck by how well the figure occupies the shallow space created by the curtain hanging behind him. His hands almost touch the picture plane whilst his head is further back – reticent and sad, yet wise and watchful.

Lord Pembroke was an especially important patron of Van Dyck. He not only commissioned the famous family group which normally hangs at the end of the Double Cube room at Wilton (at present on loan to the National Gallery, London), but also single full length portraits of himself and his brother together with a number of double portraits including that of Lord and Lady Bedford (also at present on loan to the National Gallery). He had inherited Wilton on his brother the 3rd Earl's death in 1630 and during the next decade he began extensive remodelling of both the house and gardens in a style mirroring the Royal building at Greenwich. It was at Wilton that Charles I chose to spend his summer months from 1636 to the outbreak of the Civil War. The portrait from the Boone collection shows Pembroke towards the end of that time, still a powerful courtier, a Knight of the Garter and Lord Chamberlain, but now saddened by the estrangement of his wife, the death of his eldest son and by his growing alienation from the Court which would eventually lead to his break with the King and his support for the Parliamentary cause. It was to be Pembroke who stood watching the King as he went to his execution at Whitehall in January 1649.

Portraits of the seventeenth-century Herberts included a number of Philip, 4th Earl as well as a Mytens of his brother William, 3rd Earl of Pembroke. William, like his brother the 4th Earl, took a keen interest in the arts: together they were 'The incomparable pair of Bretheren' to whom the first Folio of Shakespeare was dedicated. The portrait by Mytens, however, reveals more of the other side of William's character, a hard-living adventurous Courtier with a reputation for womanizing. He was a keen supporter of various voyages of exploration both in India and the Far East with the East India Company, and also in the Americas as an Incorporator in the North West Passage Company. In 1629 he had purchased the famous Barocci Library from Venice which he bequeathed to the The Bodleian Library in Oxford.

Mrs Boone's ancestors, the Dundas family only rose to pre-eminence in Scotland during the second half of the eighteenth century, so their portraits began at a later date than the Herberts. Historically, the most important were the portraits of Henry Dundas, 1st Viscount Melville and his first wife Elizabeth Rennie by David Martin (Figs 2 and 3). Like so many prominent Scotts families, the Dundases were lawyers. Henry Dundas, the fourth son of the celebrated judge Robert Dundas of Arniston, rose to become Law Advocate of Scotland in 1775 when he was only thirty-eight. He had become a Member of Parliament the previous year and his political fortunes prospered as he rose to the office of Home Secretary and then Secretary of State for War during the Napoleonic Wars. He was created Lord Melville in 1802. His portrait remained in the possession of his descendants from whom it was acquired by the Boones. At the sale it was appropriately bought by the National Portrait Gallery of Scotland. David Allan's delightful portrait of the Dundas children at study in their schoolroom (Fig. 4) has also returned to Scotland, while a view of Melville Castle attributed to Charles Stuart was bought by the Melville family.

A charming portrait of the Boone children by George Romney (Fig. 5) was the sole eighteenth-century family portrait in the collection. The sitters were the children of Charles Boone, a close friend and political ally of Lord Orford, Horace Walpole's cousin. They sat for Romney between March and June 1778. The Boones were outbid at auction when this picture came for sale in 1935 and it had to be hunted down by their agent to the new owner, who only parted with it for considerable profit.

James R. Herbert Boone had graduated from the John Hopkins University in 1921 and at his death made the University the beneficiary of his estate. The proceeds from the sale of Oak Hill and its contents went to form the Herbert and Muriel Boone Endowment Fund for the Humanities. Some of the principal pieces from the collection have been thoughtfully retained by the John Hopkins University and these will be on display at Homewood, a Federal house on the University campus, which has now been restored and opened as a museum.

Fig. 4
David Allan
PORTRAIT OF THE CHILDREN OF HENRY DUNDAS, 1ST VISCOUNT MELVILLE
48in by 59½in (122cm by 151cm)
London £44,000 ($83,600). 16.XI.88
From the collection of James R. Herbert Boone

Opposite
Fig. 5
George Romney
PORTRAIT OF THE CHILDREN OF CHARLES BOONE, ESQ.
59½in by 47⅝in (151cm by 121cm)
London £132,000 ($250,800). 16.XI.88
From the collection of James R. Herbert Boone

Arthur Devis
PORTRAIT OF MR AND MRS ROBERT DASHWOOD OF
STANFORD HALL, NOTTINGHAMSHIRE
Signed and dated *1750*, 44in by 38in
(112cm by 96.5cm)
London £308,000 ($563,640). 8.III.89

Cornelius Johnson and Gerard Houckgeest
PORTRAIT OF QUEEN HENRIETTA MARIA
Oil on panel, stamped with the cypher of King Charles I
on the reverse, 19½in by 16⅞in (49.5cm by 43cm)
London £94,600 ($173,118). 8.III.89
From the collection of Geoffrey Coldham

John de Critz
PORTRAIT OF RICHARD,
1ST LORD LOVELACE
Inscribed *Richard yᵉ 1ˢᵗ/
Lord Lovelace/who died 1634*;
PORTRAIT OF MARGARET,
LADY LOVELACE, HIS WIFE
Inscribed *Margaret wife/to
Richard Lᵈ/Lovelace*
A pair, each 41⅞in by 32½in
(106.5cm by 82.5cm)
London £126,500
($231,495). 8.III.89

Richard Parkes Bonington
VENICE GRAND CANAL, SUNSET
17⅛in by 24in (43.5cm by 61cm)
London £319,000 ($583,770). 8.III.89
Formerly in the collection of Sir Robert Peel

Bonington's brief visit to Venice between April and May 1826 produced some of his finest
and most atmospheric landscapes. Painted between 1827 and 1828, this painting shows the
assurance with which Bonington developed a finished composition from oil sketches and
watercolours painted while still in Venice. The influence of the Venetian painters, the
particular qualities of Venetian light and the architecture of the city continued to inspire his
drawings and oils for the rest of his short life. Bonington died at the age of twenty-seven so his
works are always scarce; in view of this it was remarkable that three of his Venetian pictures
were sold this season – two oil sketches in November and this work, one of only six finished
oils of Venice, which were acquired by Sir Robert Peel shortly after the artist's death.

Peter Tillemans
PROSPECT OF THE RIVER
THAMES AT TWICKENHAM
Signed, 23in by 47⅜in
(58.5cm by 120.5cm)
London £143,000
($271,700). 16.XI.88

Antonio Joli
PROSPECT OF LONDON FROM
A COLONNADE WITH A
DISTANT VIEW OF ST PAUL'S
AND OLD LONDON BRIDGE
41in by 45in
(104cm by 114.5cm)
London £286,000
($491,920). 12.VII.89

Antonio Joli arrived in
England in 1744 after
training as a theatrical
designer under Bibbiena
and as a vedute painter
under Panini, in Italy.
He became principal
scene painter at the
King's Theatre, Hay-
market. His ability to
combine a topographical
view with an illusionistic
setting was demonstrated
in this painting where a
capriccio foreground
acts as a setting for a
well-known view. There
is another version in the
Metropolitan Museum
of Art, New York.

Alexander Nasmyth
A PROSPECT OF LONDON, SEEN FROM THE EARL OF CASSILIS'S PRIVY GARDEN, WITH WATERLOO BRIDGE
Inscribed on the relining *painted by/Alex Nasmyth/Edinburgh 1826*, 54⅞in by 82in (139.5cm by 208.5cm)
London £374,000 ($643,280). 12.VII.89
From the collection of the British Rail Pension Fund

This magnificent panorama is taken from the Privy Garden at the foot of 1, Whitehall
Gardens, built in 1806 for Archibald Kennedy, 12th Earl of Cassilis. On the left is Robert
Adam's Adelphi Theatre and further down the river is Sir William Chambers's Somerset
House, begun in 1776. The spires of St Mary le Strand and St Clement Danes can be seen on
the horizon and the dome of St Paul's Cathedral is in the centre. The composition is
dominated by Waterloo Bridge, designed by John Rennie and opened in 1817. Archibald
Kennedy was a prominent liberal, and an important patron of Nasmyth.

John Frederick Herring, Sr
'PRIAM' BEATING LORD EXETER'S 'AUGUSTUS' AT NEWMARKET, 1831
Signed and dated *1831*, 28in by 42in (71.1cm by 106.7cm)
New York $495,000 (£319,355). 9.VI.89

Opposite
Jacques-Laurent Agasse
EMMA POWLES ON HER GREY HUNTER ACCOMPANIED BY HER SPANIEL IN A RIVER LANDSCAPE
Signed, 36in by 27¾in (91.5cm by 70.5cm)
London £407,000 ($773,300). 16.XI.88
From the collection of Peter Powles

William Turner of Oxford
A BRIDGE AND COTTAGE AT NUNEHAM, OXFORDSHIRE
Watercolour over pencil heightened with bodycolour and gum arabic, 17⅛in by 26½in
(43.5cm by 67.5cm)
London £29,700 ($51,084). 13.VII.89

This watercolour probably dates from the 1850s and is closely related to a series of
watercolours of waterlilies on the Cherwell which share the profusion of lilies and the view
point from the boat. The view shown in this watercolour is a backwater of the Thames at
Nuneham with a bridge crossing to an island. The cottage is one of a group known as the
Lock cottages, some of which are still standing.

Thomas Girtin
NEAR BOLTON ABBEY, YORKSHIRE
Watercolour over pencil on laid paper, signed; inscribed on the reverse of the mount *opposite Bolton Abbey/Yorks.*, 13in by 20½in (33cm by 52cm)
London £231,000 ($397,320). 13.VII.89

This hitherto unrecorded watercolour was worked up from sketches made on Girtin's tour of the north of England in 1801. He sketched extensively along the beautiful Valley of the Wharfe, making several drawings of the medieval ruins at Bolton Abbey. This view has its origins in a sketch now in the British Museum, and is related to a second finished watercolour, *Stepping Stones on the Wharfe*. The painting is one of a series of watercolours of similar dimensions in which Girtin responds to the grandeur of northern England's landscape with monumental compositions and broad, deep-toned washes.

David Roberts, RA
EL DEIR, PETRA
Watercolour over pencil
heightened with
bodycolour on buff paper,
signed and dated *El Deir.*
Petra./March 8th 1839.
13⅝in by 19⅝in
(34.5cm by 50cm)
London £37,400
($64,328). 13.VII.89

William Alexander
CHINESE MILITARY POST ON
THE RIVER EU-HO
Watercolour over pencil,
signed with initials and
inscribed with the title,
19 October 1793, and in a
later hand *At every interval*
of a few miles (on the Eu ho
River)/we saw military Posts
where soldiers are stationed/to
protect the internal Commerce
of the Provinces/as well as
travellers from pirates
robbers./Staunton . . . ps Vol 2
p. 365, 11⅞in by 18½in
(30cm by 47cm)
London £29,700
($57,321). 17.XI.88

Joseph Mallord William Turner, RA
A CASTLE ON A HEIGHT NEAR GENEVA
Watercolour with pencil heightened with scratching out on paper
prepared with grey wash, 6⅛in by 9in (15.5cm by 23cm)
London £55,000 ($94,600). 13.VII.89

This watercolour has been dated to Turner's Swiss tour of
1836, when he accompanied his patron H.A.J. Munro to
Geneva, Bonneville, Chamonix and the Val d'Aosta.
Characteristic of a number of watercolours from this tour is
the strong, dark palette and extensive scratching out. In this
work Turner has made much vigorous use of this technique.
If not from the 1836 tour, it dates from a later journey to the
Alps, probably the 1841 trip.

Right
Joseph Mallord William Turner, RA
THE PASS OF GLENCOE
Watercolour over pencil, 5¾in by 4⅜in (14.5cm by 11cm)
London £37,400 ($68,068). 9.III.89

John Dunstall

STUDIES OF WALNUTS AND HAZELNUTS

Pen and brown ink over metalpoint outlines on vellum, signed, inscribed *This piece is drawn/with Pen &*
Inke. and dated *1666*, $7\frac{7}{8}$in by $11\frac{3}{8}$in (20cm by 29cm)
London £73,700 ($134,134). 9.III.89

Only two other drawings by Dunstall are known, both of which are in the British Museum
and both are in watercolour over pencil on vellum. Born in Sussex, Dunstall was probably
working in London by the early 1660s and George Vertue records him as living 'in the
Strand a small professor and teacher of drawing as by a title in a book of flowers drawn and
etched by him 1662'. In his will, Dunstall describes himself as a schoolmaster. He etched a
number of sets of plates, intended no doubt as copybooks, with such subjects as houses,
flowers, fruit and trees, several being published by Peter Stent. This drawing was previously
unknown.

Cornelius David Krieghoff
THE BLIZZARD
Signed and dated *Quebec 58*, 1858, 13in by 17¾in (33cm by 45cm)
London £132,000 ($246,840). 2.XI.88

Right
Edward Pierce
DESIGN FOR A DOORCASE FOR THE FISHMONGERS' COMPANY, LONDON
Pen and brown ink and grey wash, signed with initials,
15½in by 9¼in (39.5cm by 23.5cm), from a folio of architectural
drawings and designs collected by John Talman, 151 designs,
ninety-nine leaves, almost all with gilt borders, all stamped with a
collector's mark
London £88,000 ($159,280). 27.IV.89
From the collection of Philip Robinson

John Brett's *Val d'Aosta*

Simon Taylor

When John Brett's painting was exhibited at the Royal Academy in 1859, Ruskin devoted some 1,100 words of his *Academy Notes* to describe the scene. The importance he gave to this painting is understandable, as Brett had painted perhaps the greatest of all Pre-Raphaelite landscapes and one which embodied the artistic theories of Pre-Raphaelitism which Ruskin had developed.

The Pre-Raphaelites rejected the classical tradition which had permeated Western European painting from the death of Raphael in favour of a fresh, deliberately naive reproduction of the visible world. As a student of the Royal Academy, Brett would have been aware of Ruskin's championship of the Pre-Raphaelite Brotherhood, but it was through his meeting, in Switzerland, with J.W. Inchbold, a protégé of Ruskin's, that he was 'converted' to the Pre-Raphaelite doctrine of truth to nature. In June 1858, Brett arrived in Val d'Aosta and set up his portable easel facing the peaks of Testa du Rutor and Mont Paramont, and without any precedents to fall back on, began to paint exactly what he saw. His eye denied the convention of aerial perspective (colours becoming thinner and paler in the distance), and instead he felt his way to his own optical perspective. Likewise he reversed the normal conventions of landscape painting by which the foreground is carefully drawn, with a broader brush used further back. One can pick out his feathery strokes in the lichen on the foreground rock, but the background haziness is achieved by a myriad of molecular dots. Unlike the usual Pre-Raphaelite technique of painting on a wet, white ground, he mixed pure pigments with white, applied almost dry, to create a completely smooth, powdery surface. He described in a letter to his sister a special technique he had used to render the sky: 'The blue I put in with a sharp tool bouncing it down on its point perpendicularly, driving the paint into the grain, using no medium [. . .] and laying the paint securely [?]. You can get it beautifully flat this way.'

Ruskin's article was largely laudatory, but in a characteristically perverse conclusion, he deemed the painting devoid of genuine emotion: 'Mirror's work, not Man's', while in a later article he described it as 'mere photography of physical landscape'. Further disappointment came for Brett when his masterpiece failed to find a buyer. It was finally acquired by Ruskin himself for £200, less than half the original price.

Ruskin's dismissal of Brett's masterpiece must seem unfair and superficial today. Both the intensely worked surface and the chosen view, squarely facing a cross etched into the hillside, which is directly echoed in the iron cross around the neck of the sleeping goat girl, reinforce the impression of spiritual depth. Sadly, Brett was discouraged by its poor reception. His next painting, *The Hedger* was an enclosed woodland scene, and he would never again work with the same intensity.

John Brett, ARA
VAL D'AOSTA
Signed and dated *1858*,
34½in by 26¾in (87.6cm by 68cm)
London £1,320,000 ($2,191,000). 20.VI.89
From the collection of Sir Richard Cooper

Opposite

Sir Edward Coley Burne-Jones, ARA
PHILIP COMYNS CARR
Signed with monogram, inscribed *London* and
to CAJ, titled and dated *1882*,
28in by 19in (71cm by 48.5cm)
London £407,000 ($675,620). 20.VI.89

This is among Burne-Jones' first portraits.
Philip was the son of Joseph Comyns Carr,
managing director of the Grosvenor Gallery,
where the painting was exhibited in 1883.
Many subsequent portraits by Burne-Jones
followed this composition of a simply dressed
sitter against a dark background. The half-
length format, the illusionistically painted
label and the Botticelli-like angelic features
of the boy owe much to *quattrocento* painting.
Above all the portrait has a sense of classical
balance, the complex knot of little fingers
creating an almost abstract counterweight to
the pale face. The reviewer for *The Art
Journal*, 1883 criticised Burne-Jones for
showing only 'slight sympathy with the zest
of a boy's life', but this was not his intention.
'Of course my faces have no expression in the
sense in which people use the word,' he told
his wife Georgina. 'The moment you give
what people call expression you destroy the
typical character of the heads and degrade
them into portraits which stand for nothing'.
According to *Mrs J. Comyns Carr's
Reminiscences*, Philip exhausted the patience
of the painter who exclaimed: 'Oh, Phil, I
think you are the very worst little sitter I
ever had.' The boy, who been standing day
after day, shifting from one foot to the other,
replied: 'Sitter! Do you call this sitting, Mr
Burne-Jones?' Despite this, the artist made
use of Philip again to pose as one of the page-
boys in his *King Cophetua and the Beggar Maid*,
exhibited at the Grosvenor Gallery the
following year.

Sir Edward Coley Burne-Jones, ARA
FLAMMA VESTALIS
Signed with monogram and dated *August 1896* on the artist's label on the stretcher,
25½in by 16⅞in (65cm by 43cm)
London £341,000 ($566,060). 20.VI.89

This is the second and smaller version of *Flamma Vestalis*, exhibited at the
Grosvenor Gallery, London in 1886. It was modelled from the artist's
daughter, Margaret.

James-Jacques-Joseph Tissot
READING THE NEWS
Signed, *circa* 1874, 34in by 20½in (86.4cm by 52cm)
New York $1,375,000 (£881,410). 23.V.89

Sir John Everett Millais,
PRA
PORTRAIT OF LOUISE
JOPLING
Signed with monogram
and dated *1879*, 49¼in by
29⅞in (125cm by 76cm)
London £220,000
($420,200). 22.XI.88

Philip Wilson Steer, OM
A GIRL RECLINING ON A SOFA
Signed and dated *92*, 24in by 30in (61cm by 76cm)
London £187,000 ($351,560). 9.XI.88

The subject of this provocative pose, semi-reclining with her arms behind her head, is
Rose Pettigrew, Steer's favourite model in the early 1890s. In an autobiographical essay,
Miss Pettigrew states that she met Steer in 1888. Sir William Eden bought this canvas and it
subsequently appeared in Steer's exhibition at Goupil's Gallery in 1894.

Opposite
Dante Gabriel Rossetti
BEATA BEATRIX
Pastel, signed with monogram and dated *1872*, 34¼in by 27⅛in (87cm by 69cm)
London £220,000 ($365,200). 20.VI.89

This is a later version of the oil painting *Beata Beatrix*, *circa* 1864-70 in the Tate Gallery,
London.

Sir Alfred Munnings, PRA
STUDY: JOCKEYS AT THE START, NEWMARKET
Oil on canvas board, signed 20in by 24in (50.8cm by 61cm)
New York $341,000 (£220,000). 9.VI.89

Sir Alfred Munnings was President of the Royal Academy from 1944–49.

Opposite
Sir James Jebusa Shannon, RA
IN THE SPRINGTIME
Signed and dated *1896*, 50in by 40in (127cm by 101.6cm)
New York $687,500 (£388,418). 27.X.88

Walter Richard Sickert, ARA
UN COIN DE LA PLACE SAINT MARC A VENISE
Signed, 1902, 17⅞in by 25⅛in (45.5cm by 64cm)
London £77,000 ($136,290). 10.V.89

Opposite
Duncan Grant
SELF PORTRAIT
1925, 18⅛in by 15in (46cm by 38cm)
London £77,000 ($136,290). 10.V.89
Formerly in the collection of Lord Clark of Saltwood

Painted in 1925, probably at Charleston, this painting was acquired by Lord Clark who
became a patron and friend of both Duncan Grant and Vanessa Bell in the 1930s.

Joseph Crawhall
THE SPANGLED COCK
Watercolour heightened with bodycolour on linen, signed, 1903, 17½in by 23in (44.5cm by 58.5cm)
Hopetoun House £176,000 ($318,560). 25.IV.89

Francis Campbell Boileau Cadell
AFTERNOON, 1913
Signed; dated *1913* on the reverse, 40in by 50in (101.5cm by 127cm)
Gleneagles £214,500 ($383,955). 30.VIII.88

Francis Campbell Boileau Cadell (1883–1937) trained at the Académie Julien in Paris
between 1899 and 1903 and did not return to Scotland until 1909. In 1910 his sponsor
Sir Patrick Ford, who was later to be of such encouragement to John Lavery, financed a trip
to Venice. This produced the shimmering, rapidly painted panels of which *Florians, St Marks,
Venice* is a perfect example (*Art at Auction 1987–88*, p.96). Cadell's *Afternoon*, painted three
years later, is a superb indication of his early maturity. Its dazzling use of bright flashes of
lime, pink and orange against a startling white background shows that Cadell had, in terms
of colour, learnt the lessons of recent French painting arguably better than any contemporary
British painter.

Nineteenth-century European paintings

Johann Jakob Biedermann
A FARMER PLOUGHING BY LAKE LUCERNE
Signed and dated *1813*, 28⅞in by 38⅛in (73.5cm by 97cm)
Zurich SF550,000 (£205,224:$322,770). 1.VI.89

Eduard Schleich the Elder

A YOUNG BOY RESTING
Signed and dated *1833*,
14in by 18½in
(35.5cm by 47cm)
Munich DM143,000
(£44,898: $75,066).
10.V.89

Ferdinand Georg Waldmüller

GRANDFATHER'S BIRTHDAY
Signed and dated *1849*,
22⅞in by 31¼in
(58cm by 79.5cm)
London £1,485,000
($2,465,100). 20.VI.89
Formerly in the Reichert collection

John Frederick Lewis, RA
THE KIBAB SHOP, SCUTARI, ASIA MINOR
Oil on panel, signed and dated *1858*, 21in by 31in (53.3cm by 78.7cm)
New York $1,100,000 (£628,571). 22.II.89

Lewis travelled through a considerable portion of Asia Minor in the summer of 1841, having
spent most of the spring sketching the mosques of Constantinople. In November of the same
year he sailed for Egypt, where he remained for ten years. Upon his return to England,
armed with a vast number of sketches, studies and unfinished pictures, Lewis began to
concentrate on oil painting, exhibiting Eastern scenes at the Royal Academy from 1855.

    The Kebab Shop was included in the 1858 exhibition and in his *Academy Notes*, Ruskin
describes it as 'a very notable picture', adding that the animal life was 'nearly perfect' and
'the kid making up its mind to butt the pigeons especially delightful'. In his view, 'there
never, perhaps, in the history of art was work so wholly independent as Lewis's. He worked
with the sternest precision twenty years ago, when Pre-Raphaelitism had never been heard
of [...] There is not another picture in all this Academy which I believe to have been painted
wholly without reference to the Pre-Raphaelite dogmas [...] but John Lewis paints as he
would have painted had no such school, no such dogmas ever existed'.

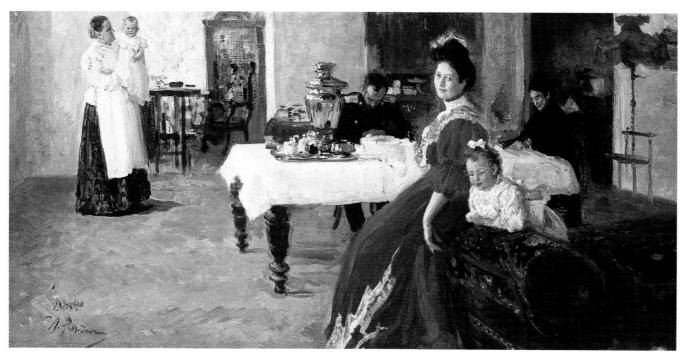

Ilya Efimovich Repin
FAMILY PORTRAIT: THE ARTIST'S DAUGHTER, TATYANA, AND HER FAMILY
Signed in Cyrillic, 1905, 34½in by 70¾in (87.6cm by 179.7cm)
New York $1,100,000 (£705,128). 23.V.89

This work depicts Repin's younger daughter with her husband Nicolai Genadiewich Yazeff, her two daughters and their nurse. The woman seated at the right of the table is Nicolai Yazeff's mother. The setting is the artist's apartments at the Academy of Arts, St Petersburg, where he served as director from 1898–99, and professor and head of the Higher Art School affiliated with the Academy from 1894–1907.

This family scene exemplifies the domestic genre of realism which Repin, as Russia's foremost national artist, championed. He continued to devote much time to portraits in his later years, both formal portraits of prominent writers and musicians and more intimate depictions of his family circle.

Frederik Hendrik Kaemmerer
THE BEACH AT SCHEVENINGEN, HOLLAND
Signed, 1874, 27½in by 55in (69.9cm by 139.7cm)
New York $1,320,000 (£745,763). 27.X.88
From the collection of the Corcoran Gallery of Art, Washington, DC

The Dutch artist Frederik Hendrik Kaemmerer initially worked as a landscape painter, but after he moved to Paris in 1865 his work changed dramatically. There he turned to elegant genre pictures such as this beach scene. Painted in 1874, it was exhibited to great acclaim at the Paris Salon of that year, and the artist was awarded a *médaille de troisième classe*. The fashionably dressed man seated at the right of the composition is a self-portrait of the artist.

The Corcoran Gallery of Art is the legacy of the Washington banker and philanthropist William Wilson Corcoran, who founded the gallery in 1869 with his personal collection of paintings and sculpture. William Macleod's *Catalogue of the Corcoran Gallery of Art*, 1887, mentions Kaemmerer's painting: 'This remarkable work is by a native of Holland, but now one of the resident artists of Paris. [...] The subject is painted with a peculiar open-air effect, startling at first, but true to nature. [...] The technical skill of the artist is successfully shown in his way of grouping together so many objects of the lightest colour – the white dresses, white chairs, and white wagons, without confusion, and in proper relief.'

Opposite
Gustave Doré
ANDROMEDA
Signed and dated *1869*, 101in by 68in (256.5cm by 172.7cm)
New York $577,500 (£330,000). 22.II.89

Jules Breton
LA FEMME A L'OMBRELLE; BAIE DE DOUARNENEZ
Signed and dated *1871*, 25⅝in by 35¾in (65cm by 90.8cm)
New York $1,650,000 (£942,857). 22.II.89

This painting depicts the artist's wife, Elodie, seated amongst the pines on the Bay of
Douarnenez, Brittany, where Breton and his family spent the summer months between 1865
and 1875. The artist started work on this composition in the summer of 1870, beginning with
a small oil sketch. He used this and a much larger drawing, squared for transfer, to enable
him to finish the painting on location, probably in the summer of 1871.

Opposite, above
Odoardo Borrani
LA MIA TERRAZZA, FIRENZE
Signed and dated *1865*, 21¼in by 32in (54cm by 81.5cm)
London £242,000 ($401,720). 20.VI.89

This painting was almost certainly painted at 20, Via delle Ruote in Florence, where the
artist was living with his parents. Carlotta Meini, his future wife, lived on the floor below.
Her father died on Easter Sunday 1865, and this picture probably depicts her shortly after
his death.

Below
Mosé Bianchi
SALTIMBANCHI
Signed, 19in by 29⅜in (48.5cm by 74.5cm)
Milan L474,600,000 (£209,722:$329,812). 1.VI.89

Nikolai Astrup
APPLE TREES IN BLOOM
Signed, 21¼in by 34⅝in (54cm by 88cm)
London £297,000 ($543,510). 14.III.89

Opposite
Anders Zorn
IN SCOTLAND (MRS SYMONS)
Watercolour, signed and dated '87, 1887, 39⅜in by 26in (100cm by 66cm)
London £902,000 ($1,650,660). 14. III.89

The best Scandinavian painters are notable for the way they incorporate the most-up-to-date developments in the painting of their time, but interpret them in a very distinctive manner. Anders Zorn is a good example. The most famous turn-of-the-century Swedish painter, his work is closely paralleled by that of John Singer Sargent and Joaquin Sorolla y Bastida. Zorn was both a highly esteemed portrait painter and a painter of figures in a landscape, in the tradition of the French Impressionists. *In Scotland (Mrs Symons)* was painted in 1887, at a time when Zorn was producing his finest paintings. It was commissioned by Sir Ernest Cassel and was executed at Dunkeld in Perthshire. It is an exceptional work for a number of reasons. It is one of Zorn's largest watercolours and one which he regarded to be among his best works in that medium. It is both a portrait and a landscape painting, combining the two most characteristic aspects of Zorn's work, unusual in his œuvre. Reflections in water fascinated Zorn, and are an important element in many of his major works.

Sigrid Hjertén
TEATIME
Signed and dated *1915*, 60in by 63in (152.5cm by 160cm)
London £528,000 ($966,240). 14.III.88

Opposite
Vilhelm Hammershøi
INTERIOR WITH A GIRL AT THE CLAVIER
Signed with initials, 22in by 17⅜in (56cm by 44cm)
London £242,000 ($401,720). 20.VI.89

Impressionist paintings from the collection of the British Rail Pension Fund

Michel Strauss

In the mid 1970s the British Rail Pension Fund perplexed their pensioners and stunned fund managers by announcing that they would invest in art. Although bold, the decision was far from unconsidered – at the time inflation was very high, the stock market low, the property market uncertain. Art seemed a viable alternative. The fund spread its risk over a wide area which included French furniture (see pp 388–96) and Chinese art (see pp 284–87). The Impressionist collection formed 10% of the total amount invested in art. The Fund's strategy was proven successful on 4th April 1989, when the twenty-five paintings, drawings and sculpture from this part of the collection (cost to the Pension Fund: £3.4 million) sold for a total of £35.2 million. The investment had therefore grown at a rate of 20.1% per annum (11.9% after inflation). A portfolio of shares invested at the same time could have expected to have yielded 7.5% per annum after inflation. The figures prove that in this case art was a valid long-term investment.

There were three rules in making recommendations. The collection should include paintings, drawings and sculpture and should therefore cover a wide range of prices. All pieces should be of outstanding quality and condition; and finally, the expert's personal taste played a large part in discerning good works of art from the point of view of investment. An excellent eye for quality and an awareness of the general public's perception of 'quality', as well as an understanding of the shifting nature of that opinion were essential.

The sale of the collection yielded some remarkable insights into major changes that have taken place in our approach to Impressionist and modern art. The highest price of the sale was paid for the Renoir (Fig. 1). Painted in 1870, early in Renoir's career, it appeared more than two years before Monet painted *Impression: Soleil levant* and four years before the first exhibition of Impressionist paintings in 1874. In the mid 1970s early works by Renoir would probably have made less than works painted in his maturity. Now with the increasing desire to give works a historical context, both early and late works by major artists fetch increasingly high prices. The new status of the early work is confirmed by the fact that it was bought by an institution, the J. Paul Getty Museum, Malibu, California.

British Rail were fortunate that their quest coincided with the sale of some superb collections, among them the Robert von Hirsch Collection sold at Sotheby's in 1978. From it came Camille Pissarro's *Paul Cézanne* (Fig. 2), the earliest portrait of Cézanne by another artist, painted in 1874 when the two painters were working together at

Fig. 1
Pierre-Auguste Renoir
LA PROMENADE
Signed and dated '70, 1870,
32in by 25⅜in
(81.3cm by 65cm)
London £10,340,000
($18,715,400). 4.IV.89
From the collection of the
British Rail Pension Fund

Pontoise. The portrait is without flattery and conveys Cézanne's vision and determination. It is also a good likeness judging by Lucien Pissarro's description of Cézanne at this period: 'He wore a cap, his long black hair was beginning to recede from a high forehead, he had large black eyes which rolled in their orbit when he was excited.'

Not only is it a very fine, characterful portrait, but it is an important art historical document. Cézanne is shown against a background of paintings and posters: one of Pissarro's landscapes, and a caricature of the Realist painter Courbet, who influenced both Pissarro and Cézanne. The portrait was accompanied by Renoir's rather more suave portrait of Cézanne in city dress, 1880. It was the first time that these two portraits had been seen together and happily they were bought by the same buyer.

A Van Gogh drawing and a large Cézanne watercolour also came from the Von Hirsch Collection. Van Gogh's sinuous reed-pen drawing, *Mas à Saintes-Maries* (Fig. 3), contrasts the neat lines of cottages with burgeoning summer foliage showing his powerful response to the heat and colour of the Mediterranean. Van Gogh travelled to Saintes-Maries de la Mer, near Arles for the first time in June 1888. Just before leaving he wrote to his brother Theo, 'I must draw a great deal. Things have so much line. . . . I want to get my drawing more spontaneous, more exaggerated . . .'. Later he wrote, 'I am convinced that I shall set my individuality free simply by

Fig. 4
Paul Cézanne
NATURE MORTE AU MELON VERT
Watercolour and pencil, 1902–1906, 12¾in by 18¾in (31.5cm by 47.5cm)
London £2,530,000 ($4,579,300). 4.IV.89
From the collection of the British Rail Pension Fund

staying here.' Large size watercolours have also acquired new status; Cézanne's *Nature Morte au Melon Vert* (Fig. 4) painted between 1902 and 1906 in Aix-en-Provence, is one of the several large watercolour still lifes that are among the last works produced by the artist.

Monet's *Santa Maria della Salute et le Grand Canal, Venise* (Fig.5) is another late work. It is a very personal interpretation of a city that had captured so many imaginations through the centuries. In the present climate the familiarity of the subject would enhance its status and value (the Pension Fund paid £253,000 ten years ago). Monet, by 1908 a highly successful painter, stayed at the Palazzo Barbaro with Mr Curtis, a friend of John Singer Sargent. Afterwards he moved to the Grand Hotel Brittania, on the Grand Canal, opposite the Salute. In the works of this period, Monet moved away from his earlier objectivity to evoke an iridescent dream city as dazzling and romantic as a Turner.

Fig. 5
Claude Monet
SANTA MARIA DELLA SALUTE ET LE GRAND CANAL, VENISE
Signed and dated *1908*, 28⅜in by 35⅞in (72cm by 91cm)
London £6,710,000 ($12,145,100). 4.IV.89
From the collection of the British Rail Pension Fund

Claude Monet
NYMPHEAS
Signed and dated *1908*, 36¼in by 35in (92cm by 89cm)
London £5,720,000 ($11,096,800). 29.XI.88

Edgar Degas
LE BAISSER DU RIDEAU
Pastel on joined paper, signed, 1880, 21¼in by 29⅛in (54cm by 74cm)
New York $7,975,000 (£4,480,337). 11.XI.88

Performances at the Opéra were an important part of sophisticated Parisian social life
during the latter half of the nineteenth century. Subscribers, or *abonnés*, were welcome
throughout the theatre, not only in the boxes and stalls but also backstage and in the wings.
By the late 1860s Degas was a familiar figure to the dancers. Suzanne Mante, a student
recalled that he stood 'at the top or bottom of the many staircases in the building, drawing
the dancers as they rushed up and down. He used to ask them to stop in order that he could
make quick sketches of them.'

The result of this scrutiny is a large body of paintings and sculpture, drawings and studies
that captures the poses and gestures of the dance and the character of more intimate
moments off stage. Although Degas worked in many media – wax, oil charcoal, gouache,
monotype, pastel and frequently in combinations of these – the ephemeral quality of pastel
seemed especially suited to the equally evanescent nature of his subject. *Le Baisser du Rideau*
captures part of the nightly cycle of the ballet – the finale as the curtain falls.

Paul Gauguin
TE FARE HYMENEE (LA MAISON DES CHANTS)
Oil on burlap, signed, inscribed *TE FARE HYMENEE* and dated *'92*,
19¾in by 35⅜in (50.3cm by 90cm)
London £6,600,000 ($11,946,000). 4.IV.89

Although Tahiti is undoubtedly Gauguin's most famous subject matter, paintings from this
period are rarely seen on the market. This was produced during Gauguin's first Tahitian
stay from 9th June 1891 to 4th June 1893, and can be dated to before the end of April 1892.
In Chapter IV of *Noa Noa*, Gauguin's personal record of his first journey to the South Pacific,
written in 1894 on his return to Paris, he describes a 'Maison des Chants': 'They all assemble
in a sort of communal house to sing and talk. They start with a prayer; an old man recites it
first very carefully, and everyone else repeats it as a refrain. Then they sing. On other
occasions they tell stories to make each other laugh.'

Opposite
Paul Cézanne
ARLEQUIN
Circa 1890-95, 24½in by 18½in (62.2cm by 47cm)
London £4,400,000 ($8,536,000). 29.XI.88

Paintings from the collection of Jaime Ortiz-Patiño

The eight Impressionist and Post-Impressionist paintings sold in New York on 9th May represent just one aspect of a collection that is extremely diverse and highly select in character. The owner, Jaime Ortiz-Patiño, is a member of the third generation of a family of distinguished collectors that included his grandfather, Simon I. Patiño, his uncle, Antenor Patiño, and his mother, Graziella Patiño. Bolivian in origin, this family has always had close ties with France, and their respect for French civilisation has had a profound impact on Señor Ortiz-Patiño's collecting attitudes. In his magnificent house in Vandoeuvres, near Geneva, he has assembled several collections of great quality, particularly Medieval and Renaissance manuscripts, fine bindings of the eighteenth century, miniatures and enamelled snuffboxes, and above all, French and English silver.

His taste for the exquisitely-crafted object was equally expressed in the paintings he chose to complement the very beautiful Renoir portrait, *Jeune Fille au Chapeau garni de Fleurs des Champs* (Fig.1), which he inherited from his mother. The legacy started its owner in a promising new direction, and in less than eight years, Señor Ortiz-Patiño succeeded in acquiring seven equally significant works of the Impressionist period. Hanging with this charming Renoir were examples from the early period of Impressionism by Monet and Pissarro and fully developed, mature statements by the major artists of the Post-Impressionist period, Cézanne and Gauguin. In this carefully chosen group, Señor Ortiz-Patiño achieved a remarkably strong image of one of the most enchanting periods of French art.

Garden House on the Banks of the Zaan (Fig.4), a lovely riverside scene by Monet, has recently been identified as a view of the Luchthuis at Westzijde 78 on the Zaan. On his arrival in Zaandam in June 1871, Monet found the Dutch landscape much more beautiful than he had expected. 'This is a marvellous place for painting', he wrote to Pissarro. 'There are the most amusing things everywhere. Houses of every colour, hundreds of windmills and enchanting boats.'

Imposing works by Cézanne and Gauguin represent the liberation of form which came in the wake of the Impressionist liberation of colour. Cézanne's still life of 1893–94 (Fig.2), shows him at the height of his achievements in this genre. Similarly, Gauguin's richly coloured *Mata Mua* ('In Olden Times'; Fig.3) is among the most important of his Tahitian paintings, one in which he synthesized elements of Tahitian landscape and legend to create his own vision of paradise lost.

Fig. 1
Pierre-Auguste Renoir
JEUNE FILLE AU CHAPEAU
GARNI DE FLEURS DES CHAMPS
Signed and dated *80*, 1880,
21⅝in by 18⅛in
(54.9cm by 46cm)
New York $13,750,000
(£8,233,533). 9.V.89
From the collection of
Jaime Ortiz-Patiño

Fig. 2
Paul Cézanne
PICHET ET FRUITS SUR UNE TABLE
Oil on paper laid down on panel, *circa* 1893–94, 16½in by 28½in (41.9cm by 72.4cm)
New York $11,550,000 (£6,916,168). 9.V.89
From the collection of Jaime Ortiz-Patiño

This is one of the most lyrical of Cézanne's still lifes of the mid 1890s. By the late 1880s he began to abandon strict frontality in the still lifes in favour of more complex spatial arrangements. The relatively unusual elongated format of the painting allowed Cezanne to space out the jug, dish and fruit so that there is little overlapping. The apparent simplicity of the work is deceptive; Cézanne's formal liberties serve to give it remarkable vigour. The cloth seems to weigh down the left edge of the table, warping it and distorting the perspective. The rim of the white plate between the two apples is omitted and, most surprising of all, the plate of fruit in the background seems to float in the air, echoing the shape of the dish on the table.

Opposite
Fig. 3
Paul Gauguin
MATA MUA ('IN OLDEN TIMES')
Signed, titled and dated *92*, 1892, 34¾in by 25¾in (88.3cm by 65.4cm)
New York $24,200,000 (£14,491,017). 9.V.89
From the collection of Jaime Ortiz-Patiño (jointly owned with Baron Heinz-Heinrich Thyssen-Bornemisza)

MATA MUA

P Gauguin 92

Fig. 4
Claude Monet
GARDEN HOUSE ON THE BANKS OF THE ZAAN
Signed, 1871, 21½in by 29in (54.6cm by 73.7cm)
New York $11,000,000 (£6,586,826). 9.V.89
From the collection of Jaime Ortiz-Patiño

Pierre-Auguste Renoir
BAIGNEUSE (FEMME EN JUPE ROUGE S'ESSUYANT LES PIEDS)
Signed, *circa* 1888, 26in by 20in (66cm by 50.8cm)
New York $8,525,000 (£4,789,326). 11.XI.88

Yo Picasso, a self-portrait

In 1901, when he painted the famous *Yo Picasso*, Picasso was only twenty years old, an age at which the work of even the most gifted artists is generally more illuminating for what it predicts than for what it actually accomplishes. Yet this is a work of startling genius, boldly executed and penetrating in its psychological analysis of the young painter who would establish a dominating position in the art of the twentieth century.

The steady growth in Picasso's sense of self can be traced through the fairly frequent self-portraits of the latter part of the 1890s, but none predicted the blazing self-assurance of this work. On one level, as a result of his frequent travels and rapid assimilation of all that he found new and interesting, Picasso had the technical means to express whatever he chose. On another, more personal level, away from Spain and the heavy burden of family pressure and social conformity, Picasso was free to develop in as yet unknown directions.

Patricia Leighten has given a fascinating explanation of the monosyllabic *Yo* inscribed in the midnight-blue paint above the signature. In the circle in which Picasso moved, the philosophy of Friedrich Nietzsche was highly regarded, particularly his anti-intellectualism and exaltation of genius. In Spain, these beliefs were encapsulated in the word *Yo*, the ego:

A dash follows the *Yo*, distinctly separating it from the much smaller cursive signature below. The dash and the difference in their appearance show that these words do not constitute a sentence, *Yo Picasso* ('I am Picasso'), which would manifest an as yet undeserved and egotistical proclamation of achievements and at the same time a humour inappropriate to the drama of the image. Rather, the *Yo-* above Picasso's signature announces the fact of his genius, its potential and his intention to allow its voice to flow through him unhindered: an act not of hubris but of genuine bravery in his social and artistic setting.

Yo Picasso was included in Picasso's first Parisian exhibition, which opened at the Galerie Vollard on 24th June 1901. Organized by Petrus Mañach and with a catalogue preface by Gustave Coquiot, the exhibition was favourably reviewed by Félicien Fagus in *La Revue Blanche*: '[Picasso] is the brilliant newcomer . . . like all pure painters, he adores colour . . . Each influence is transitory . . . one sees that Picasso's haste has not yet given him time to forge a personal style; his personality is in his haste, this youthful impetuous spontaneity. I understand he is not yet twenty, and covers as many as three canvases a day.'

In 1912, *Yo Picasso* was acquired by the great Austrian poet and librettist Hugo von Hofmannsthal, using the proceeds of his first royalties from his opera *Der Rosenkavalier*, written in collaboration with Strauss.

Pablo Picasso
YO PICASSO
Signed and inscribed *Yo*,
1901, 29in by 23⅞in
(73.7cm by 60.6cm)
New York $47,850,000
(£28,652,694). 9.V.89

Georges Braque
TETE DE FEMME
Charcoal and collage, signed on the reverse at a later date, 1912, 24in by 18½in (61cm by 47cm)
London £2,420,000 ($4,017,200). 28.VI.89

Fernand Léger
MOTEUR II
Signed, titled and dated *11-18* on the reverse, 18⅛in by 21¼in (46cm by 54cm)
London £1,320,000 ($2,389,200). 4.IV.89

This painting is a smaller, horizontal version of *Moteur I* of 1918. A year later Léger used the same mechanical elements but this time added the figure of the mechanic on the right hand side and titled it *Le Mécanicien*. The *Moteur* paintings have been described as the culmination of the machine themes of 1918.

Gino Severini
PRINTEMPS A MONTMARTRE
Signed and dated *MCMIX;* titled and inscribed *ce tableau est de moi et a été fait en 1909 à Paris G. Severini*
on the reverse, 28⅜in by 23⅝in (72cm by 60cm)
London £770,000 ($1,393,700). 4.IV.89

Opposite
Alexandra Exter
COMPOSITION (GENOA)
Signed in Cyrillic, 1912, 45½in by 34in (115.5cm by 86.5cm)
London £759,000 ($1,373,790). 6.IV.89

Wassily Kandinsky
HERBSTLANDSCHAFT
Signed and dated *1911*, 28in by 39in (71.1cm by 99cm)
New York $3,960,000 (£2,371,257). 9.V.89
From the collection of Lora F. Marx

This painting, also known as *Herbst I,* is an important work in the development of Kandinsky's
new form of pictorial expression. It was painted in 1911 during the time the artist lived in
Murnau, near Munich; a transitional period in his career when he was formulating ideas
that would eventually lead to abstraction.

Oskar Kokoschka
DRESDEN, NEUSTADT I
Signed with initials, 1919, 32in by 44⅛in (81.3cm by 112cm)
New York $2,970,000 (£1,778,443). 9.V.89
From the collection of the Art Institute of Chicago

Kokoschka arrived in Dresden in December 1916 for medical treatment but it was not until
August 1918 that he signed a contract for a professorship at the Dresden Academy to run for
seven years. In the autumn he moved into a new studio at the Brühlsche Terrasse above the
River Elbe from which he painted a number of views. This series of city-scapes was to be
among Kokoschka's most popular works in the ensuing years.

Opposite
Pablo Picasso
TETE DE FEMME
Pastel, signed, 24⅜in by 18⅞in (62cm by 48cm)
London £4,070,000 ($7,895,800). 29.XI.88

Amedeo Modigliani
L'HOMME AU VERRE DE VIN
Signed, *circa* 1918–19, 36⅜in by 21½in (92.5cm by 54.5cm)
London £3,520,000 ($5,808,000). 27.VI.89

Modigliani spent a considerable proportion of his working life in cafés and on café terraces, but this is the only known painting of such a subject.

Odilon Redon
THE BIRTH OF VENUS
Signed, 1912, 56½in by 24½in
(143.5cm by 62.2cm)
New York $1,650,000 (£988,024). 9.V.89
From the collection of the Kimbell Art
Foundation

Marc Chagall
FLEURS DANS LA RUE (LA MAISON DE MON ENFANCE)
Signed and dated *1935*, 35½in by 46in (90.2cm by 116.7cm)
London £2,090,000 ($3,448,500). 27.VI.89

In paintings of this period Chagall often placed bunches and vases of flowers in the middle of
street scenes or shooting out of the sky. Here the street is reminiscent of Vitebsk where
Chagall spent his childhood.

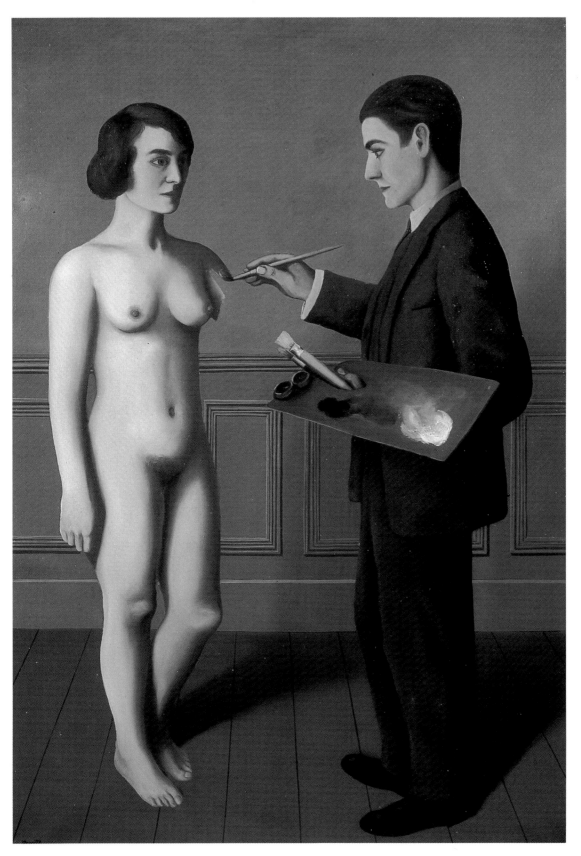

René Magritte
TENTATIVE DE
L'IMPOSSIBLE
Titled on the
reverse, 1928,
45½in by 31⅞in
(115.5cm by
81.1cm)
London £880,000
($1,452,000).
27.VI.89

Opposite
Gustave de Smet
LE CANAPE BLEU
Signed, 1928,
57in by 45¼in
(145cm by 115cm)
London £550,000
($913,000).
28.VI.89

Joan Miró
MURAL (FOR JOAQUIM GOMIS)
Oil on fibre-cement, 1948, 49¼in by 98⅜in (125cm by 250cm)
Madrid Ptas385,696,000 (£1,911,752: $3,026,253). 7.VI.89

Opposite
Pablo Picasso
PORTRAIT DE JACQUELINE
A unique hand-painted and glazed ceramic plate, dated *10.2.56.IV;* stamped *Madoura Plein Feu* on the
reverse, diameter 9⅞in (25cm)
London £68,200 ($126,170). 19.X.88

Picasso produced some of the most innovative twentieth-century ceramics. It was in 1946
that he befriended Georges and Suzanne Ramié, who owned and ran the Madoura pottery
at Vallauris. The following summer he took up working with ceramics seriously, setting up a
studio for himself with the Ramié family and working there regularly until 1966.

   The strength of Picasso's ceramics lay not only in his ability to use his techniques, material
and shapes to create his pottery, but in the way he transformed a plate, pot or vase into a
painting or sculpture without losing sight of the object with which he was working.

Paintings from the collection of Mr and Mrs Victor W. Ganz

Twelve paintings – six by Picasso and two each by Jasper Johns, Robert Rauschenberg and Frank Stella – were selected for the sale in November 1988 in New York to convey the unique character of the Ganz collection, a group that is widely acknowledged as one of the finest and most idiosyncratic collections of twentieth-century art. In the depth of his commitment to a small number of artists, Victor Ganz differed significantly from the great majority of collectors whose aims are more encyclopedic. Mr Ganz purchased the first work, the poetic *Dream* by Picasso, in 1941, and focused on that artist exclusively for the next twenty years, building a collection that is unmatched in its depth and quality. Nonetheless, he also maintained a keen interest in the development of contemporary American art, ultimately incorporating works by Johns, Rauschenberg, Stella and several younger artists – Eva Hesse, Mel Bochner and Dorothea Rockburne among them – from the 1960s onwards. Significantly, these young Americans did not supplant the Spanish Colossus; rather the perspectives they provided added depth to the character of the original collection.

The Picassos in the sale encompassed aspects of his work from the 1920s to the late 1950s. The earliest, *La Cage d'Oiseaux* (Fig. 1), painted in Paris in 1923, is a major statement of the theme of a still life in an interior that the artist had previously treated on a much smaller scale and in gouache. In the intricacy of its geometry and its high-keyed palette, the painting may be seen as the culmination of the Synthetic Cubist style, a manner that was largely superseded as Picasso's later still lifes became increasingly curvilinear and decorative.

Three of the other Picassos date from the 1950s. Vital precursors of what is now viewed as a genuine late style rather than a sad decline, these paintings bear testimony to the amazing vitality of Picasso's art even in his seventies. *Les Femmes d'Alger*, 1954, (Fig. 2) is a variation on the painting by Delacroix that had long fascinated Picasso; Françoise Gilot recalls that he often took her to the Louvre to look at it. As early as 1940 he made studies of the composition and individual figures and of the colours but it was not until December 1954, however, that Picasso began the first of his studies of the painting. The death of Matisse and the resemblance between Jacqueline Roque and the woman seated on the right in Delacroix's masterpiece have been cited as catalysts in Picasso's decision to undertake a series of variations on this theme; he ultimately produced fifteen canvases and two lithographs. Victor Ganz purchased the entire group from Galerie Louise Leiris in June 1956, and this version, painted on 28th December was the third in the suite. Entirely different in style was the multifaceted *Femme Nue Assise* of 1959 (Fig. 3) which in its inventiveness and humour surely ranks with Picasso's work at its very best.

Fig.1
Pablo Picasso
LA CAGE D'OISEAUX
Signed, 1923,
79¼in by 55¼in
(201.3cm by 140.3cm)
New York $15,400,000
(£8,651,685). 10.XI.88
From the collection of
Mr and Mrs Victor W.
Ganz

Left
Fig. 2
Pablo Picasso
LES FEMMES D'ALGER
(VERSION 'C')
Signed; dated *28 Dec. 54* on
the reverse, 21¼in by 25⅝in
(54cm by 65cm)
New York $962,500
(£540,730). 10.XI.88
From the collection of
Mr and Mrs Victor W.
Ganz

Representing the second phase of Mr Ganz's collecting were works of comparable significance by Rauschenberg, Johns and Stella. Each of these artists in his own way is indebted to Picasso. In their treatment of surface and use of collage and 'found' objects, both Johns and Rauschenberg recall Picasso's innovations with *papier collés* whereas Stella's Polish village series reveals a strong debt to Synthetic Cubism.

Both *Rebus*, 1955 (Fig.4), and *Winter Pool*, 1959, aptly evoke Rauschenberg's famous comment 'Painting relates to both art and life. Neither can be made. (I try to act in the gap between the two).' Both are known as 'combine' paintings, works which combine the various materials and techniques of contemporary painting – dripped paint, collage cloth, comic strips, photographs and so forth. Widely considered a seminal work in Rauschenberg's career, *Rebus* can be seen as a turning point in the 'combine' series in which the imagery has become more impersonal and less nostalgic. No central image dominates the painting. Instead the individual elements and images function like those of a rebus to build an overall notion of content, image by image or syllable by syllable. *Winter Pool* is an example of Rauschenberg's mature combine paintings of the late 1950s in which he introduced 'found' objects – doors, chairs, stuffed birds, coke bottles and tyres. The ladder functions both as a recognizable object and as an element in the formal composition, perhaps occupying Rauschenberg's gap between life and art.

Opposite
Fig. 3
Pablo Picasso
FEMME NUE ASSISE
Signed; dated
*14.2.59/18.2.59/19.22/
8.-9.-3.-59* on reverse,
1959, 57½in by 45in
(146cm by 114.3cm)
New York $6,050,000
(£3,398,876). 10.XI.88
From the collection of
Mr and Mrs Victor W.
Ganz

Jasper Johns's *Grey Rectangles* (Fig.5) belongs to a series of monochromatic grey paintings that began with works such as *Tango* in 1955. Yet, as Roberta Bernstein points out (see pp 144–49), the subtle introduction of colour at the edges of the inset canvases makes it a transitional work in his œuvre, an early step towards the vibrant paintings of 1959 in which colour becomes the subject of the work.

As a collector, Victor Ganz was recognized for his exceptional eye and the group of paintings he chose has a remarkable coherence. David Sylvester has noted their dark palette and their difficult, inaccessible, even violent character. But more telling is his observation that all the artists who interested Mr Ganz 'made or make art which is notable for its powerful interplay between a passionate intensity and a very sharp intelligence.'

Fig. 4
Robert Rauschenberg
REBUS
Oil, pencil, fabric and paper collage on canvas, 1955, 96in by 131in (243.8cm by 332.7cm)
New York $6,325,000 (£3,553,371). 10.XI.88
From the collection of Mr and Mrs Victor W. Ganz

Fig. 5
Jasper Johns
GREY RECTANGLES
Encaustic on canvas, 1957, 60in by 60in (152.4cm by 152.4cm)
New York $4,290,000 (£2,410,112). 10.XI.88
From the collection of Mr and Mrs Victor W. Ganz

Contemporary art

Morris Louis
UNTITLED
Magna on canvas, 1959–60, 98¼in by 140½in (249.5cm by 356.9cm)
New York $1,017,500 (£571,629). 10.XI.88

Frank Stella
QUATHLAMBA
Metallic powder in polymer emulsion on canvas, 1964, 77½in by 178¾in (196.9cm by 454cm)
New York $1,320,000 (£785,714). 2.V.89
From the collection of Carter Burden

Lucio Fontana
LAGUNA DI VENEZIA
Signed and titled on the reverse, 1961, 59in by 59in (150cm by 150cm)
London £396,000 ($772,000). 1.XII.88

Opposite
Jackson Pollock
NUMBER 8, 1950
Oil, enamel and aluminium paint on canvas mounted on board, signed; signed, titled and dated *50* on
the reverse, 56in by 39in (142.2cm by 99cm)
New York $11,550,000 (£6,875,000). 2.V.89

Jasper Johns:
False Start, 1959

Roberta Bernstein

Jasper Johns
(Photograph by Lizzie
Himmel).

Fig. 1
Jasper Johns
FALSE START
1959, 67½in by 53in
(171.5cm by 134.7cm)
New York $17,050,000
(£9,578,652). 10.XI.88
From the collection of
Mr and Mrs François de
Menil

'False Start' is a brilliant title for a painting so full of new ideas. Its self-disparaging tone immediately contradicts the confident, celebratory aura of the painting's multi-coloured, explosive surface. An additional ironic twist comes from *False Start*'s pivotal role in a body of work where Johns deliberately set out to break the very habits that led to the instant recognition he received after his first exhibition at the Leo Castelli Gallery in 1958. A 'false start' means jumping the gun at the start of a race, with all the tension and anticipatory excitement such a move suggests. Given Johns's new-found prominence in the New York art world, it is not insignificant that he chose a title implying competition and that he took it from a racing print he saw at the Cedar Street Tavern, an artist's bar identified with Abstract Expressionism, the style his work was seen to reject. Further, the word 'false' fits perfectly with the way Johns used words to confuse the viewer's perception of what is 'true' and 'false' regarding colour, the painting's main theme.

False Start (Fig. 1) appears initially to contradict everything Johns held sacred in his earlier works. Yet in it, he initiates a way to expand his political vocabulary without undermining the integrity of the art object he had established during the past five

years. This change required opening up the range of colour and allowing his brush-work more fluidity and flexibility. The extent of the break from his early encaustics is evident when *False Start* is compared with *Grey Rectangles*, 1957 (see Fig. 5; p. 139). Here the entire surface is covered in a subtly modulated grey, Johns's preferred monochrome, used to reinforce the literalness of his paintings and to avoid what he called 'all the emotional and dramatic quality of colour.' Each of the three small panels set into the larger canvas is painted in a primary colour that, upon close inspection, shows through the grey. Red, yellow, and blue are established early on by Johns, as by Mondrian, to impart an objective look to his art. The short, tight brushstrokes reinforce the mute flatness of the surface, while the inserted panels establish the painting as a self-contained, three-dimensional construction.

False Start, Johns's first major oil painting and his first with a non-descriptive title, is done with a kind of open, gestural brushwork that signals a new approach to marking the surface. For the first time, there is no predetermined design to organise and unify the surface. Here, Johns rejects the ordered, symmetrical, and complete compositions characteristic of his previous work and instead creates an all-over, amorphous composition of agitated brushstrokes and misaligned words, cropped at the edges. He also moves away from his rigorous position of defining the painting as object by using only literal space. In *False Start*, a layer of illusionist space is created by overlapping and intersecting brushstrokes and advancing and receding colours. Even the printed words that establish the flatness of the canvas surface simultaneously participate in the spatial illusionism by interacting with the brushstrokes whose colours, scale, and placement they parallel. This new approach to picture space has to do with Johns's evolving exploration of the nature of painting by casting doubt on its status as object. From this point on, the issue of what is real and what is illusionary takes on a more complex presence in Johns's art.

In *False Start* Johns openly acknowledges the central role of colour in painting. In doing so, he lets loose with the range of colour and applies paint freely throughout the surface. Building on his earlier language paintings of alphabets and words, Johns introduces their names. The stencilled words, printed with varying degrees of legibility, add a strong conceptual dimension that is played against the sensuous and expressive impact of the painted surface. What appears initially to be an arbitrary interplay of colours and words is actually a calculated scheme with purposefully ambivalent relationships between the two, creating what Max Kozloff called 'a tissue of conflicts between what is read and what is seen'.

False Start includes the full complement of primaries and secondaries and black, white and grey, a scheme Johns has since employed with variations in both encaustics and oils. However, those that predominate are his 'classical' red, yellow, and blue, along with orange, a colour he had used in two *Flags on Orange Field*, 1957 and 1958, and a small oil, *Alley Oop*, 1958. Of the neutral tones, grey and white appear most, with fewer traces of black, green and violet. The number of times a colour's name is repeated corresponds approximately to its predominance in the painting, to the extent that only the 'v' of 'violet' and the 'b' of 'black' are found among the words. Overall, the words function as labels and in some cases words even label specific areas, such as 'blue' on blue (near the lower right). However, the relationship of words to colours intentionally confuses what the eye and mind perceive as 'true' and 'false'. Most of the names are printed across patches of different colours such as 'red' against blue or 'blue' against orange. In addition, the letters of the words themselves

Fig. 3
Jasper Johns
PERISCOPE (HART CRANE)
1963, 67in by 48in (170.2cm by 121.9cm)
(Reproduced courtesy of the Leo Castelli
Gallery).

participate in the complicated interplay, since all possible combinations are presented, including 'white' in red on yellow, 'blue' in blue on blue, and so forth.

Johns's involvement with the art and thought of Marcel Duchamp starting in 1958/59 is an important factor in many new directions in his work at this point, including a more intensified focus on language. In a 1960 review, Johns wrote that the notes for the *Large Glass* reveal Duchamp's 'brilliantly inventive questioning of visual, mental and verbal focus and order'. It is this aspect of Duchamp's work that reinforced Johns's own interest in using words to explore the interaction of the visual and conceptual aspects of perception.

False Start initiates Johns's focus on colour present in other works of the same year. In a black and white companion piece to *False Start*, called *Jubilee* (Fig. 2), he tackles a colour scheme favoured by the Abstract Expressionists, and one he had earlier avoided, because, as he said, 'Black and white is very leading. It tells you what to do or say.' In *Jubilee*, Johns makes the viewer more aware of the mental pictures words evoke, because only 'black', 'white', and 'grey' function as labels, while the other colours named in the painting are present only in the barest traces, if at all. The pairing of *False Start* and *Jubilee* recalls Duchamp's suggestion 'to reach the impossibility of sufficient visual memory to transfer from one like object to another the memory imprint,' a passage from Duchamp's notes, cited by Johns in a published statement from 1959. While the two paintings look initially as if they are 'like objects', one with colour, one without, their surface details are completely different. Johns has made no attempt to imitate the brushstrokes nor the placement of words from one to the other. In Johns's next painting with colour names, *Out the Window*, the all-over arrangement of words in *False Start* and *Jubilee* is abandoned for a more

Fig. 4
Jasper Johns
DECOY II
1972, 47in by 29½in (119.4cm by 74.9cm)
(Reproduced courtesy of the Leo Castelli
Gallery).

structured format where the words, 'red', 'yellow', and 'blue' appear only once, each centred in its own horizontal panel. Another 1959 painting, *Thermometer*, calls attention to properties associated with colour, as the real thermometer fictively measures the 'temperature' of the painting's 'warm' and 'cool' colours.

False Start marks the beginning of many new directions for Johns, some taken up immediately, others later. The most important image spawned by *False Start* is that of the colour names which become a central motif for the artist during the next decade. By the mid 1960s, the words 'red', 'yellow', and 'blue' are so identified with the artist that he uses them to frame his photograph in the two *Souvenir* paintings from 1964. The primary colour names are used in a series of works that include *Periscope (Hart Crane)*, 1963 (Fig. 3), where the words continue to focus on the idea of colour, but become expressive devices as well, as they float in space, flip upside-down and backwards, and fly out of the field, while letters shift scale, replicate themselves, and fall apart. Although the format of *Out the Window* serves as the basis for this series, it is the disorientation and fragmentation of words in *False Start* that foretells the break up of structure found in *Periscope* and the other paintings in this group. By the time the colour names appear for the last time in *Decoy II*, 1972 (Fig. 4), they form part of a complex, self-referential painting, whose title, like *False Start*, calls attention to what is true and false. By now the full spectrum of primary and secondary colour names has been reintroduced and the words have gone through many incarnations as printed signs, three-dimensional objects, and photographic reproductions. *Decoy* serves as a summarising piece, a coda perhaps, for the myriad devices Johns had employed since *False Start* in his continuing inquiry into the fundamental issues of the relationship between art and reality.

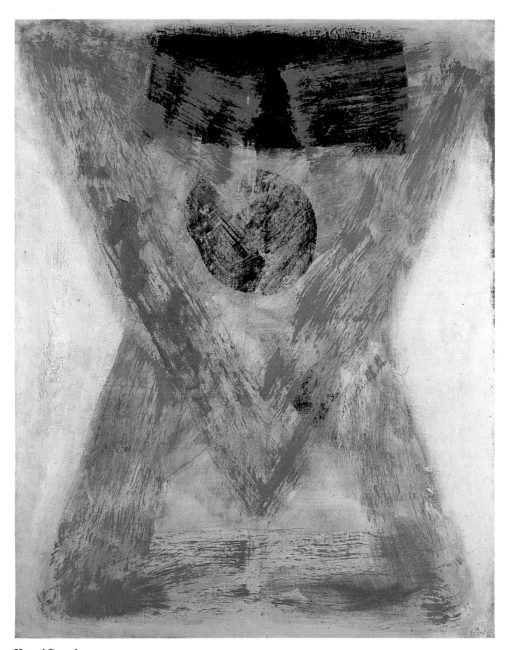

Kumi Sugai
YOROKOBI
Signed and dated '59; signed, titled and dated *1959* on the reverse, 67in by 51in (170cm by 129.5cm)
London £88,000 ($139,000). 29.VI.89

Opposite
Jean Dubuffet
LE PRINCIPE DANSANT DE L'HOURLOUPE
Signed and dated '63; signed, titled and dated *Aout '63* on the reverse, 78in by 59in
(198.2cm by 149.8cm)
London £858,000 ($1,356,000). 29.VI.89

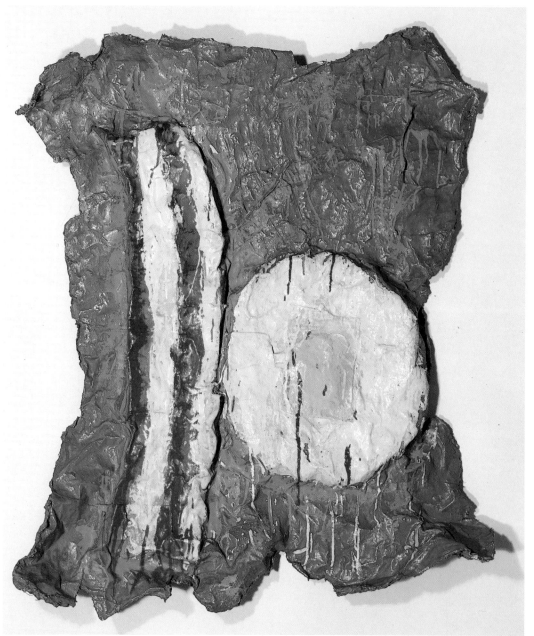

Opposite
Alberto Burri
BIANCO
Mixed media, collage and
oil on canvas, signed on the
reverse, 1952,
39in by 33⅞in
(99cm by 86cm)
London
£440,000 ($695,000).
29.VI.89

Claes Oldenburg
BACON AND EGG
Muslin and fabric soaked in plaster over wire frame, painted with enamel, signed with initials and
dated *1961*; signed with initials and dated *1961* on the reverse,
42½in by 35in by 6½in (108cm by 88.9cm by 16.5cm)
New York $495,000 (£294,643). 2.V.89
From the collection of the late Karl Ströher

Opposite
Francis Bacon
STUDY FOR PORTRAIT OF
VAN GOGH II
Inscribed *On the Road to Tarascon* on
the reverse, 1957, 78in by 56in
(198cm by 142.3cm)
New York $5,830,000
(£3,470,238). 2.V.89
From the collection of the late
Edwin Janss, Jr

Andy Warhol
MARILYN MONROE (TWENTY TIMES)
Synthetic polymer hand-painted
and silk-screened on canvas, signed
and dated *62* on the reverse,
76¾in by 44¾in
(195cm by 113.7cm)
New York $3,960,000
(£2,224,719). 10.XI.88
From the collection of Mr and Mrs
François de Menil

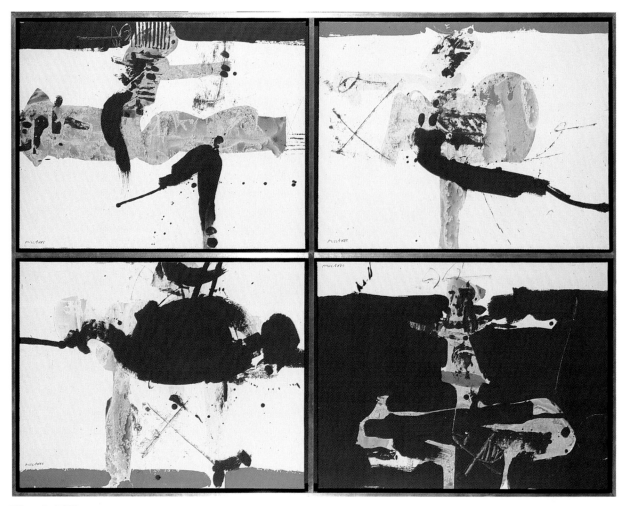

Manolo Millares
LES QUATRE GENERAUX
Gouache on paper laid down on canvas, each signed, 1966, each panel 19⅝in by 25⅛in (50cm by 64cm)
London £121,000 ($203,000). 25.V.89

Opposite
Hans Hartung
T 56-13
Signed and dated '*56*; titled on the stretcher, 70⅞in by 54in (180cm by 137cm)
London £286,000 ($452,000). 29.VI.89

Opposite
David Hockney
A GRAND PROCESSION OF
DIGNITARIES IN THE
SEMI-EGYPTIAN STYLE
Signed, titled and dated
1961, 84in by 144in
(213.4cm by 365.8cm)
New York $2,200,000
(£1,309,524). 2.V.89
From the collection of the
late Edwin Janss, Jr

Lucian Freud
GIRL IN A WHITE DRESS
Conté crayon and pastel on buff paper, 1947, 22⅜in by 18⅞in (57cm by 48cm)
London £308,000 ($487,000). 29.VI.89

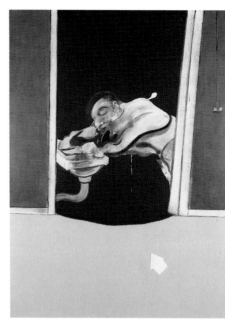

Francis Bacon
TRIPTYCH MAY-JUNE
Signed, titled and dated *1973* on the reverse of each panel, each panel 78in by 58in (198.1cm by 147.3cm)
New York $6,270,000 (£3,732,143). 2.V.89
From the collection of Saul P. Steinberg

American art

Frederic E. Church
HOME BY THE LAKE (SCENE IN THE CATSKILL MOUNTAINS)
Signed and dated *1852*, 32in by 48¼in (81.3cm by 122.6cm)
New York $8,250,000 (£5,254,777). 24.V.89
From the collection of the Walker Art Center

Opposite, above
Albert Bierstadt
PLATTE RIVER, NEBRASKA
Signed and dated *1863*, 36in by 57½in (91.4cm by 146cm)
New York $2,640,000 (£1,681,529). 24.V.89
From the collection of the Jones Library, Inc.

Below
George Inness
DELAWARE WATER GAP
Signed with monogrammed initials and dated *1857*, 32in by 52in (81.3cm by 132cm)
New York $935,000 (£595,541). 24.V.89

Martin Johnson Heade
HUMMINGBIRDS AND PASSION FLOWERS
Signed, *circa* 1875–85,
20in by 12¼in (50.8cm by 31.1cm)
New York $1,100,000 (£700,637). 24.V.89

Opposite
John Frederick Peto
THE WRITER'S TABLE: A PRECARIOUS MOMENT
Signed and dated '92,
27½in by 22¼in (69.9cm by 56.5cm)
New York $418,000 (£225,946). 1.XII.88

William Merritt Chase
YOUNG GIRL ON AN OCEAN STEAMER
Pastel on paper, signed and stamped *P.P*, *circa* 1884, 29in by 24in (73.7cm by 61cm)
New York $836,000 (£451,892). 1.XII.88

John Singer Sargent, RA
THE HON. MRS CHARLES RUSSELL
Signed and dated *1900*, 41⅜in by 29⅛in (105cm by 74cm)
London £418,000 ($798,380). 22.XI.88
From the collection of Sir Charles Russell

New York in the 1890s: the cityscapes of Childe Hassam

Kathleen Burnside

Childe Hassam (Reproduced courtesy of the archives of the American Academy and Institute of Arts and Letters, New York).

Fig. 1
Childe Hassam
BROADWAY AND MADISON SQUARE, FROM A BALCONY, IN MAY
Signed and dated *1890*, 14in by 10¾in (35.6cm by 27.3cm)
New York $1,265,000 (£683,784). 1.XII.88

In an interview with A.E. Ives in *The Art Amateur* (October 1892), Childe Hassam described his predilection for painting the urban street scene:

There is nothing so interesting to me as people. I am never tired of observing them in every-day life, as they hum through the streets on business or saunter down the promenade on pleasure. Humanity in motion is a continual study to me. The scientific draughtsman who works long and patiently may learn to draw correctly from a model a figure in repose; but it takes an artist to catch the spirit, life, I might say poetry, of figures in motion.

His interest in capturing the vitality of the city is evident throughout his career, from the evocative renditions of his native Boston, executed during the mid-1880s, such as his *Boston Common at Twilight* (Museum of Fine Arts, Boston), to the flag series, a group of vivid Impressionist renderings of the liberty parades held along Fifth Avenue in New York during World War I.

Many of Hassam's most beautiful and inventive works in this genre were painted in New York during the 1890s, just after his return from three years of study in Paris. Two superb examples were sold at Sotheby's in December 1988: *Broadway and Madison Square, from a balcony in May*, 1890 (Fig. 1), and *A Spring Morning, circa* 1890–91 (Fig. 2). Individually these works present two distinct aspects of the artist's Impressionism and together, they convey the prosperity and optimism that prevailed

in America in the late nineteenth century, a spirit that was especially concentrated in New York and perhaps best captured by Hassam.

Drawing upon the precedents set by such artists as Edgar Degas and Gustave Caillebotte, as well as J.A.M. Whistler, Hassam developed an urban genre that was compared in its time to the work of Jean Béraud, Giuseppe de Nittis, and Jean François Raffaelli, as well as to the paintings of Edouard Manet and Claude Monet. In style and subject, Hassam's New York cityscapes were an extension of the paintings and watercolours he had executed in Paris between 1886 and 1889. While receiving instruction in drawing at the Académie Julien, he also began to produce an independent body of work that depicted the genteel and picturesque of Parisian life: the flower sellers and shopkeepers of Montmartre, the public parks, and the broad boulevards crowded with four-in-hand carriages.

During the 1890s, Hassam rendered more than fifty images of Manhattan's streets and parks. These scenes were overwhelmingly centred in the most elegant and fashionable sections of New York in the Gilded Age – Lower Fifth Avenue, Washington and Madison Squares, and the esplanades and by-ways of Central Park. Although other American painters of this period such as William Merritt Chase and Paul Cornoyer focused on aspects of city life, perhaps no other artist was as strongly identified with this genre as Hassam. In these works, he merged his virtuoso technique with a driving desire to depict what was, in his words, 'aesthetic and fitting' in modern urban life.

Four such canvases were presented at the 1890 Autumn Exhibition of the National Academy of Design, and two were singled out by a reviewer in *The Critic* (29th November 1890):

Mr Childe Hassam, who, for some years, has been experimenting on our city streets, scores a success in his 'Winter Morning, Union Square' . . . His 'Broadway and Madison Square, from a balcony, in May', with its string of red umbrellas swaying in the breeze from the cornice of a high building, its red geraniums and blue hydrangeas in the balcony in the foreground, is nearly as good.

Broadway and Madison Square, subsequently acquired by a New York family, was not exhibited again until it appeared at Sotheby's last December. It is a view looking north across Madison Square with the bustling traffic of Broadway and Fifth Avenue looming in the distance. Across the square is Worth Monument, an obelisk erected in 1858 to commemorate General William Worth, a hero of the Mexican War. Behind stands the Victoria Hotel, which, along with the Fifth Avenue Hotel, the Brunswick, and several others, made Madison Square the centre of elegant hostelry. The red umbrellas which provide such a pleasing visual accent at the right of the canvas are actually a type of awning commonly seen on hotels at that time.

Although Hassam had occasionally adopted a raised vantage point in his earlier cityscapes of Boston and Paris, it was not until the 1890s that he began to produce a more panoramic vision of the city. Together with *Spring Morning in the Heart of the City*, 1890 (Metropolitan Museum of Art) and *Union Square in Spring*, 1896 (Smith College Museum of Art), *Broadway and Madison Square* is one of a select group that illustrates the artist's experiments with a more expansive city view.

Fig. 2
Childe Hassam
A SPRING MORNING
Signed, *circa* 1890-91,
27½in by 20in
(69.8cm by 50.8cm)
New York $2,310,000
(£1,248,649). 1.XII.88
From the collection of
Jean Cullen

Beyond providing the means for portraying New York as a potent symbol of the modern city, these elevated views also supplied a compositional technique that was an ideal vehicle for Hassam's style of Impressionism. Although he frequently denied the direct influence of his French predecessors, preferring to align himself with the English landscape tradition of Constable and Turner, the artist's mature style, characterised by broken strokes and use of pure pigments, undoubtedly reflects his response to their work. In particular, the fluid and free translation of nature into paint exhibited in *Broadway and Madison Square, from a balcony, in May* marks one of his most daring uses of oil. Its inventiveness and success within the Impressionist idiom may be rivalled only by a series of watercolours, including *Flower Garden, Isles of Shoals* (Fig. 3), executed during the same period at the rural retreat of Appledore Island, off the Maine–New Hampshire coast.

In contrast to the verve and excitement of Hassam's bird's-eye views are works such as *A Spring Morning*, which exhibit a more static and controlled Impressionism, equally typical of the artist. In the degree of finish, compositional strategy and cheerful vernal palette *A Spring Morning* compares directly to several other major New York canvases, notably to *The Washington Arch*, 1890 (Phillips Collection, Washington, DC). Through its direct, almost frontal point of veiw, *A Spring Morning* creates an iconic emblem of genteel urban life in the Gilded Age. Elegantly dressed women descend the steps of a townhouse on 20th Street, near Fifth Avenue, and cross the side-walk to their waiting carriage. Rising above them is the gold-domed roof that crowned the Sixth Avenue store of Hugh O'Neill, who first owned and quite possibly may have commissioned the painting. There can be few images that celebrate the wealth and optimism of New York more fully than this highly finished, brilliantly painted canvas.

Hassam's views of New York in the 1890s were greeted by a particularly receptive audience. During this period, America began to understand its strength fully and to trumpet its coming of age as a world power. As Albert Stevens Crockett noted in *Peacocks on Parade*, published in 1931, 'For decades we had been boasting but on unproved bases. Now we knew. We began to be sure of ourselves. We had something to boast about. An industrial giant had obtained manhood.' This national self-awareness was mirrored and intensified in New York, the pre-eminent commercial centre of an industrial country. Contemporary publications, especially popular illustrated magazines such as *Harper's Weekly* and *Scribner's Magazine* (for which Hassam did a significant amount of artwork during the 1890s), repeatedly record evidence of the rise of New York as a cosmopolitan centre. Hardly an article on the rapid development of the city appeared without an implicit or explicit comparison to the important cities of Europe.

Hassam himself joined in this surge of comparative publications when *Three Cities by Childe Hassam*, a folio volume of his views of New York, Paris and London appeared in 1899. In works such as *Spring Morning* and *Broadway and Madison Square*, he succeeded in translating the urban Impressionist conception he had honed in France into a language with strong nationalistic appeal. Hassam was thus able to create a vision of New York as a sophisticated international city, one that fully supported his conviction that 'the thoroughfares of the great French metropolis are not one whit more interesting than the streets of New York.'

Fig. 3
Childe Hassam
FLOWER GARDEN, ISLES OF SHOALS
Watercolour, signed and dated *1893*, 19½in by 13¾in (49.5cm by 34.9cm)
New York $803,000 (£434,054). 1.XII.88

Worthington Whittredge
SECOND BEACH, NEWPORT
Signed, *circa* 1878–80, 30¼in by 50¼in (76.8cm by 127.6cm)
New York $1,870,000 (£1,191,083). 24.V.89
From the collection of the Walker Art Center

Opposite, above
William Merritt Chase
GRAVESEND BAY
Pastel on paper mounted on canvas, signed, *circa* 1888, 20in by 30in (50.8cm by 76.2cm)
New York $2,200,000 (£1,189,189). 1.XII.88

Below
William Merritt Chase
ALONG THE PATH AT SHINNECOCK
Oil on panel, signed, *circa* 1896, 12in by 18in (30.5cm by 45.7cm)
New York $1,100,000 (£700,637). 24.V.89

Edward H. Potthast
AT ROCKAWAY BEACH
Signed; titled on the stretcher, 24¼in by 30in (61.6cm by 76.2cm)
New York $253,000 (£136,757). 1.XII.88
From the collection of Lewis C. Thomson

Opposite, above
Maurice B. Prendergast
TELEGRAPH HILL
Watercolour and pencil on paper, signed; titled and numbered on the reverse, *circa* 1896–97,
14in by 20¾in (35.6cm by 52.7cm)
New York $1,870,000 (£1,191,083). 24.V.89

Below
Maurice B. Prendergast
SUNSET
Signed, *circa* 1917, 21in by 32in (53.3cm by 81.3cm)
New York $1,815,000 (£1,156,051). 24.V.89

Georgia O'Keeffe
YELLOW CACTUS FLOWERS
Inscribed *Georgia O'Keeffe, 1929, Yellow Cactus Flower* by Alfred Stieglitz on the backing,
30¼in by 42in (76.8cm by 106.7cm)
New York $1,320,000 (£840,764). 24.V.89
From the collection of the Modern Art Museum of Fort Worth

Opposite
Georgia O'Keeffe
DARK IRIS, NO. 2
Signed with initials and a star, titled and dated *1927* on the backing, 32in by 21in (81.3cm by 53.3cm)
New York $1,650,000 (£1,050,955). 24.V.89

Latin American, Canadian and Australian art

José Maria Velasco
ORIZABA MORNING
Signed and dated *Mexico 1892*, 40⅛in by 63in (102cm by 160cm)
New York $341,000 (£207,927). 16.V.89

Diego Rivera
NUDE WITH FLOWERS
Signed and dated *1944*, 62¼in by 47in (158cm by 119.4cm)
New York $440,000 (£268,293). 16.V.89

Lawren Stewart Harris
TORONTO HOUSES, AUTUMN
Oil on board, *circa* 1915,
15¾in by 19¾in
(40cm by 50.2cm)
Toronto CN $71,500
(£37,240:$60,084).
17.V.89

Alexander Young Jackson
NORTHERN LANDSCAPE
Signed, *circa* 1939,
41in by 49¾in
(104.1cm by 126.4cm)
Toronto CN $187,000
(£97,396:$157,143).
17.V.89

**Arthur Merric
Bloomfield Boyd**
THE SEASONS
Signed and dated '44,
24⅜in by 28⅞in
(62cm by 73.5cm)
Melbourne Aus$220,000
(£104,662:$178,862).
17.IV.89

Sir Sidney Nolan
THE KELLY GANG
Signed; titled and dated 1945 on the reverse, with sketches of Ned
Kelly's head and gun, 29⅞in by 24¾in (76cm by 63cm)
Sydney Aus $110,000 (£51,887:$94,502). 17.XI.88

Prints

Rembrandt Harmensz. van Rijn
ST JEROME BESIDE A POLLARD WILLOW
Etching and drypoint, second state of two, 1648, 7in by 5⅛in (17.9cm by 13.1cm)
New York $137,500 (£82,335). 11.V.89
Formerly in the collection of Theodore Irwin

Hendrik Goltzius
HERCULES AND CACUS
Chiaroscuro woodcut, early impression of the second state of four, 1588, $16\frac{1}{8}$in by $12\frac{7}{8}$in (41cm by 32.8cm)
London £58,300 ($96,195). 27.VI.89

Paul Signac
LES BATEAUX A FLESSINGE
Lithograph printed in colours, third state of four, signed in pencil and numbered *12*, 1895,
12¾in by 15⅞in (32.3cm by 40.2cm)
London £26,400 ($51,216). 2.XII.89

Opposite
Paul Gauguin
L'ESPRIT VEILLE
Traced monotype printed in black and ochre, signed in pencil with a drawing on the *verso* in graphite
shaded with blue crayon, *circa* 1900, sheet size 25in by 19⅞in (63.7cm by 50.5cm)
London £308,000 ($597,520). 2.XII.88

Maurice B. Prendergast
PARK PROMENADE
Colour monotype, 1901,
sheet size approximately
10in by $7\frac{7}{8}$in
(25.5cm by 20cm)
New York $181,500
(£101,966). 3.XI.88

Henri de Toulouse-Lautrec
LA CLOWNESSE ASSISE (MADEMOISELLE CHA-U-KA-O)
Lithograph printed in colours, from the *Elles* series, inscribed in ink *Série no.44*, from the edition of 100,
1896, sheet size 20¾in by 15⅞in (52.7cm by 40.5cm)
New York $330,000 (£185,393). 4.XI.88

Joan Miró
SOMNABULE
Etching, aquatint and carborundum, printed in colours, signed and numbered *HC VIII/XXIV*,
edition of 50, Maeght, Paris, 1974, 44$\frac{7}{8}$in by 29$\frac{3}{8}$in (114cm by 74.7cm)
Barcelona Ptas 15,314,400 (£76,021: $133,053). 22.II.89
From the collection of the Joan Miró Foundation

Joan Miró: the graphic work

Rosa Maria Malet

Within the general context of Joan Miró's artistic production, his graphic works have always held a prime position, not only because of their great number, but also and above all because of their quality. If we add together the 'pochoirs', the lithographs, the etchings and woodcuts and the extensive production of posters, the total number would exceed more than a thousand. Obviously such a quantity would be of no value if it were not for their quality.

It was characteristic of the artist to experiment with all the available techniques. He produced his first eight 'pochoirs' in 1928 to illustrate Lise Hirtz's book *Il était une petite pie*. This technique, using a template on which the parts to be coloured were outlined, was a preliminary step before undertaking the actual process of lithography or engraving. A year later, in 1929, he attempted his first lithographs, in solid black, to illustrate Tristan Tzara's book *L'Arbre des voyageurs*. In this process the lithographic stone is stained with ink to reproduce an image on the paper.

Four years later, in 1933, Christian Zervos ordered three etchings in black from Miró to illustrate George Hugnet's book of poems *Enfances*. These etchings give a very clear foretaste of his first engravings in which the real protagonist was to be the hand of the artist. Miró worked the copper plate with a burin (engraver's tool), as though he were using a pencil and paper. The result was a representational work that corresponded closely to the narrative.

In 1938 the cubist painter Marcoussis, a friend of Miró's, taught him the drypoint technique. The outcome of this collaboration was the *Self-Portrait* in which the image of the Catalan artist became lost among twisting and turning lines and stars. In the meantime, Miró had already done other 'pochoirs': two in 1934 for the extraordinary number of the review *D'ací d'allà*, dedicated to the art of the twentieth century, and in 1937 the famous *Aidez l'Espagne*, which was used to raise funds in aid of the Republican fighters in the Spanish Civil War. In 1939, just after the end of the civil war, Miró began work on the *Barcelona Series*, comprised of fifty lithographs in black which were not finished until 1944 due to the material difficulties involved in such a vast project. Joan Prats was the editor of the work, considered to be Miró's commentary on the disasters of war. Aggressive figures with pointed teeth, grotesque figures with trunk-shaped noses, arms resembling hooks and sharp-pointed tongues made obvious the repugnance that the recently concluded conflict inspired in the artist.

In 1947 in New York Miró met up with S.W. Hayter, the engraver with whom he had learned the burin technique in Paris. With Hayter he created the drypoints for Tristan Tzara's *L'Antitête*, to which Yves Tanguy and Max Ernst also contributed. Until 1948 Miró had not made coloured lithographs. From this date he used colour

with more and more fluency, until it took over as the major protagonist in his work while black was reserved for creating forms on the white ground of the paper, just as it was used traditionally in drawing. It wasn't until 1950, the year in which he illustrated a book on his own work for the Brazilian diplomat Joao Cabral de Melo, that he used the woodcut technique, a process in which an image was made with an ink-stained piece of boxwood carved in relief. In 1958 he used this technique again for the eighty engravings of Paul Eluard's *A toute épreuve*, doubtless his most ambitious artist's book. His first etchings in colour, *Série I*, were produced in 1952. At this time a wider collaboration began between Miró the engraver, and poets and writers. He illustrated books by Prévert, Ribemont-Dessaignes, René Crevel, Michel Leiris, René Char, Paul Eluard, André Breton, Joan Brossa and writers rehabilitated by the Surrealists such as Alfred Jarry and Lautréamont.

By the end of the 1960s Miró had attained perfect control of the traditional engraving technique; what interested him now was to search for new possibilities to achieve new textures. In 1968, cement casts in relief were used in his engravings, and in 1969, carborundum casts. Once again we can see how Miró's restless mind caused him to reject any stagnating tendencies or desire for easy success. In his last years Miró had an important engraving studio built at San Boter beside his already existing studio Son Abrimes in Palma de Mallorca, where he worked assiduously with Joan Barbarà

Opposite
Joan Miró
SAN FRANCESC D'ASSIS: CANTIC DEL SOL
One of a book of 32 colour etchings, numbered *8*
from an edition of 273, Gustavo Gili, Barcelona,
1975, 13¾in by 19¼in (35cm by 49cm)
Barcelona Ptas 4,991,360 (£24,777:$43,365).
22.II.89
From the collection of the Joan Miró
Foundation

Joan Miró
EQUINOXE
Etching, aquatint and
carborundum, printed in
colours, signed and
inscribed *HC*, edition of 75,
Maeght, Paris, 1967
Barcelona Ptas 14,747,200
(£73,205:$128,125).
22.II.89
From the collection of the
Joan Miró Foundation

in engraving and Damià Caus in lithography. From this studio came the majority of
the graphic works from the final phase of the artist's life.

A significant selection of Miró's lithographs, engravings and artists' books made
up the content of an unprecedented sale which the Joan Miró Foundation organised
on the 22nd of February 1989 under the auspices of Sotheby's. These works exemplified
clearly the phases of the artist's lithographic career outlined above which ran
parallel to his development in painting. In total there were 305 works auctioned, of
which 125 were lithographs, 156 engravings and 23 artists' books. All of them,
original works signed by Miró, were duplicates from the Joan Miró Foundation in
Barcelona, and were acquired from Miró's studio in Palma de Mallorca or the
studios where he worked in Paris and Barcelona.

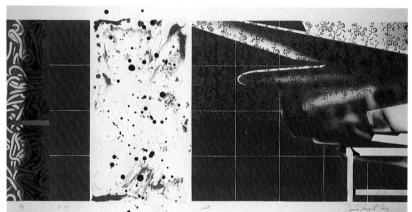

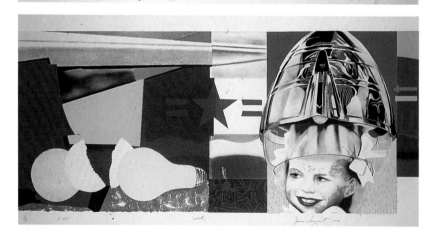

Jasper Johns
FLAG 1
Silkscreen printed in colours, signed in pencil, inscribed *I*, dated *1973*, and numbered *36/65*, published
by the artist and Simca Print Artists, Tokyo, 1973, sheet size approximately 27½in by 35in (70cm by 89cm)
New York $275,000 (£154,494). 5.XI.88

Opposite
James Rosenquist
F1–11 BOMBER: F1–11 (NORTH); F1–11 (SOUTH); F1–11 (EAST); F1–11 (WEST)
Each signed, titled and dated in pencil, numbered *45/75*, 1974, each sheet 36⅝in by 75⅛in (93cm by 191cm)
London £25,300 ($41,998). 28.VI.89

Fig. 1
William Henry Fox Talbot
LAYCOCK ABBEY
Study in the stable-yard, calotype, contemporary inscription on the album page *H.F. Talbot. Oct 14. 1840*, 6⅞in by 9in (17.5cm by 22.8cm)

Fig. 2
Hippolyte Bayard
STUDY OF ROOFTOPS, LOOKING NORTH TOWARDS MONTMARTRE, PARIS
Direct positive, 1839–40, 7½in by 7½in (19cm by 19cm)

The above images are from an album of early experimental photographs gathered by the Reverend Calvert Richard Jones between 1839 and 1844, comprising eleven photographs by William Henry Fox Talbot, sixteen calotype portraits by Antoine Claudet and two direct positives by Hippolyte Bayard. The complete album, from the collection of the Reverend Calvert R. Jones, sold for £231,000 ($415,800), in London on 14th April 1989.

Photography, 1839–1989

Philippe Garner

Photography has, through 1989, been celebrating its 150th birthday. The principle of fixing images in light sensitive chemicals had a long pre-history, but it was the rival announcements in 1839 of the first refined and practicable processes, by William Henry Fox Talbot and Louis Jacques Mandé Daguerre, which marked the beginnings of the photograph as we know it today.

The anniversary has been widely commemorated with major exhibitions, publications and conferences. These have drawn attention to the range of the medium, emphasizing the aesthetic and historic significance of the work of distinguished photographers from both nineteenth and twentieth centuries. Photography has had ardent advocates from the very beginning, and important works have been documented and preserved from as early as 1839, and, indeed, even earlier. The earliest extant photographic image, a primitive experimental plate which dates from 1826, by Nicéphore Niépce, was carefully preserved through several generations, to be rediscovered in 1952 by the historian Helmut Gernsheim. It is now in the collection of the University of Texas. Fox Talbot annotated and preserved his earliest successful negative, from 1835, now in the collection of the Science Museum, London. Certain of Daguerre's earliest plates and some key experimental images from 1839–40 by another inventor of photography, Hippolyte Bayard, were given to the Société Française de la Photographie, for the enjoyment and education of later generations.

In the wider market, until around 1970 photography had been regarded as a minor branch of the antiquarian book and print trades which meant that major institutional holdings could be amassed at relatively little expense, as often as not through gift or bequest. These have included the collection of the Société Française, the Royal Photographic Society in England, and the George Eastman Collection in the United States. The Victoria and Albert Museum in the mid nineteenth century, and again today, has followed a policy of buying contemporary work. The low market esteem has also enabled a small number of private collectors to build extensive collections on modest budgets, and has meant that, at least in Britain, much precious material has been kept in the care of descendants of the early photographers or within libraries and other archives.

In 1971, Sotheby's held its first sale of photographic material, and this initiated a regular pattern of sales which helped to develop a lively market. The 70s were golden years of rediscovery, with great works by all the major pioneers resurfacing in a profusion which belied the actual scarcity of the material. This pattern has changed during the 80s, with a marked falling off in the availability of top quality prints. The private sale to an American buyer in 1983 of the historic Harold White collection of works by Talbot and his circle, a collection put together largely in the 40s, appeared to mark the end of this rush of dispersals from major primary sources.

Fig. 3
Rev. Calvert R. Jones
PORTRAIT OF A YOUNG MAN
Calotype negative, *circa* 1845, 8¾in by 6⅝in (22.3cm by 16.9cm)
London £19,800 ($35,640). 14.IV.89
From the collection of the Reverend Calvert R. Jones

Fig. 4
Rev. Calvert R. Jones
STUDY OF THE RIGGING OF A
SAILING VESSEL, TILTED ON
ITS SIDE FOR CAREENING
Calotype, *circa* 1845,
7⅜in by 8¾in
(18.6cm by 22.3cm)
London £35,200
($63,360). 14.IV.89
From the collection of the
Reverend Calvert R. Jones

It was therefore, particularly fortuitous that the 150th anniversary year should be celebrated in London by a sale on 14th April which included a truly exceptional group of images. The majority of these, many hitherto unrecorded, were by the pioneer photographer, the Reverend Calvert Richard Jones and by his contemporaries, including Talbot, Hippolyte Bayard, the Reverend George Bridges and Antoine Claudet. The material was from the personal collection of Calvert Jones and had been passed down by descent through several generations. Family dispersals had already brought on to the market a fine album of photographs by Jones, sold on 25th June 1982 for £24,200. This was the first occasion on which Jones' work commanded a substantial price; later, on 6th November 1987 his earliest recorded photograph, a whole plate

daguerreotype from 1840, a unique, fully annotated work, sold for £14,300. This daguerreotype was eventually acquired by the National Library of Wales, affirming the strength of local as well as international interest in the achievement of this Welshman.

The competition for these two items gave a foretaste of the interest that was to be aroused by the 14th April auction. The lots from Calvert Jones' collection included a series of rare calotypes and photoglyphic engravings by Talbot, several of the former with autograph manuscript inscription; paper negatives and various types of prints by Jones himself, including calotypes from the 1840s and albumen prints from the 1850s. These included architectural and topographical studies, picturesque images and a remarkably intimate series of portraits, shedding light on a little known aspect of his work. The highlight of the collection, however, was an album of early experimental images by Talbot, Bayard and Claudet compiled and annotated by Jones. The album is a unique document, linking together the activities of four pioneering figures at the very dawn of the invention of photography.

Fig. 5
William Henry Fox Talbot
OAK TREE CARCLEW PARK, CORNWALL
Talbotype, titled in ink on the reverse, print *circa* 1845 from photogenic drawing negative of 1st June 1840, 7⅜in by 9in (18.8cm by 22.9cm)
London £27,500 ($49,500). 14.IV.89
From the collection of the Reverend Calvert R. Jones

The Talbot prints within the album dated from 1839 and 1840 (Fig. 1) and were arranged by Jones in a didactic sequence which records the evolution of Talbot's discovery in those crucial years, as well as providing a representative cross-section of his subject-matter. The two Bayard prints in the album, unique direct positives, comprise a view of the rooftops of Paris (Fig. 2) and a study of plaster casts of statuary. They also date from 1839–40 and are amongst only a handful which have survived in private hands. The Claudet calotypes date from 1844 and include two self portraits. The album sold for £231,000 ($415,800), setting a new world record for any photographic item.

Amongst the other key lots from the Jones collection were two studies by the artist himself: a calotype negative portrait of a young man and a calotype detail of a ship's rigging (Figs 3 and 4) as well as a study of an oak tree by Talbot (Fig. 5). The calotype of rigging set a new record for a British photograph at £35,200, equalled in the same sale by a superb print of Henry Peach Robinson's *She Never Told Her Love* (Fig. 6), a melancholic allegorical study of a dying girl.

Fig. 6
Henry Peach Robinson
SHE NEVER TOLD HER LOVE
Albumen print, 1857,
7in by 9in
(18cm by 23.1cm)
London £35,200
($63,360). 14.IV.89

Opposite
Eadweard Muybridge
PANORAMA OF SAN FRANCISCO
One of an album of thirteen
albumen prints, the
photographer's letterpress
copyright date legend affixed
to each image, 1877,
each print approximately
22½in by 16in
(57.2cm by 40.6cm)
New York $132,000
(£78,107). 26.IV.89

Walker Evans
ARCHITECTURAL ABSTRACTION,
NEW YORK
Silver print, *circa* 1929,
2½in by 1⅝in
(6.4cm by 4.1cm)
New York $3,575 (£2,115).
26.IV.89

Charles Sheeler
SAVOY-PLAZA HOTEL
Silver print, mid-1920s, 9½in by 7⅜in (24.1cm by 18.7cm)
New York $29,700 (£17,574). 26.IV.89

Walter Peterhans
TOTER HASE
Silver print, signed and titled in pencil in the margin, *circa* 1929, 8½in by 9⅛in (21.6cm by 23.2cm)
New York $29,700 (£17,574). 26.IV.89

Maurice Tabard
UNTITLED
Unique photocollage of silver prints and orange paper, signed and dated *30* in pencil, 1930,
12¾in by 9½in (31.4cm by 24.1cm)
New York $31,900 (£18,876). 26.IV.89

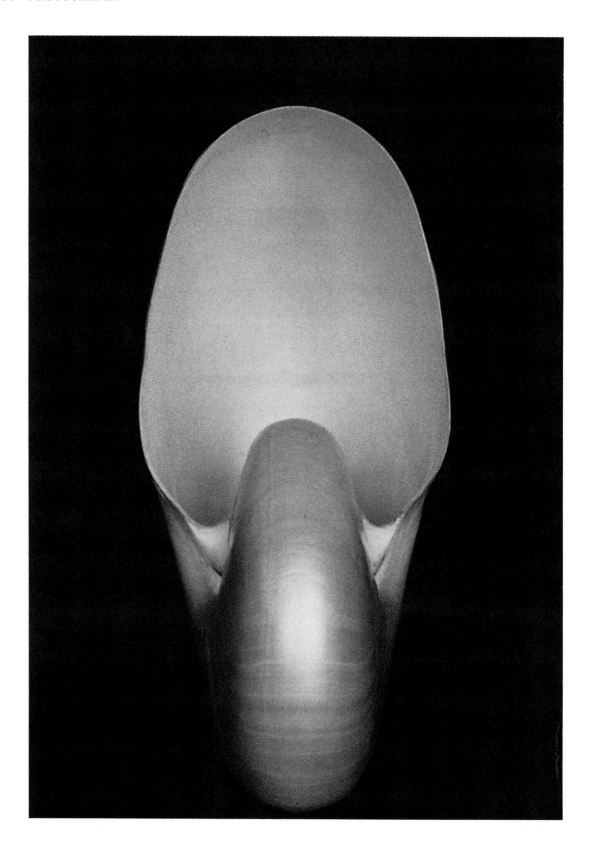

Opposite
Edward Weston
SHELL
Silver print, signed and
dated in pencil on the
mount, 1927, $9\frac{1}{2}$in by $6\frac{5}{8}$in
(24.1cm by 16.8cm)
New York $115,500
(£68,343). 26.IV.89

Laszlo Moholy-Nagy
UNTITLED
Unique photogram, silver print, signed and dated, 1929, $11\frac{3}{4}$in by $9\frac{3}{8}$in (29.8cm by 23.8cm)
New York $71,500 (£42,308). 26.IV.89

Printed books, autograph letters and music manuscripts

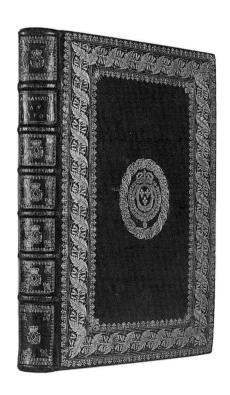

Right

Jean Nieuhoff

Ambassades Mémorables de la Compagnie des Indes Orientales
des Provinces unies vers les Empereurs du Japon,
red morocco binding with arms of Louis XIV, Jacob de Meurs,
Amsterdam, 1680
Monte Carlo FF222,000 (£21,142: $37,000) 2.XII.88

Below

Johannes Balbus

Catholicon, first edition, third issue, 373 leaves, Mainz, 1460
London £132,000 ($232,320). 27.IX.88
From the collection of the British Rail Pension Fund

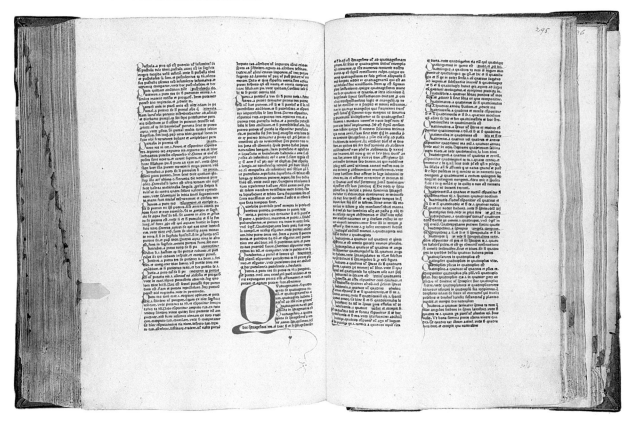

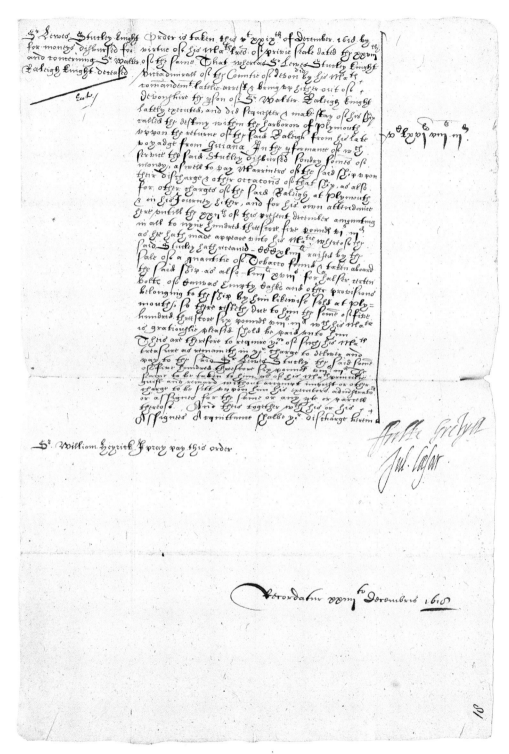

The Exchequer Papers of Sir William Herrick, one of the four tellers of the Exchequer from 1616–23,
over 2,300 documents, 28 volumes, 1608–23
London £115,500 ($221,760). 15.XII.88

Perhaps because of its 'duplicate' heading, this copy of the note never found a place in official files and was later given to William Silliman Hillyer, a friend of Grant and one of his wartime aides. It remained among Hillyer's personal papers, which were deposited at the Alderman Library at the University of Virginia by his descendants in 1985. Once Ervin Jordan, the Civil War specialist at the library, had determined its authenticity and historical significance, the family decided to offer it for sale.

'Men at rest – firing stopped'

Mary-Jo Kline

Robert E. Lee
An autograph note to
General Ulysses S. Grant,
signed *R E Lee Genl* and
dated *9th April 1865* in
pencil, with autograph
endorsement by General
O.C. Ord, approximately
8in by 10in
(20.3cm by 25.4cm)
New York
$220,000 (£125,000).
26.X.88
From the collection of
William Silliman Hillyer

A pencilled note on a slip of faded paper captures the drama of one of the most famous events in American history: the Confederate General Robert E. Lee's surrender to General Ulysses S. Grant at Appomattox Courthouse, Virginia, on 9th April 1865, a moment which marked the symbolic, if not the actual, end of the American Civil War. In it, Lee requests a 'suspension of hostilities' until a formal surrender could be arranged. The page also bears an endorsement from the Union lines by General Edward O. C. Ord, commander of the Northern infantry: 'April 9th 11.55 am the within read . . . acted on . . . men at rest – firing stopped.' Another copy was sent to the Union lines in the east, to General Meade which was duly forwarded to the War Department, and was for many years proudly displayed in the treasure room of the National Archives.

Lee's decision to surrender came after a desperate flight following the fall of the Confederate capital at Richmond on 2nd April. Pursued by Union armies, Lee vainly sought a route of escape to the west. His last chance was to reach a rail line south of Appomattox Courthouse. The arrival of Ord's infantry reinforcements on the morning of 9th April convinced Lee that his cause was hopeless, and he sent word to Grant that he was ready to surrender.

It was nine o'clock when Lee dispatched his first message to Grant, but almost three hours passed before it was received. Long before Grant learned of his triumph, the news spread along the Confederate and Union lines. Flags of truce fluttered on both sides, and firing began to die away. Unfortunately, neither Union nor Confederate field commanders were sure whether Lee's offer of surrender allowed any of them to declare a cease-fire. Lee's first note to Grant had not mentioned a cessation of hostilities, and Grant's whereabouts remained a mystery.

After Lee had prepared a second message to reassure Grant, a two hour cease-fire was declared. Quiet descended and the 'suspension of hostilities' inspired by Lee's pencilled notes become a reality. The men of the grandly-named Armies of Northern Virginia, of 'The James,' and of North Carolina were 'at rest.' The 'rest' later became peace.

The original note to Grant that commemorates this event came to auction through a combination of idiosyncratic military filing, family pride, and archival detective work. The new owner is Malcolm Forbes, the famous American publisher and founder of the Forbes Collection, which includes many of the most important documents recording the events of American history, particularly those related to the Civil War.

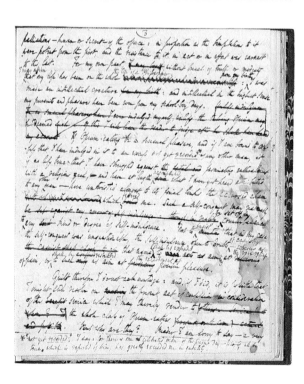

Above, left
Ian Fleming
A notebook containing autograph notes for *You Only Live Twice*, 39 pages,
6in by 4in (15.2cm by 10.2cm)
London £13,200 ($22,704). 20.VII.89

Right
William Blake and Edward Young
The Complaint and the Consolation, or *Night Thoughts*, 43 pictorial borders
designed and engraved by William Blake and hand-coloured, R.Noble
for R. Edwards, 1797
London £33,000 ($55,440). 1.VI.89

Left
Thomas de Quincey
The autograph manuscript of the first part of *Confessions of an English
Opium-Eater*, which was sent in instalments to the publisher John Taylor
and used by his printer, C. Baldwin of New Bridge Street, for its original
appearance in the issue of the *London Magazine* for September 1821,
approximately 50 pages, written at 4, York Street, Covent Garden, 1821
London £28,600 ($50,336). 27.IX.88
From the collection of the British Rail Pension Fund

Jane Austen
The autograph manuscript of
the novel *The Watsons*, first
draft, approximately 75 pages,
Bath, 1804–1805
London £99,000 ($174,240).
27.IX.88
From the collection of the
British Rail Pension Fund

This is the earliest surviving
manuscript of a novel by
Jane Austen. *The Watsons*
was her only literary
composition between the
completion of *Northanger
Abbey* in 1799 and the
commencement of *Mansfield
Park* in 1811. It was begun in
1804, but her father died
early in 1805 and it was
never finished. Because of
the heavy working revisions,
the manuscript throws
exceptionally revealing light
on the creative processes
involved in the composition
of a novel by Jane Austen.

Jemand mußte Josef K. verleumdet haben denn
ohne daß er etwas Böses getan hätte, wurde er eines
Morgens verhaftet. Die Köchin der Zimmervermieterin
die ihm jeden Tag gegen acht Uhr früh das Frühstück
brachte kam diesmal nicht. Das war noch niemals geschehn.
K. wartete noch ein Weilchen, sah von seinem Kopfkissen
aus die alte Frau die ihm gegenüber wohnte und
die ihn mit einer an ihr ganz ungewöhnlichen
Neugierde beobachtete dann aber, gleichzeitig befrem-
det und hungrig, läutete er. Sofort klopfte es
und ein Mann, den er in dieser Wohnung noch
niemals gesehen hatte trat ein. Er war schlank
und doch fest gebaut, er trug ein anliegendes schwarzes
Kleid, das ähnlich den Reiseanzügen mit verschiedenen
Falten, Taschen, Schnallen, Knöpfen und einem Gürtel
versehen war und infolgedessen ohne daß man sich
darüber klar wurde, wozu es diene, besonders
praktisch erschien. Wer sind Sie? fragte K.
Der Mann aber ging über die Frage hinweg, als
müsse man seine Erscheinung hinnehmen und
sagte seinerzeit: Sie haben geläutet? Anna
soll mir das Frühstück bringen, sagte K. und
versuchte zunächst stillschweigend durch Überlegung

Franz Kafka's 'The Trial'

Dr Susan Wharton

Franz Kafka,
photographed in 1914, at
the age of 30, at about the
time he wrote 'The Trial'.

Fig. 1
Franz Kafka
The opening page of the
first chapter, from the
autograph manuscript of
Der Prozess (The Trial),
in ten chapters with five
unfinished 'fragments',
316 pages, late July – late
December 1914
London £1,100,000
($2,123,000). 17.XI.88

'Some one must have been telling lies about Joseph K., for without having done anything wrong he was arrested one morning'. If we add 'and executed exactly one year later', we have a summary of one of the most important and influential novels of the twentieth century: Franz Kafka's *The Trial*. In November 1988 it also became the most expensive, when the autograph manuscript was sold in London for £1.1 million, four times the previous record for a modern literary manuscript (Fig. 1).

Franz Kafka (1883–1924) must rank alongside James Joyce and Marcel Proust as one of the leading novelists of the twentieth century. *The Trial* is his acknowledged masterpiece. Kafka's work has been translated into all the major languages, including Japanese, and the corpus of critical writing devoted to Kafka is comparable in size only to those on Goethe or Shakespeare. The characteristics of his writing, the deceptively simple style, the fantastic situations, the nightmarish inexorability of events, are now so familiar that the adjective 'kafkaesque' has been coined to describe them. As Georg Lukács put it, 'Franz Kafka is the classic example of the modern individual's arrest by blind and panic-stricken *Angst* in the face of reality'.

The manuscript consists of 316 pages, written in ink on both sides of the page. The work is arranged in ten chapters, with five unfinished chapters or Fragments. It is very much a working manuscript: words and phrases are deleted and substitutes inserted, whole paragraphs are crossed through, names are abbreviated, sentences are hastily scribbled down in shorthand. It is the only manuscript of the work; there was no fair copy or typescript. It was written, according to Kafka's custom, in quarto-sized note-

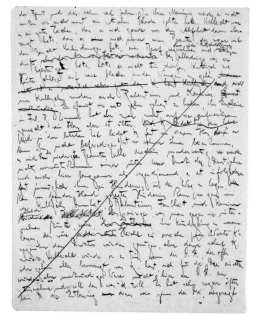

Fig. 2
Franz Kafka
Part of the unfinished fragment 'Fahrt zur Mutter' from the autograph manuscript of *Der Prozess (The Trial)*.

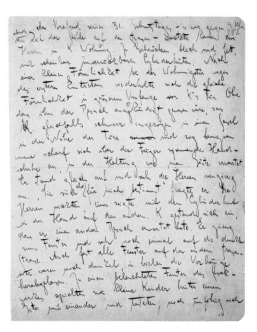

Fig. 3
Franz Kafka
The opening page of the final chapter of the autograph manuscript of *Der Prozess (The Trial)*.

books with black covers. The same notebook might be used for more than one piece of writing, one starting at the beginning, another at the end. Once a section was complete, Kafka would tear it out of the notebook and keep it separately, with a loose sheet on top giving a summary of its contents. This was his practice with *The Trial;* the various chapters were grouped together with a sheet giving a brief title, but no number. The fact that Kafka did not number the chapters of *The Trial* has led to endless scholarly controversy about the order in which they were published (see Figs 2, 3 and 6).

The history of this work is one of survival against almost impossible odds. It is indeed little short of miraculous that Kafka's novels have survived at all. Kafka left no will, but his friend and literary executor Max Brod (Fig. 4) found among his papers after his death two notes addressed to himself. One instructed him to burn everything without exception. The second, apparently from a later date, expressed a similar wish with regard to his unpublished work, diaries and letters, but excepted the works which had been published during Kafka's lifetime. Brod decided, however, that he could in conscience ignore this wish, basing his decision in part on a conversation they had had during Kafka's lifetime in which he had told Kafka that he would never carry out such a request. Indeed after Kafka's death Brod's first priority was to publish as much of Kafka's work as he could, for only a small fraction had appeared during his lifetime. *The Trial* was published in 1925, with the other two novels *The Castle* and *America* appearing in succeeding years. Brod was at that time still living in Kafka's native city of Prague. In 1933 Kafka's work was banned by the

Fig. 4
Max Brod, Kafka's friend
and literary executor.

Nazis, and Brod, as its custodian, was consequently in a hazardous position. He attempted to emigrate to America in 1939, by offering Kafka's papers to any institution which would give him a position as its curator. Thomas Mann's letter of recommendation to H.M. Lydenberg, Director of the New York Public Library, on 27th February 1939, explains his situation:

Dr Max Brod, the German-Czechoslovakian novelist and dramatist . . . is a gifted and cultured man; but now, because he is a Jew, he is no longer permitted to write what he thinks and believes, and is being ridiculed and vilified in the German press. As a young man Dr Brod became an intimate friend of Franz Kafka. When Kafka died, leaving his work unfinished and incomplete, Dr Brod, as executor, undertook the editing of his friend's books. His scholarly and devoted work led to the publication of many of Kafka's books, such as the novels The Castle, The Trial, etc, which have been translated into English. Dr Brod is anxious to leave Czechoslovakia and come to the United States . . . He writes that he is willing to give his collection of the books and manuscripts of Franz Kafka to any institution of repute which would accept it and in return offer him a position to act as assistant or curator of the collection and so make possible his entry into this country . . . Perhaps you will agree with me that the possibility of acquiring the manuscripts and books of so well known a writer as Franz Kafka is an opportunity deserving of consideration quite apart from the human tragedy of the individual for whom the collection represents the one real chance of escape from an intolerable situation.

This plan, however, for whatever reason, came to nothing. In March 1939 Hitler entered Prague; the previous night Brod had fled the city, taking Kafka's manuscripts in his hand luggage and leaving his own papers to follow as and when they could. For the manuscript of *The Trial* this was the beginning of an odyssey which was to last for almost half a century. Brod travelled through Romania and the Dardanelles to Palestine, where the manuscripts remained until the time of the Suez crisis, and they were then taken to Switzerland for safekeeping. A few years before Brod's death, the bulk of Kafka's literary estate was deposited in the Bodleian Library in Oxford. *The Trial* however did not form part of this consignment. Unlike the others, it had been given to Brod by Kafka during his lifetime and was thus of especial sentimental value. It remained in private hands after Brod's death in 1968, until it came to London in 1988 to be catalogued for sale. Before going under the hammer, the manuscript travelled almost round the world, being taken east to Japan and Hong Kong, west to New York and to Europe to be exhibited to prospective purchasers and lovers of Kafka's work. For many it would be their only chance of seeing an original manuscript in the hand of Kafka.

The sale itself generated enormous excitement, and the atmosphere in the Grosvenor Gallery as lot 244 ('Kafka, Franz. The autograph manuscript of his novel *Der Prozess* . . .') came under the hammer was electric. Nine television cameras were ranged along one side of the room to record the event, as well as numerous newspaper correspondents and radio reporters crouched beneath the rostrum with their microphones directed at the auctioneer. In thirty-two seconds the hammer had fallen and the record broken. The successful bidder was a German dealer who had purchased the manuscript on behalf of the German Literary Archive at Marbach near Stuttgart. In December 1988 the manuscript's wanderings finally came to end when it was taken from London to Marbach, which was to be its final resting place.

Although *The Trial* is not literally an autobiographical work, it is inextricably bound up with Kafka's life. Indeed it is possible to trace its origins to a specific event, namely his relationship with Felice Bauer. *The Trial*, together with his letters to Felice (which, by coincidence, were sold in New York in 1987) form two halves of a diptych, inspired by the same event but differing in form and emphasis.

Fig. 5
Kafka and his fiancee Felice Bauer, at the time of their second engagement in 1917.

Kafka first met Felice Bauer in August 1912, at the home of Max Brod's father. Felice was distantly related to the Brod family. At this first meeting she and Kafka talked for about an hour; Kafka's diary entry suggests that she had not made much of an impression ('. . . she . . . looked to me like a maidservant. What is more, I was not at all curious to know who she was but simply put up with her . . .'), but on the strength of this acquaintance Kafka began a correspondence with her which was to last some five years and comprise over three hundred letters. Since Felice lived in Berlin, they met only infrequently, but in late May 1914 they became formally engaged to be married. Kafka described the event in his diary thus: 'I was bound like a criminal. If they had tied me with real chains and put me in a corner with real policemen before me and only let me look on in that way, it could not have been worse. And that was my engagement.' Already the themes of crime and punishment can be seen which are central to *The Trial*. The parallel is even clearer at the time this first engagement is ended: Kafka describes the ceremony (which took place in a Berlin hotel in the presence of Felice's father and sister and two other friends) baldly as 'a court of law'. Kafka and Felice were briefly engaged for a second time in 1917 (see Fig. 5), though the correspondence continued unabated. Their relationship finally came to an end in September 1917, and in 1919 Felice married a Berlin banker.

Unsatisfactory as this relationship was on a sentimental level, it triggered in Kafka a frenzy of creative activity. Shortly after writing his first letter to Felice in September 1912, Kafka wrote the short story *The Judgement* in a single sitting between ten at night and six the following morning. The crisis provoked by the termination of their first engagement produced, in the space of six months, both *The Trial* and the short story *In the Penal Colony*. Kafka documents in his diary his progress with the novel: the entry for 29th July 1914 includes a short fragment about a character called Josef K. In August the work is first referred to by the title 'Prozess', and in September he read the first chapter aloud to Max Brod. Kafka worked continuously at the novel during the following six months, and by December 'several chapters' were finished. In January the following year he declares himself incapable of continuing work on the novel, and as far as is known he never returned to the manuscript. Those seeking specific auto-biographical clues in the novel do not have far to look. The initials of the protagonists Josef K. and Fräulein Bürstner (the latter generally abbreviated in the manuscript to F.B.) are obvious pointers to Kafka and Felice Bauer. Joseph K. is the same age as his creator. Franz, one of the warders who arrests K., shares both Kafka's first name and his physical appearance. More ingenious critics have found countless parallels between Kafka's novel and his life, but the most fundamental link centres on the theme of guilt. Josef K. is guilty from the very first page, though he is never told of what crime; Kafka himself is racked with guilt over his treatment of Felice, who is an innocent and unwitting victim of his self-tormenting and contradictory desire for, and terror of, marriage. Kafka's guilt has its origins in his profoundly unsatisfactory relationship with his father, a distant and tyrannical figure who enforced his authority

Fig. 6
A loose sheet giving a brief title and summary of the contents of the chapter. The letter 'P' in the top left-hand corner is for 'Prozess'. The sheets Kafka used for this purpose were in fact part of a carbon copy of the typescript of his short story *Der Heizer*, which he had published in 1913.

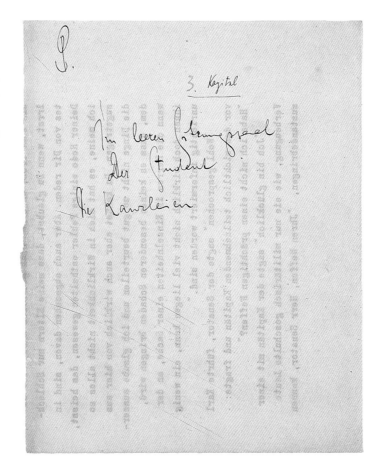

severely and arbitrarily. It was the arbitrary nature of the father's authority which had such a profound effect on Kafka as a child and it is this feature of the distant and shadowy regimes in *The Trial* and *The Castle* which is the essence of the nightmare world now termed 'kafkaesque'. Much has been written on this problematical relationship between father and son, inevitably focusing on its Oedipal aspects. In the *Brief an den Vater* which Kafka wrote in 1919, he describes his writing as 'a long-drawn-out leave-taking' from his father: 'my writing was all about you'. Kafka even quotes, with reference to himself, the words 'he is afraid the shame will outlive him', which he had used as the last sentence of *The Trial*. The father-figure in his story *The Judgement* so tyrannises his son that the son jumps from a bridge to his death on his father's orders. Kafka was familiar with psychoanalytical concepts, and he shared Freud's view of the importance of early life and upbringing. One critic has even dubbed him the Dante of the Freudian age. However, he rejected psychoanalysis as therapy. Life was the disease, and the only cure was death.

The Trial has inevitably been subjected to a wide variety of interpretations, from the Freudian to the Existentialist, and the Marxist to the theological. The work has variously been seen as autobiography, as a parable, a dream and a prophecy of Naziism, and its hero as a modern Everyman. It is a measure of its greatness that no single interpretation can encompass all its richness.

-21-

ANNOUNCER TWO

Ladies and gentlemen, I have a grave announcement to make.
Incredible as it may seem, both the observations of science and the
evidence of our eyes lead to the inescapable assumption that those
strange beings who landed in the Jersey farmlands tonight are the
vanguard of a n invading army from the planet Mars. (LONG PAUSE)

ANNOUNCER

The battle of Grovers Mill has ended in one of the most startling
defeats ever suffered by an army in modern times; Seven thousand men
armed with rifles and machine guns pitted against a single fighting
machine of the invaders from Mars. 120 known survivors. The rest
strewn over the battle area from Grovers Mill to Plainsboro crushed
and trampled to death under the metal feet of the monster, or burned
to cinders by its heat-ray. The monster is now in control of the
middle section of New Jersey, has effectively cut the state through
its center. Communication lines are down from Pennsylvania to the
Atlantic ocean. Railroad tracks are torn and service from New York
to Philadelphia discontinued except for the Pennsylvania Railroad
which is routing its trains through Allertown and Phoenixville.
Airplanes flying high over the area report innumerable forest fires
and a score of villages and cities in flames, including Hopewell
and Hightstown. Princeton is standing untouched...a ghost city of
mute spires and deserted streets. Highways to the north, south, and
west, are clogged with frantic human traffic. Police and army
reserves are unable to control the mad flight. By morning fugitives
will have swelled Philadelphia, Camden and Trenton to twice their
normal population. The Red Cross, working with local and state
relief agencies, are attempting to feed and house the overflow. (MORE)

Above

Sir John Tenniel

An ink and watercolour drawing of Alice standing between the
gryphon and the mock-turtle on a rocky shore, reading from a paper,
the only parody by the artist of his own work, made for the cartoon
Alice in Bumbleland, reproduced in *Punch*, 8th March 1899, signed with
monogram, 6⅜in by 6in (16.3cm by 15.4cm)
London £9,900 ($19,206). 2.XII.88

Above, right

Sir Edward Coley Burne-Jones

An extensively illustrated series of over three hundred autograph
letters to Olive Maxse, containing approximately 140 drawings, all
from The Grange, 49 North End Road, West Kensington,
October 1894 to October 1896
London £176,000 ($302,720). 20.VII.89

Right

Michelangelo Buonarroti

An autograph manuscript, listing sums of money paid for quantities
of marble for the façade of San Lorenzo, Florence, 1½ pages, in
Italian, 24th January to 28th March 1519
New York $66,000 (£36,066). 14.XII.88

Opposite

The original radioplay typescript of *The War of the Worlds*, written by
Howard Koch, read by Orson Welles, 46 pages, New York, broadcast
on 30th October 1938
New York $143,000 (£78,142). 14.XII.88
From the collection of Howard Koch

Wolfgang Amadeus Mozart
An autograph manuscript of the aria *Schon lacht der holde Frühling*, for soprano and
orchestra, notated in brown ink, 26 pages, 17th September 1789
London £104,500 ($180,785). 19.V.89

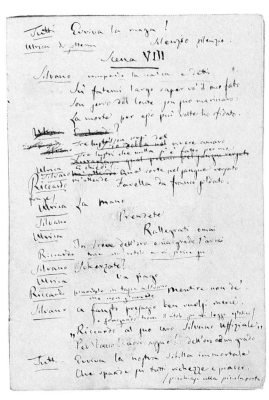

Giuseppe Verdi
An autograph working manuscript of the complete libretto of *Un Ballo in Maschera*,
the first two acts in Verdi's hand, act three transcribed by his wife, 52 pages, 1858
London £88,000 ($152,240). 19.V.89

Above
John Gould
The Birds of Australia, 8 volumes, 681 hand-coloured
lithographed plates by John and Elizabeth Gould and
H.C.Richter, printed by Hullmandel (& Walton) or Walter,
R. and J.E. Taylor (Taylor and Francis), published by the
author, 1848–69
London £187,000 ($329,120). 27.IX.88
From the collection of the British Rail Pension Fund

Above, right
Priscilla Susan Bury
*A selection of Hexandrian plants, belonging to the natural orders
Amaryllidae and Liliacae*, first edition, 51 aquatint plates partly
printed in colours and finished by hand by Robert Havell, Jr
from drawings by Mrs Bury, Robert Havell, 1831–34
London £33,000 ($61,380). 20.X.88

Right
Johann Wilhelm Weinmann
Phytanthoza iconographia, a complete set of 1,025 engraved and
mezzotint plates, printed in colours and finished by hand by
J.J. Haid, J.E. Ridinger and B. Seuter after drawings by
G.D. Ehret, N. Asamin and others, 4 volumes, Zacharias
Romberg, Amsterdam, 1746–48
London £33,000 ($59,400). 13.IV.89

Fig. 1
John James Audubon
The Carolina Parrot from *The Birds of America*, first edition, four volumes in five, 435 hand-coloured
etched plates with line engraving and aquatint, by W.H. Lizars of Edinburgh, and Robert Havell,
father and son, of London, published by the author, London, 1827–38,
approximately $38\frac{1}{4}$ by $25\frac{5}{8}$in (97.2cm by 65cm)
New York $3,960,000 (£2,522,293). 6.VI.89
From the library of H. Bradley Martin

The ornithological library of H. Bradley Martin

Selby Kiffer

François Levaillant
Le Perroquet jaune écaillé de rouge, from *Histoire naturelle des perroquets*, first edition, two volumes, 145 plates, after Jacques Barraband, printed in colour by Langlois, Levrault frères, Paris, 1801–1805, 19in by 12½in (48.3cm by 31.8cm)
New York $231,000 (£146,203). 7.VI.89
From the library of H. Bradley Martin

Ornithology was only one component of the magnificent library assembled by H. Bradley Martin during a lifetime of collecting, but it was the logical choice to begin the series of sales at Sotheby's New York that, from June 1989 through June 1990, will disperse his books and manuscripts to other private and institutional collections around the world. The ornithological collection was probably the most widely known aspect of the Martin Library. With some 5,000 volumes, it was certainly the largest, eclipsing other private collections of the subject and rivalling in number, scope, and condition those at Yale University, the University of Kansas, McGill University, Trinity College, and the Field Museum of Natural History.

Fig. 2
Prideaux John Selby
Purple Heron, original
signed watercolour for
Plate 2.3 of *Illustrations of
British Ornithology*, London,
1819–34, 21⅝in by 15⅝in
(54.9cm by 39.7cm)
New York $55,000
(£35,032). 8.VI.89
From the library of
H. Bradley Martin

Moreover, many of the most beautiful and desirable books in the Martin Library were in this section. Finally, ornithology was the favourite subject of Mr Martin, who had been introduced to bird-watching as a young man by an earlier bird-book collector, John E. Thayer.

The first three sales from the Martin Library focused on illustrated bird books of the nineteenth century, that pivotal period during which such artists as François Levaillant, Edward Lear, John Gould, Daniel Giraud Elliot, Josef Wolf, Joseph Smit, Prideaux John Selby, and, especially, John James Audubon expanded ornithological illustration from rigid stylization to realistic art.

Sir Sacheverell Sitwell has written that 'there is nothing in the world of fine books quite like the first discovery of Audubon. The great energy of the man, and his power

Fig. 3
Eleazar Albin
Watercolour No. 55 of *The Natural History of Birds*, the first English colour-plate bird book,
three volumes, 300 watercolour paintings, one signed *Eliz Albin, circa* 1730–40,
11¼in by 9in (28.6cm by 22.9cm)
New York $264,000 (£167,089). 7.VI.89
From the library of H. Bradley Martin

T. 13.

Quercus Castanea foliis, procera Arbor Virginiana. Pluk: Alma.
Chefnut Oak.

Picus varius major, alis aureis
The golden Wing'd Woodpecker.

of achievement and accomplishment, give to him something of the epical force of a Walt Whitman or a Herman Melville.' The superb set of *The Birds of America* (Fig. 1), originally subscribed for by John Heathcote of Conington Castle, gave even those viewers who were very familiar with Audubon a renewed sense of that first discovery. Each of its five double-elephant folio volumes stood over three feet tall, and its 435 brilliantly hand-coloured etched plates were in the finest possible condition, many on completely untrimmed sheets. When the bidding ended with *The Birds of America* selling to an anonymous private collector for $3,960,000 (£2,522,293), the previous auction record for Audubon's magnum opus had been more than doubled. The Auduboniana also included the frontier naturalist's signed autograph manuscript journal for May to December 1826. This highly important document is intimately connected with *The Birds of America*, for it recounts Audubon's voyage to England in search of both subscribers to his work and an engraver competent to produce it. The journal was also closely allied with another prize of the Martin ornithology collection because in his entry for 19th December, Audubon recounts tutoring Prideaux John Selby in his own style of drawing birds.

Selby had conceived a plan very similar to Audubon's: to publish a book illustrating every British species of bird at its full life-size. He began issuing his work eight years before Audubon's first *Wild Turkey* plate appeared, but, like several other fine artists, Selby had the misfortune of being a contemporary of the great Audubon, and his work has always been somewhat overshadowed.

In the mid 1950s Mr Martin made the extraordinary acquisition of all of the 277 known surviving original watercolours for Selby's *Illustrations of British Ornithology*, including 50 images either omitted from the printed work or combined with others to form a single etched plate. Selby painted 217 of these watercolours himself, while 55 were by his brother-in-law Robert Mitford, four by Sir William Jardine, and one by Edward Lear. The drawings, principally watercolour, gouache, and grey and brown washes, often over graphite underdrawing, were little known either before or after they entered the Martin Library.

The watercolours were offered individually and three of them sold for more than any complete copy of the printed work ever had at auction – with the single exception of Mr Martin's own copy. Selby's magnificent rendering of a *Great Eared Owl*, drawn from a live specimen lent to him by Jardine, made $57,750 (£36,783), and his graceful and delicate *Purple Heron* brought $55,000 (£35,032; Fig. 2). But the high price of the group went to Edward Lear's portrait of the *Great Auk*, which sold for $66,000 (£42,038). Like all the best of his ornithological work, the *Great Auk* is a wonderfully successful blend of whimsy and cold accuracy.

The books that made up the 'Magnificent Colour-Plate Ornithology' section best demonstrated Mr Martin's personal taste and technique in collecting, and his knowledge of the field and connoisseurship were fully endorsed during the auction, when both estimates and records were not simply exceeded but shattered. Mr Martin's collection of the sumptuous folio works of John Gould, the most prolific and certainly the most commercially successful of the nineteenth-century ornithologist-publishers, made a total of $978,450 (£619,241), or nearly half again as much as Gould's own set of his works had fetched at Sotheby's in 1987 – and this despite the fact that Mr Martin's fine copy of Gould's most extensive and most valuable work, *The Birds of Australia*, was retained by the family.

Fig. 4
Mark Catesby
The golden Wing'd Woodpecker, from *The Natural History of Carolina, Florida and the Bahama Islands*, first edition, two volumes in three, 220 hand-coloured etched plates, after and by Catesby, with three plates by G.D. Ehret, published by the author, London, 1729–47, 20⅜in by 14in (51.8cm by 35.6cm) New York $407,000 (£257,595). 7.VI.89 From the library of H. Bradley Martin

The sale did feature the earlier suppressed, and consequently much rarer, *Birds of Australia, and the Adjacent Islands* (London, 1837–38). Gould had predicted that this cancelled work would eventually be of value – to book collectors, not naturalists – and on a per-plate basis it was in fact the most expensive of Gould's works in the Martin sale, with its 20 hand-coloured lithographs selling for $66,000 (£41,772). Other works of Australian interest did exceptionally well, particularly William Lewin's *Birds of New South Wales, with their Natural History* (Sydney, 1813), the first natural history book printed in Australia, which made $396,000 (£250,633). Lewin's work is not only extremely important as the first Australian edition of the first illustrated book on Australian birds, but it is also a legendary rarity. Mr Martin at one time owned two of the eleven copies known to exist; he donated his other copy to a benefit auction for the Grolier Club of New York in 1980.

The theme of this part of the sale quickly became extraordinary prices for extraordinary books. A magnificent subscriber's copy of *The Natural History of Carolina, Florida, and The Bahama Islands* (London, 1729–47; Fig. 4) by Mark Catesby, 'the father of American ornithology,' achieved $407,000 (£257,595); one of just four known copies of Jean Théodore Descourtilz's *Oiseaux brillans du Brésil* (Paris, 1834) sold for $121,000 (£76,582) and the only known copy with the plates in two states, hand-coloured and black and white, of *Locupletissimi rerum naturalium thesauri* (Amsterdam, 1734–65), Albertus Seba's astonishing illustrated record of his cabinet of natural history specimens and curiosities, was sold for $143,000 (£90,506). Manuscripts were also eagerly competed for: a magnificent series of watercolours, with text, for Eleazar Albin's *The Natural History of Birds* (English, *circa* 1730–40; Fig. 3), the first colour-plate bird book, made $264,000 (£167,089) and a fair copy of the manuscript for the unpublished third and fourth volumes of Louis Jean Pierre Vieillot's *Histoire naturelle des oiseaux de l'Amérique septentrionale* (Paris, 1807–10), with sixteen original watercolours by Jean-Gabriel Prêtre, fetched $187,000 (£118,354).

But again it is perhaps the work of Edward Lear that best conveys the tenor of the first series of sales from the Martin Library. As with a number of great books, Mr Martin had acquired two copies of Lear's *Illustrations of the Family of Parrots* (London, 1830–32), justly recognized as one of the greatest achievements of one of the most gifted artists of the nineteenth century. One was a perfectly fine copy and the other a perfectly wonderful copy. In addition to 42 very fine hand-coloured lithographed plates after and by Lear, the 'wonderful' copy included two preliminary lithographs not included in the published work and two of the very rare pictorial front wrappers from the book's original issue in parts. In addition, it had belonged to Sir William Jardine, the noted ornithologist and an original subscriber, with his signature on the title-page. This was clearly one of the key books in the ornithology collection, and keen bidding pushed the price to $209,000 (£132,278), more than double the auction record for this work.

The next lot was the 'fine' copy of Lear's beautiful work (Fig. 5). With a new price level for the *Parrots* having just been established, and any number of bidders evidently regretting that they had given up the chase on the preceding lot, Mr Martin's secondary copy was sold for $231,000 (£146,203), yet another record in an auction of records.

Fig. 5
Edward Lear
Macrocercus Aracanga (Red and Yellow Maccaw), from *Illustrations of the Family of Psittacidae or Parrots*, first edition, 42 hand-coloured lithographed plates, after and by Lear, London, 1830–32, $21\frac{1}{4}$in by $14\frac{1}{2}$in (54cm by 36.8cm)
New York $231,000 (£146,203). 7.VI.89
From the library of
H. Bradley Martin

This is the second of two first edition copies of Lear's magnificent work sold from the library of H. Bradley Martin. It is a scarce book, for Lear destroyed the lithographic stones from which the plates were printed in order to protect his 124 subscribers. It has been said of Lear that he was 'the first bird artist to appreciate the aesthetic possibilities in the grain of the lithographic stone, how it would be used to vary tone and sharpness of line, to render subtle textures and the gradation of closely-packed feathers'.

Stanislaw Lubieniecki
Theatrum cometicum, three parts in one volume, 81 plates, first edition, D. Baccamude for F. Cuperus, Amsterdam, 1666–68
London £49,500 ($87,120).
27.IX.88
From the collection of the British Rail Pension Fund

Opposite, above
An Italian composite atlas formerly belonging to the Doria family, comprising 104 Italian maps and views dated between 1535 and 1570, including some by the celebrated Giacomo Gastaldi, a woodcut wall map of Spain by Vincentus Corsulensis dated 1551, several Viennese maps mostly by Wolfgang Lazius, together with seventeenth-century additions, probably Venice, *circa* 1570
London £247,500 ($435,600).
27.IX.88
From the collection of the British Rail Pension Fund

Below
Georg Braun and Franz Hogenberg
Civitates orbis Terrarum, six volumes in three, 355 engraved plates, Latin edition, Cologne, 1576–1617
London £51,700 ($93,060).
13.IV.89

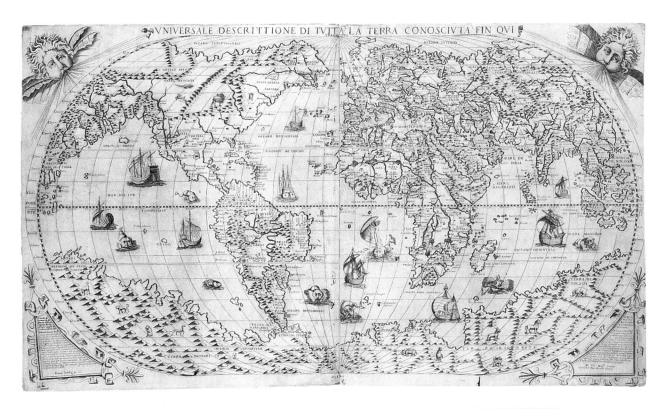

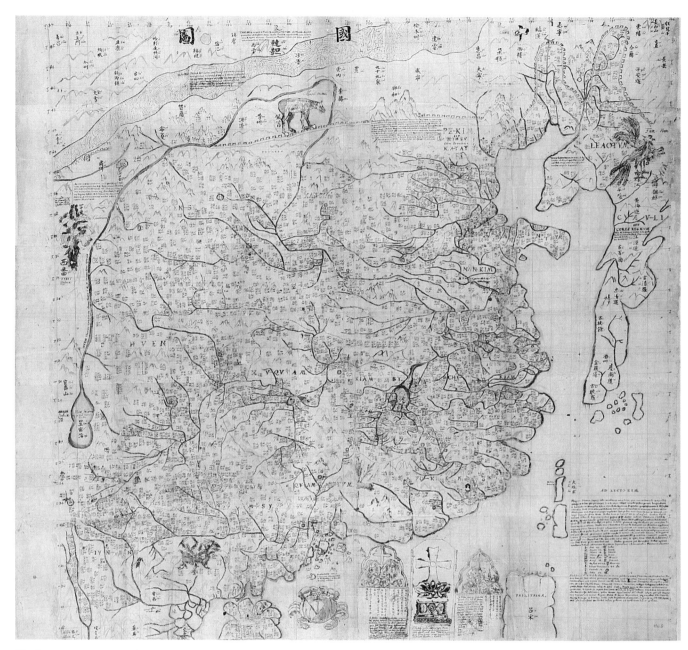

Fig. 1
Michal Piotr Boym
One of three known copies of the map of the 'Middle Kingdom', the first map produced by the Jesuits
with a view to conveying their knowledge of the country to Europeans, ink and colour on European
paper, approximately 4ft 10⅝in by 5ft 3in (149cm by 160cm), possibly Rome, *circa* 1652
London £66,000 ($126,060). 22.XI.88
From the Philip Robinson Chinese Collection

A treasury of Chinese maps

Dr Helen Wallis

'The Great Maps' in the Chinese Collection of Philip Robinson, auctioned on 22nd November 1988, rank among the most remarkable of the sixteenth and seventeenth centuries. They represent the finest examples of the cartographic works of the Jesuit missionaries to China and their Chinese associates and show the dramatic confrontation between the new and the old, the East and the West, as Europeans introduced into China the scientific learning of the Renaissance.

The first of the missionaries, and the pioneer map maker, was the Italian Jesuit Father Matteo Ricci, called by the Chinese *Hsi-ju*, or 'Wise Man from the West'. 'In Ricci, the civilization of the Far West was for the first time meeting that of the Far East', wrote the late Father Pasquale d'Elia, S.J., 'It was a happy meeting of minds.' When Ricci entered China from Macao in 1583, he saw the propagation of Western science as a means of promoting the Christian faith. The European maritime discoveries of the fifteenth and sixteenth centuries had revealed the five continents and the oceans of the terraqueous globe. With the help of his circle of learned Chinese friends Ricci converted this western knowledge into an oriental idiom. He found in China a deep reverence for geographical studies. From the earliest times the Chinese had appreciated the need for exact knowledge of the country's geography. They could claim a continuous tradition of map making extending over some 2,000 years, from at least the fifth century BC. In technical skills, moreover, the Chinese were ahead of Europe. Their oldest printed map dates from about AD 1155, three centuries earlier than its European equivalent.

Ricci made his first world map some time before the end of 1584. Between 1600 and 1603 he went on to construct three further maps, each one larger than the last. His third world map, published at Peking in 1602, is preserved as his surviving masterpiece. The finest of the four known examples is that previously in the Philip Robinson Collection (Fig.2). With printing techniques so advanced and in response to the heavy demand, the map was repeatedly printed in 'many thousands' of copies. Ricci constructed the map on the oval projection popularized by Abraham Ortelius's world map of 1570. This is believed to be the map which Ricci fixed to the wall of his mission room in 1583 and for which he prepared a Chinese version as his first map in 1584. Ricci, however, in 1602 centred his map on the meridian of 170°E, which passes east of New Guinea, so giving China pride of place.

Ricci's scholarly friends showed in their prefaces to his maps how much they appreciated his efforts. In a preface to the fourth map, 1603, made to meet the still unsatisfied demand, Feng Ying-Ching wrote:

Many … will see this map in China. Some will get from it the pleasure of travelling while reclining at their ease; others seeing it will enlarge their administrative plans; others seeing the great size of other countries will rid themselves of petty sentiments of excessive provincialism …

An official who had already enlarged his administrative map in the light of the new knowledge was Liang Chou, 'a man from Ssu, and education official of Wu-hsi County in Ch'ang-Chou Prefecture' of Jiangsu Province. A unique example of his 'comprehensive map delineating heaven and earth and the myriad of countries and modern human affairs', published at Nanking in 1593, is one of the treasures from the Robinson Collection (Fig.3).

The map serves two purposes. As an administrative map of China made for mandarin officials it contains detailed statistical information on administrative areas, such as numbers of families and population and products. At a first glance it appears to be a map of these Chinese territories, but it is also a map of the world. Liang Chou writes in a preface:

after seeing the drawings of the Hsi-t'ai scholar [Ricci] and the European engraved maps and the six scrolls engraved by some gentlemen in Nanking I began to realize that the world was extremely large and contained a multitude of places. For this reason I combined all the maps and produced this one, utilising both the knowledge of the Chinese and that of foreigners.

Although it provides some evidence of what Ricci's lost map of 1584 was like Liang Chou's map is still a picture of the world as seen by a typical conservative Chinese official. Describing the reactions of the Chinese to Liang Chou's map in his mission room, Ricci made some very stern comments on this somewhat traditional style of map-making:

Fig. 2
Matteo Ricci
One of four, or possibly five, known copies of the first issue of the third world map or 'Map of the ten thousand countries of the earth', printed on six sheets of native Chinese paper, overall size 6ft 1$\frac{7}{8}$in by 7ft 5$\frac{3}{4}$in (187.5cm by 228cm), Peking, 17th August 1602 London £209,000 ($399,190). 22.XI.88 From the Philip Robinson Chinese Collection

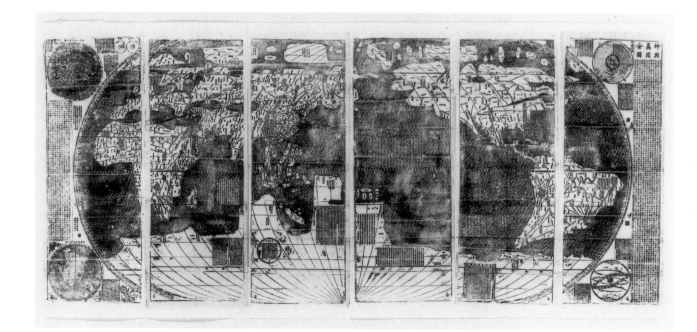

True, they had charts somewhat similar to this one, that were supposed to represent the whole world, but their universe was limited to their own fifteen provinces, and in the sea painted around it they had placed a few little islands to which they gave the names of different kingdoms they had heard of. All of these islands put together would not be as large as the smallest of the Chinese provinces. With such a limited knowledge, it is evident why they boasted of their kingdom as being the whole world, and why they called it Thienhia, meaning, everything under the heavens.

The new geographical information was incorporated in a traditional Chinese manner, with foreign lands situated peripherally to the great, central landmass of the Chinese empire. Canada, the Appalachian country, Africa and America (marked

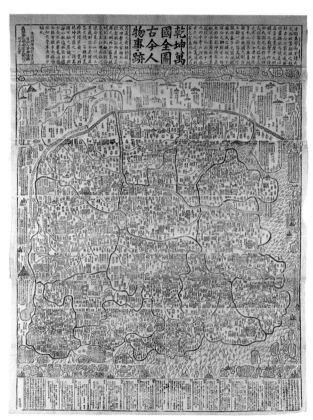

Fig. 3
Liang Chou
The only known copy of the first Chinese world map to incorporate geographical information brought into China by the Jesuits, based on Matteo Ricci's first world map of 1584 (now lost), printed on native Chinese paper, 5ft 7⅞in by 4ft 4¼in (172.5cm by 132.5cm), Nanking, 1593
London £110,000 ($210,100). 22.XI.88
From the Philip Robinson Chinese Collection

Fig. 4
A world map, with references to 'Liang's old map' showing it to be a derivation of the world map in traditional form by Liang Chou (see Fig. 3), printed on native paper, hand-coloured, overall size 4ft 3in by 5ft 6⅜in (129.5cm by 168.5cm)
China, *circa* 1743
London £14,300 ($27,313). 22.XI.88
From the Philip Robinson Chinese Collection

for the first time on a Chinese map) appear as small islands to the north-east (upper right), Brazil, Magellanica, the kingdom of women (Amazons) and other South American places are shown to the south-east (lower right). Liang Chou was following a well-established tradition in adopting this lay-out. One of the monuments of medieval Chinese cartography is the *Hua I Thu*, 'Map of China and the Barbarian Countries', which was carved in stone in 1137, and probably dates from about 1040. This shows the 'barbarian' or foreign countries round the edge of the map. Another notable map in the same style is the *Ti Li Thu*, 'General Map of China', which was engraved on a stone stele at Suchow by Wang Chih-Yuan in 1247.

A much later world map sold from the Philip Robinson Collection, published in or after 1743, proves to be a derivative of Liang Chou's, and carries an explicit reference to 'Liang's old map' (Fig.4). It is similar in style and content, with the western lands appearing as islands around the central continent comprising Chinese territories. As late as 1819 maps were still being produced in this traditional form. The influence of Liang Chou's map thus proved more enduring than Ricci's, from which it was derived, appealing to the Chinese preference for a sino-centred universe.

Ricci's successors in the China mission carried on the good work. Father Francesco Sanbiasi, known to the Chinese as Bi Fangji, came to China in 1613 and produced a simplified version of Ricci's world map. Philip Robinson's example is one of two or perhaps three maps by Sanbiasi now known (Fig.5). Sanbiasi assisted the Ming emperor during the Manchu invasion, and was in Canton in 1647 when the city was captured. His map was published there, probably in 1648. The name of China is given as *Zhonghua* 'Middle Glorious', in place of Ricci's *Da Ming* 'Great Ming', as a compliment to the new Qing (Manchu) dynasty established in 1644.

The two most famous missionaries among Ricci's successors were Father Schall von Bell the German Jesuit, who came to China in 1619, and Father Ferdinand

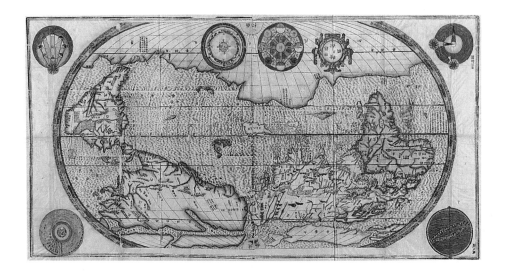

Fig. 5
Francesco Sanbiasi
A simplified version of the world map by Matteo Ricci, drawn on an oval projection with China at the centre, incorporating various improvements made in the light of later knowledge, printed on native paper, hand-coloured,
overall size 2ft 2in by 4ft 2in (66cm by 127cm),
Canton, *circa* 1648
London £49,500 ($94,545). 22.XI.88
From the Philip Robinson Chinese Collection

Verbiest who took over as head of the China Mission after Schall's death in 1666. They brought to China western mathematics and astronomy. Some of the rarest of their astronomical maps are preserved in the Philip Robinson Collection.

A Jesuit of a very different outlook was the Pole Michal Boym, who entered China in 1643 and returned to Europe as Chinese ambassador to Venice and Rome from 1652 to 1656. His concern was to promote knowledge of Chinese science and philosophy in Europe. Described in recent years as the first sinologist, he reversed the flow of information, showing how much Europe could learn from the Orient. His manuscript map of China in the Philip Robinson Collection is one of three such maps known, of which only two now survive: the present example (Fig.1) and another in the Vatican. Place names are given in romanized form and in Chinese characters, an innovation which was to become standard practice. The romanized names are identified as in Boym's hand, while the Chinese characters were presumably drawn by the Chinese scholar Andreas Chên, whom Boym brought with him to Italy as his assistant. In content the map is a remarkable record of Chinese geography, complete with flora, fauna and mineral resources. The key to the symbols for minerals ranks as the first given both in Chinese characters and Latin script. Four large drawings embellish the map, showing the phoenix (in Korea), musk deer, rhubarb (in Tibet), and ginger, *Radix sinica*. The drawing depicting rhubarb may be one of the earliest European representations of the plant. Boym's map of China became widely known through its publication in an edited and reduced version by Nicolas Sanson in 1670. The manuscript map in the Philip Robinson Collection may well be the original, made about 1652, probably in Rome.

These maps from the Philip Robinson Chinese Collection comprise a corpus of great historical interest. Except for Boym's map, they are all printed on native Chinese paper and are in excellent condition. Boym's map, in contrast, is drawn on European paper and bears signs of considerable use. The maps have survived as a group known as 'Phillipps 1986'. How the collection was made and finally reached the salerooms in November 1988 is an intriguing story.

When Philip Robinson and his brother Lionel purchased in 1946 the library of the great collector and bibliophile Sir Thomas Phillipps, Bt, they found among the voluminous papers a modest bundle described in Phillipps's catalogue as '1091 Fragmenta Sinica Historica'. On the wrapper Phillipps had added the pencil note, 'the original papers of the Jesuit Verbiest, the Astronomer in China. They were bought at the Meerman sale and came originally from the Jesuit College at Clermont.' Phillipps had attended in person the sale of the collections of the Dutch dealer Gerard Meerman at the Hague in 1824, and there had purchased the Chinese maps as lot 1091. The most famous of Meerman's acquisitions was the great library of the Jesuit College of Louis Le Grand at Clermont, near Paris, which was sold in 1764 following the suppression of the Society of Jesus in 1762. How and when the maps came to the College remains unknown. Phillipps's belief that they were all from Father Verbiest may have been his own inference.

Whatever their earlier provenance, these 'Chinese fragments' have proved to comprise one of the finest collections of Chinese Jesuit maps now known. They survive as a memorial to a remarkable exchange of spiritual and wordly wisdom between West and East.

Left

Blaise Cendrars and Sonia Delaunay

La prose du Transsibérien et de La Petite Jehanne de France, with watercolour illustrations by Sonia Delaunay, folded into 42 panels, presentation copy to Alexander Archipenko, inscribed by the author *aux Archi Penk O Madame et Monsieur le poème de le beau chemin de fer que l'a est peut-être en [.] ain de délivrer [?]/Blaise Cendrars/Nice, janv. 1918*, Editions des Hommes Nouveaux, Paris, 1913
New York $99,000 (£54,098). 14.XII.88

This is the first French modern illustrated book; it holds a unique place as the precursor of the modern *livre d'artiste*. It is one of only 60 copies completed, of a proposed edition of 150. The extraordinary format of the *Transsibérien* is related to the Delaunays' fascination with the Eiffel Tower. For the 150 proposed copies of the book, each unfolded to its full two metres and floated end to end, would have risen to the height of the tower. Sonia Delaunay's original oil painting for the large pochoir illustration is preserved in the Musée National d'Art Moderne, Paris.

Marie Laurencin and le comte de Comminges
Dans son beau jardin, original wrappers, uncut, decorated throughout with 39 watercolour drawings by Marie Laurencin, inscribed by the artist for Madame Robert Ellissen, Paris, 1930
London £30,800 ($60,060). 1.XII.88

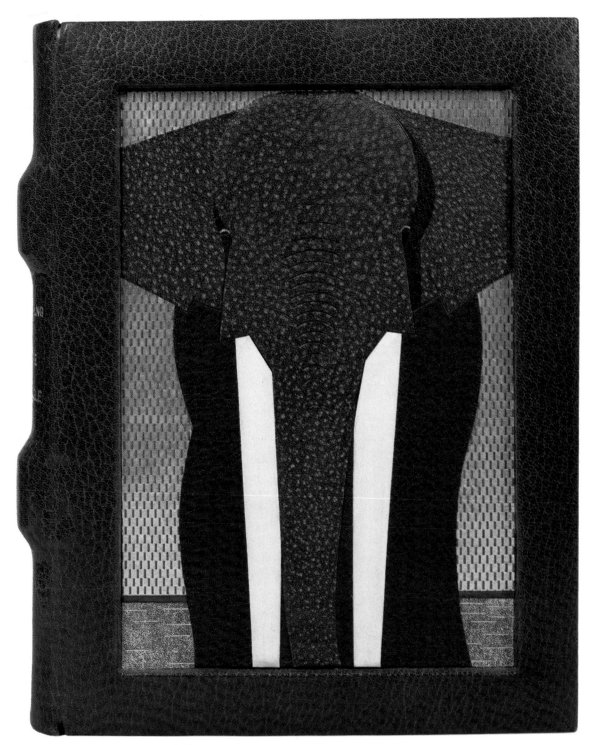

Paul Jouve and Rudyard Kipling
Le Livre de la Jungle, 127 drawings by Paul Jouve, 17 of which engraved in wood by F.L.Schmied, the
green morocco binding by Henri Creuzevault, Le Livre Contemporain, Paris, 1919
Geneva SF69,300 (£24,750: $36,474), 14.XI.88

Manuscripts

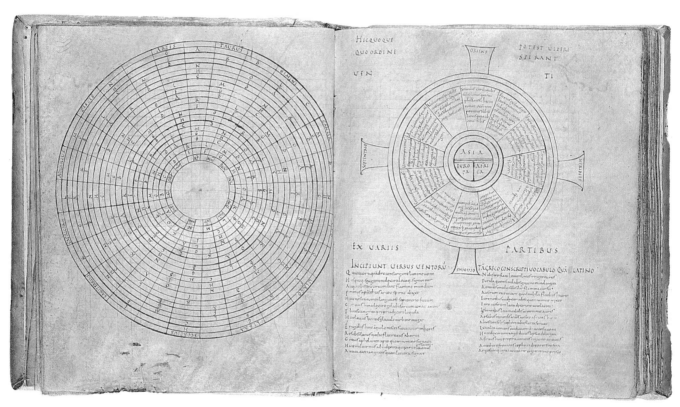

Bede
De Natura Rerum; *De Temporibus*; *De Temporum Ratione*, and other works comprising the entire corpus of
the scientific work on chronology and the nature and structure of the earth, together with works on the
calendar and the zodiac, cosmography, meteorology, mathematics and world history, including the
original manuscripts of the *Annales Laudunensis* and the *Annales Trevirensis*, an illustrated manuscript on
vellum, in Latin, with a few words in Old English and Greek, 97 leaves, Rheims or Laon, first half
ninth century, 10¼in by 8⅞in (26cm by 22.5cm)
London £616,000 ($1,213,520). 6.XII.88
From the collection of the J. Paul Getty Museum, Malibu, California

Bede died at Jarrow in 735, about a century before the present manuscript was written.
His three principal scientific texts, *De Temporibus*, on the nature of time, written in 703;
De Temporum Ratione, the foundation text for the Western calendar, promoting the theory
that years should be numbered from the birth of Christ, *anno domini*, written in 725, and
De Natura Rerum, written around 700, form part of this magnificently written and illustrated
manuscript with twenty-four diagrams and tables as well as a simplified world map. It was
written in north-east France, probably at Rheims, or at Laon following a Rheims exemplar.

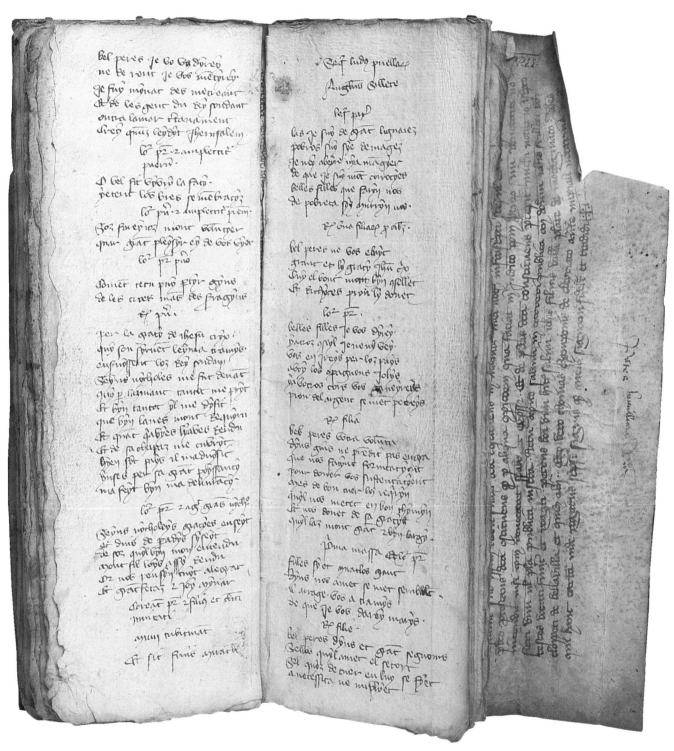

Ludi Sancti Nycholi, eight miracle plays on the Life of St Nicholas, a manuscript on paper, in a long thin
pocket-shape format suggesting actual use in public performances, in French, with stage directions in
Latin, 25 leaves, eastern France, possibly Aubepierre, early fifteenth century,
11¾in by 4⅛in (29.8cm by 10.5cm)
London £115,500 ($227,535). 6.XII.88

Equi
pfidi
est ear
de ura
dommo
abscodatis consilium quo
rum sunt in tenebris opi

et graut. Quis undet nos.
Et quis nouit nos. Per
uersa est hec uestra excita
tio quasi si lutum contra
figulum cogitet et dicat op
factori suo. non me fecisti. et
sapientiam dicat factor

The library of the late Major J.R. Abbey

There is a long tradition of manuscript collecting in England. In the first half of the twentieth century a whole generation of wealthy collectors became inspired by the persuasive enthusiasm of Sir Sydney Cockerell, Director of the Fitzwilliam Museum. Major John Roland Abbey began his book collection in 1929 and bought his first medieval manuscript in 1934, noting in his acquisitions ledger 'Sydney Cockerell approved'. He was fortunate to buy manuscripts at a time when a number of old collections were still being dispersed and acquired books from the libraries of Helmingham Hall, Sir Thomas Phillipps, Sir Robert Shafto Adair and Lord Peckover, as well as from his contemporaries. He bought widely and would seek manuscripts of importance not only for their text, but in conjunction with significant bindings, miniatures and provenances.

His own library has been dispersed over twenty-five years in a series of sales of which the eleventh and final session took place in June 1989. Among the 44 items in the sale was Major Abbey's greatest manuscript, the Monypenny Breviary (Fig. 1). Medieval liturgical manuscripts for Scottish patrons are extremely rare, owing to the vigorousness of puritanism in Scotland. The Monypenny Breviary has survived because it was made in France for a Scottish family living abroad. Sir William Monypenny (fl. 1460–88) was a Scottish ambassador in France who married Katherine Stewart by whom he had two sons. The younger, William, took holy orders succeeding to the abbacy of the convent of Saint-Satur in Berry *circa* 1489. He probably commissioned the Breviary for his elder brother, Sir Alexander Monypenny, councillor and chamberlain to Louis XII.

The Breviary is exceptionally rich with over 120 miniatures and a lavish sixteenth-century binding, probably by the royal binder, Claude de Picques. It was made in Bourges near Abbot William's monastery and illuminated by two well-known artists, Jean de Montluçon and his son and successor Jacquelin. Many manuscripts have been attributed to the Montluçons on stylistic grounds, but the Monypenny Breviary is the only one signed by Jacquelin and its borders bustle with the 'wild men' of the Montluçon shop sign.

The only English manuscript from this part of the collection was the Clarence Hours (Fig. 2). One of the surprisingly few really luxuriously illuminated English Books of Hours, it was made in London for Margaret, Duchess of Clarence (d.1439), the widow of Thomas, Duke of Clarence, second son of Henry IV. The Duke was killed in battle on Easter Eve, 1421 and one of the miniatures shows his funeral mass in Canterbury Cathedral. Two principal hands are distinguishable in the miniatures, one of which has been tentatively identified with the artist who worked on Queen Elizabeth's Book of Hours in the British Library.

Fig. 1
The Monypenny Breviary,
an illuminated manuscript
on vellum, in Latin, use of
Rome, 822 leaves, Bourges,
circa 1490–95, 9⅛ by 5¾in
(23.2cm by 14.5cm)
London £1,870,000
($3,048,100). 19.VI.89
From the library of the
late Major J.R. Abbey

ncipunt quindecim psalmi anti.
Pater dñe. psalmus
d dominum cum tribu
lara damani.
euaui oculos meos in montes.
etatus sum in hys que dicta.
d te leuaui oculos meos qui.
hsi quia dominus erat in nobis.

Opposite
Fig. 2
The Clarence Hours,
an illuminated manuscript
on vellum, in Latin, use of
Sarum, 120 leaves, London,
circa 1421–30, $9\frac{5}{8}$ in by $6\frac{3}{4}$ in
(24.4cm by 17.1cm)
London £286,000
($466,180). 19.VI.89
From the library of the
late Major J.R. Abbey

The Wodhull-Haberton Hours (Fig. 3), so named after two previous British owners, is by one of the finest of all late Dutch miniaturists. His costumes and exquisite landscapes, and his sense of colour and spatial depth belong to the realm of Netherlandish panel painting. He may well have been trained in Ghent or Bruges, although the distinctive red and blue penwork borders of the manuscript are characteristic of Delft workmanship.

With a total of just on 200 miniatures, a thirteenth-century Italian Bible (Fig. 4) was one of the most delicate and rich Italian Gothic manuscripts to appear on the market for many years. Amongst other curiosities were a book signed by the archbishop of Florence who was later canonized as St Antoninus and a miniature showing the relics in the treasury of Sainte-Chapelle in Paris before their destruction in the French Revolution. The final sale of this remarkable collection marks the end of one of the great ages of English bibliophily. It is unlikely that a private library of comparable scope and quality could ever be assembled again.

Fig. 3
The Wodhull-Haberton Hours, an illuminated manuscript on vellum, in Dutch, use of Utrecht, 245 leaves, Delft, *circa* 1480–90, $7\frac{1}{4}$ in by $4\frac{7}{8}$ in (18.5cm by 12.5cm)
London £572,000 ($932,360). 19.VI.89
From the library of the late Major J.R. Abbey

Incipit plogus ge-
neralis sci ieronim
pbri sup totam bibli-
otecam.

FRater ambrosius m
tua munuscula p-
ferens. detulit simul
⁊ suauissimas literas.

regna pertranuit ⁊ ad extremu latissi-
mo phylon amne transmisso puen ad
bracmanas. ut hiarcam in throno se-
dentem aureo. ⁊ de tantali fonte potate. int
paucos discipulos de natura de moribus. ⁊ cur-
su dierum ⁊ syderum audiret docentem. Inde
p elamitas. babylonios. chaldeos. medos. as-
syrios. partos. syros. phenices. arabes. pa-
lestinos. reuersus ad alexandria. perrex et in
ethyopia. ut gignosophistas ⁊ famosissimam
solis mensam uideret in sabulo. Inuenit il-
le uir ubiqꝫ quod disceret. ⁊ semp proficiens. semp
se melior fieret. Scripsit sup hoc plenissime
octo uoluminibus. philostratus.

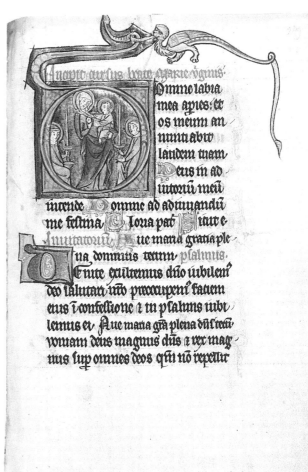

Psalter and Book of Hours, an illuminated manuscript on vellum, in Latin, with a few words in German, 316 leaves, seven full-page miniatures, Flanders, probably Brussels, *circa* 1250–75, 5⅛in by 3¾in (13.1cm by 9.5cm)
London £440,000 ($730,400). 20.VI.89

This is one of the earliest surviving Books of Hours, and belongs to the intermediate period when the offices around the Hours of the Virgin, following a Psalter, were becoming more important than the Psalter itself, and so became worthy of a separate prayerbook.

Opposite
Fig. 4
Bible, with prologues, interpretation of Hebrew names, and a calendar, an illuminated manuscript on vellum, in Latin, 514 leaves, north-east Italy, probably Bologna, *circa* 1250–62, 10¾in by 7¾in (27.5cm by 19.8cm)
London £836,000 ($1,362,680). 19.VI.89
From the library of the late Major J.R. Abbey

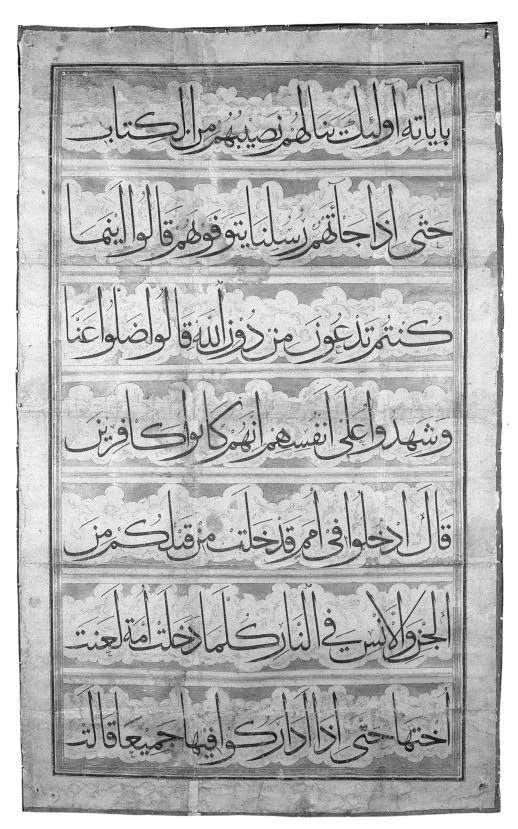

A large Qur'an leaf in
muhaqqaq script, attributed
to Baysunqur ibn Shah
Rukh ibn Timur, Herat,
circa 1420-30,
72½in by 45¼in
(184cm by 115cm)
London
£159,500 ($288,695).
10.X.88

A leaf from Baysunqur's great Qur'an

David James

Fig.1
The gigantic Qur'an stand (230cm by 200cm) in the courtyard of the Bibi Khanum Mosque, Samarkand.

The leaf from a huge copy of the Qur'an which sold on 10th October 1988, for a world record price for a single page, is one of a small number of folios surviving from a manuscript reputedly written by the famous Persian bibliophile and calligrapher, Prince Baysunqur-Mirza. It is traditionally thought to have been written for the great mosque of Samarkand, the so-called Bibi Khanum mosque. In the courtyard of the mosque is a gigantic Qur'an reading stand, the measurements of which correspond rather well with the dimensions of the Baysunqur Qur'an. It measures 230cm by 200cm while most of the surviving pages of the manuscript measure 184cm by 115cm, thus an open copy would fill the stand almost exactly. The Qur'an stand was commissioned for the mosque by Ulugh Beg (1409-49) and was moved to its current location in the centre of the courtyard in 1875 (Fig.1).

The mosque was built by Baysunqur's grandfather, Timur, or Tamberlaine, the last of the Central Asian warlords to deserve the title 'Conqueror of the World'. Timur's armies ravaged Iran, Russia and India in the east while in the west he invaded Anatolia and captured Damascus, where the famous Arab historian Ibn Khaldun met him in 1401. Timur died in 1405, during the journey to China, which he had planned to attack. His body was taken back to Samarkand and buried at Gur-i Mir, a mausoleum built by him for his grandson in 1403 (Fig.2).

By a strange paradox, the Timurid dynasty which the conqueror established in

Iran and Central Asia was one of the most cultivated and enlightened ever to rule in those parts. The Timurids are often compared to the Medicis, and like their Italian contemporaries, were great patrons of literature, architecture, music and painting. Baysunqur was one of the best known of the Timurids in this respect, particularly famous for his wonderful library which he established and for which large numbers of illustrated manuscripts were commissioned, of which some still survive today. He is known to have recruited scribes and artists on a vast scale; at least forty scribes were employed on a full-time basis, including some of the finest calligraphers of the time.

In addition to being a great patron of the arts, Baysunqur was himself an outstanding calligrapher. He was taught by Shams al-Din Muhammad ibn Husam al-Harawi. The same man copied out a Qur'an for his royal pupil, based on an original by the famous Yaqut, and this is now in the Turkish-Islamic Museum in Istanbul. Baysunqur was adept at all the classical hands of Islamic calligraphy, but was particularly renowned for his mastery of *thuluth* and *muhaqqaq*. While still a young man he produced a magnificent inscription in *thuluth* for the archway of the Gawhar Shad Mosque in Mashhad, which is proof that he was certainly capable of working on a large scale; it is signed on the lower left: 'Baysunqur son of Shah Rukh son of Timur'. Like all the Timurids he was proud of his descent.

This great Qur'an, copied in *muhaqqaq*, has text on only one side of the page. Like most other surviving examples the reverse is covered with a crude 'collage' of nineteenth-century paper, evidently added for support. The verses are from the *surah Al-A'raf* (VII), vs 37-38 and are written in panels which have been partially gilded and illuminated in the nineteenth century. There is no rosette marking the division between the verses as there is on other folios but this one is in very good condition, considering its history. The manuscript was probably not intended to be bound. It has been suggested that this is because it was in the form of a roll, but this seems unlikely, considering the enormous size which the final roll would have been.

To have worked on such a large scale over several hundred pages with such breath-taking precision must have required an inordinate amount of mental, not to mention physical, discipline. It is strange to think that Baysunqur went on to dissipate his energies in the hedonistic excess that brought about his death in 1433-34, at the age of 35, in Herat, where he had spent most of his life surrounded, as the chroniclers tell us, by artists and literati 'from all over Iran and Turan'.

There is written evidence of another huge Qur'an dating from the time of Timur, but this was copied by 'Umar Aqta'. He was said to have produced it after Timur refused a tiny version which he had copied, so small that it could fit under a signet ring. After the Conqueror declined the gift 'Umar set about writing another Qur'an which was so large that it had to be brought to Timur on a cart. This pleased him much more and he rewarded the calligrapher handsomely. What became of the Qur'an we do not know, but the Baysunqur manuscript was evidently in Samarkand until Nadir Shah captured the city in the eighteenth century. While the Afshar warlord was trying unsuccessfully to prise open the tomb of Timur (according to an article by Y. Zoka in the *Journal of the Regional Cultural Institute*) his men were stuffing the pages of the huge Qur'an into their saddle-bags, as treasured relics or soldiers' mementoes. Nadir Shah is said to have tried to recover the pages but could only lay his hands on some. However, according to M. Bayani in *Ahwal wa Athar-i Khushnavisan*,

Fig.2
Gur-i Mir, Samarkand,
the mausoleum built for
Timur, 'Conqueror of the
World'.

it was Nadir Shah himself who removed the manuscript from Samarkand. The fate of the pages in subsequent years is uncertain. Some were put in the tomb of Sultan Ibrahim ibn 'Ali ibn Musa al-Rida at Quchan, which was destroyed by an earthquake. Those folios that were later recovered from the ruins were taken to Mashhad.

By various unknown routes a number of pages, partial pages and fragments found their way into different public and private collections in Iran, while an even smaller group were taken to the West. No complete list of the surviving portions of the manuscript exists, but there are known to be pages or fragments in the following places: The Gulistan Palace Library and the Malik Library, both in Tehran: four pages and four half-pages; The Iran-Bastan Museum and the National Library of Iran: one page and twelve fragments; the Astan-i Quds Library in Mashhad: twelve pages; a private collection in Geneva: one page; The David Collection in Copenhagen: one fragment acquired from a London dealer who had two; a private collection in London: one half-page; the Metropolitan Museum in New York: one fragment; a private collection in Houston, Texas: two conjugate pages. There were four private collectors in Iran who had portions several years ago. The fate of these is unknown, but three fragments which were being offered for sale in London in 1988 may have been part of them.

Qur'an, Arabic manuscript
on paper in *muhaqqaq* script
in alternating blue and
gold, 294 leaves, Safavid,
circa 1550, 14½in by 10in
(37cm by 25.5cm)
London £115,500
($207,900). 10.IV.89
From the collection of the
Nature Conservancy,
Arlington, Virginia.

Opposite
*A performance of the Mevlevi
ritual at Galata on 24th July
1888*, gouache with gold
on paper, with inscription
in Ottoman Turkish
identifying the characters
in the painting and giving
the date of the performance,
Ottoman, *circa* 1888,
31⅛in by 22in
(79cm by 56cm)
London £15,400
($27,720). 10.IV.89

A zebra facing left, Court of Jahangir, Mughal, *circa* 1620, 5⅜in by 7¾in (13.8cm by 19.7cm)
New York $93,500 (£54,046). 22.III.89

A zebra was presented to the Emperor Jahangir in March 1616, by Mir Ja-far. Jahangir's
Memoirs state, 'at this time I saw a wild ass, exceedingly strange in appearance, exactly like
a tiger. From the tip of the nose to the end of tail, and from the point of the ear to the top of
the hoof, black markings, large or small, suitable to their position were seen on it. . . . As it
was strange, some people imagined it had been coloured.'

Opposite
The emperor Shah Jahan watching the elephants Bhishma Dil and Jang Jodha from a window of the Khas Mahal in
the Red Fort at Agra, illustration to the *Padshah-nama*, gouache with gold on paper, Mughal, dated
1049 [1639–1640, 13¾in by 9⅝in (34.8cm by 24.4cm)
New York $143,000 (£82,659). 22.III.89
From the collection of Alita D. Weaver

Judaica

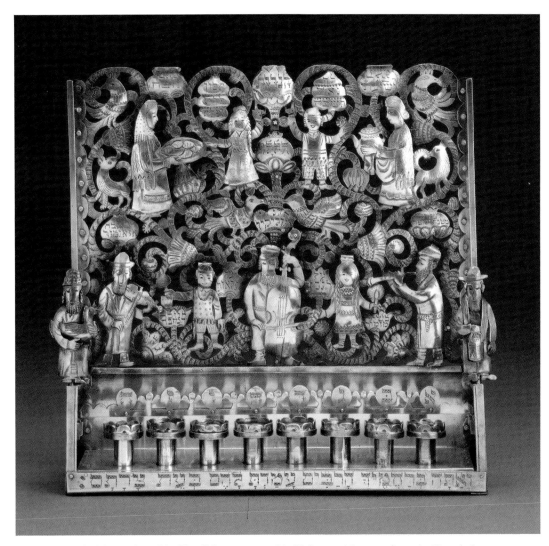

A silver Hanukah lamp signed by Ilya Schor, engraved in Hebrew with verses from the Hanukah song
Ma'o tsur, dated *1958*, height 10⅞in (27.6cm)
New York $132,000 (£71,739). 12.XII.88
From the collection of Jacob Shulman

Opposite, above
Eugen Bracht
A PANORAMIC VIEW OF JERUSALEM
Signed and dated *1912*, 31⅞in by 67¾in (81cm by 172cm)
Tel Aviv $50,600 (£29,941). 30.IV.89

Below
Seder T'fillot Le' Kol Yom U'Le' Leil Shabbat, an illuminated manuscript on vellum, written in Spanish
Hebrew script, 140 leaves, Spain or Portugal, *circa* 1450–75, 3¼in by 2⅜in (8cm by 6cm)
New York $165,000 (£89,674). 12.XII.88

Islamic art

Above
One of three Seljuk lustre-painted Mihrab tiles, Kashan, first half thirteenth century, heights approximately 15in (38cm)
New York $126,500 (£68,011). 2.XII.88
From the collection of James R. Herbert Boone

A Seljuk lustre-painted bowl, Kashan, early thirteenth century, diameter 8⅛in (20.6cm)
New York $19,800 (£12,612). 23.VI.89

A set of eight Iznik tiles, with inscriptions in *thuluth* script, *circa* AD 1565, diameters approximately 10½in (26.8cm)
London £143,000 ($261,690). 12.X.88

Each of the tiles is inscribed with a different Holy name. The practice of decorating Ottoman buildings with ceramic roundels bearing such names can be seen in the mosque of Rustem Pasha in Istanbul. In the Süleymaniye mosque, roundels bearing the same eight names were painted by Hasan Celebi, the pupil of the famous Ottoman calligrapher Ahmet Karahisari. Scalloped roundels are characteristic of Mamluk decoration, a significant influence on Ottoman art. The relief red on the tiles is thinly applied and has a blood red transparency, a feature of the transitional phase of Iznik pottery, from the 'Damascus' to the polychrome style.

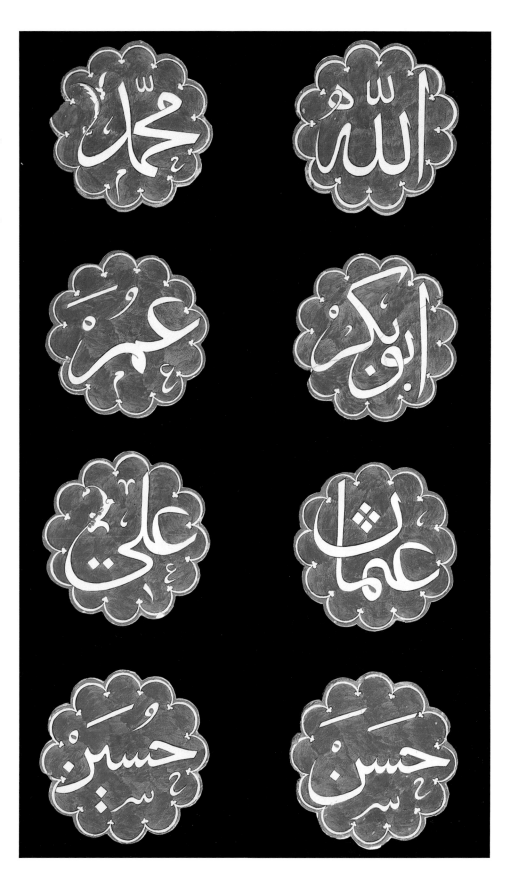

Above
An Ottoman gold inlaid hardstone bowl, first half
sixteenth century, diameter 4⅞in (12.3cm)
London £103,400 ($189,222). 12.X.88

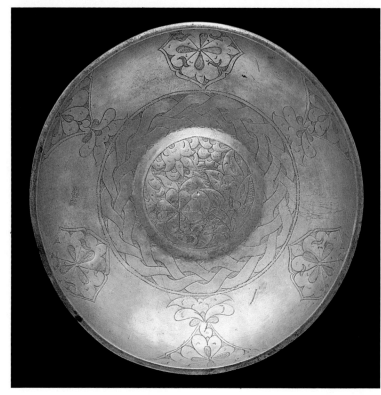

An Ottoman silver-gilt bowl, marked with the *tughra* of
Süleyman I, 'the Magnificent', 1520–66,
diameter 6in (15.4cm)
London £38,500 ($69,300). 12.IV.89

An Ottoman silk and metal thread embroidered barber's apron, eighteenth century,
6ft 2in by 3ft 8in (189cm by 112cm)
London £8,580 ($15,444). 12.IV.89

This work shows the effect of increasing European influence on Ottoman embroidery during the eighteenth century, as the strong colours of the sixteenth and seventeenth centuries gave way to a taste for pastel colours and naturalistic drawing.

A 'Mohtashem' rug, Kashan, mid nineteenth century,
approximately 6ft 8in by 4ft 8in (203cm by 142cm)
New York $52,250 (£28,091).3.XII.88
From the collection of James R. Herbert Boone

An Ottoman carpet, Cairo, seventeenth century,
approximately 26ft 8in by 12ft 3in (813cm by 373cm)
New York $93,500 (£50,269). 3.XII.88

The Mamluk Empire was overthrown by the
Ottomans in 1516–17. By the mid sixteenth century
elements of Ottoman design had found their way
across the empire into carpet weaving centres far
from Istanbul. Weavers in Cairo gradually
adopted organic decorative elements such as
curling leaves and tulip and hyacinth blossoms,
typical of Ottoman textiles, ceramics and
architectural ornamentation of the time, while
maintaining their traditional Mamluk palette.
This carpet is one of the group of carpets woven in
Cairo during the height of the Ottoman Empire.

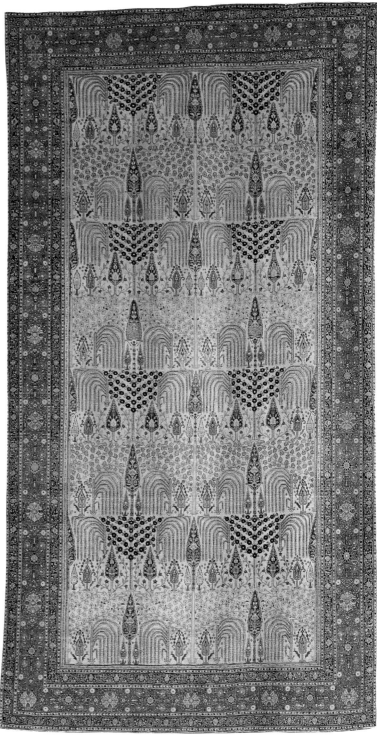

A Tabriz carpet, north-west Persia, last quarter nineteenth century,
approximately 19ft 10in by 10ft 9in (604cm by 328cm)
New York $101,750 (£63,594). 3.VI.89

Japanese art

Unkoku Togan
WILD HORSES
A pair of six-fold screens, ink and light colour on paper, each signed *Sesshu Matsuryu Togan hitsu*,
('painted by Togan, Descendant of Sesshu'), with artist's seals,
each screen 65¼in by 24½in (165.7cm by 62.2cm)
New York $473,000 (£255,676). 8.XII.88

A half-inch refracting telescope, stamped with V.O.C. monograms, second half eighteenth century,
extended length 42in (106.7cm)
London £23,100 ($42,042). 13.III.89

'V.O.C.' ('Vereenigde Oostindische Compagnie': Dutch East India Company) is found on
ceramic dishes but appears to be unrecorded on a telescope of this type.

A gold lacquer *norimono*, complete with carrying pole, the interior of *nashiji* lined with Tosa school
paintings of birds and flowers, Edo period, length excluding pole 54¾in (139cm)
London £82,500 ($150,150). 13.III.89

A lacquer *Suzuribako* depicting the Tatsuta River, Yamato
Amsterdam DFl 51,750 (£14,455:$23,958). 9.V.89

An ivory *netsuke* of a fox, eighteenth century, 3¼in (8.3cm)
New York $68,200 (£39,195).
8.II.89
From the collection of Madelyn Hickmott

A three-case lacquer *inro* by Kajikawa, nineteenth century, inscribed *Koka ni nen kinoto mi haru, Kiso setsukei zu Ichiryusai Hiroshige ga*, ('In the spring of 1854 from the snowscape scene of Kiso Gorge as painted by Ichiryusai Hiroshige'), 3in (7.7cm)
New York $71,500 (£38,649). 9.XII.88

A three-case lacquer sheath *inro* by Tokoku, nineteenth century, signed, 4⅛in (10.5cm)
New York $60,500 (£32,703). 9.XII.88

A wood *netsuke* of a man struggling with a giant eel by Sosui, signed, 2¼in (5.7cm)
New York $27,500 (£15,805). 8.II.89
From the collection of Madelyn Hickmott

A wood and ivory *netsuke* of a boy and horse by Tokoku, signed, late nineteenth century, 4¼in (10.8cm)
New York $22,000 (£12,644). 8.II.89
From the collection of Madelyn Hickmott

Opposite, above
Hiroshige
KANBARA: SNOW AT NIGHT
From the series 'The Fifty-three Stations
on the Tokaido Road', signed, *Oban yoko-e*,
9¼in by 14in (23.5cm by 35.6cm)
London £52,800 ($101,376). 15.XII.88

Below
Kiyochika
ILLUMINATIONS
A print depicting citizens admiring
a new gas light in the shape of a
chrysanthemum, at the First National
Trade Fair held at Ueno, Tokyo in 1878,
signed, *Oban yoko-e*, 9¼in by 14in
(23.5cm by 35.6cm)
London £55,000 ($96,250). 15.V.89

One of a pair of Kakiemon jars and
covers, late seventeenth century,
height 12⅜in (31.5cm)
London £396,000 ($645,480). 19.VI.89
From the collection of Dr Herman
Lindberg

Chinese art

An engraved parcel-gilt silver bowl, Tang Dynasty, diameter 9$\frac{3}{8}$in (24cm)
London £187,000 ($302,940). 13.VI.89

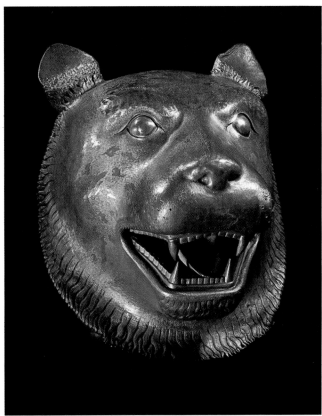

Above, left to right
A bronze head of a horse, Qianlong, height 15in (38.1cm)
£181,500 ($294,030)
A bronze head of a tiger, Qianlong, the character *wang* ('king') on its
forehead, height 12½in (31.9cm)
£137,500 ($222,750)

Right
A bronze head of an ox, Qianlong, height 14½in (36.9cm)
£148,500 ($240,570)

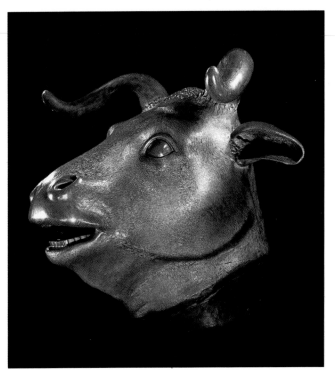

These three bronze heads were sold in London on 13th June
1989. They are part of a group of twelve bronze heads of zodiac
animals designed by Giuseppe Castiglione and executed by
Michel Benoist, for the horological water fountain, built
between 1747 and 1759 for the Emperor Qianlong, at the old
Imperial Summer Palace, the ruins of which lie outside Peking.
Only three years after its completion the hydraulic machinery
of the fountain fell victim to its own complexity and without the
attention of Benoist, who died in 1774, it ceased to work. The
fountain was destroyed in 1860; it seems likely that the heads
were taken to Paris at this time. Two other heads from this
fountain, the monkey and the boar, were sold in New York in
October 1987 and were illustrated in *Art at Auction 1987-88*,
p.271, together with an engraving of the assembled fountain.

A carved cinnabar lacquer dish, mark and period of Yongle, diameter 13½in (34.3cm)
Hong Kong HK$2,860,000 (£202,837:$366,197). 17.XI.88

An unglazed pottery figure of a caparisoned Fereghan stallion, Tang Dynasty,
height 35¼in (89.5cm)
London £484,000 ($934,120). 13.XII.88

This exceptionally large pottery horse appears to be one of only six of equivalent size ever
recorded – one of which, its companion, was sold in the same sale (£231,000:$445,830). Both
horses have a sculptural quality and naturalistic modelling which is otherwise found only on
much smaller models.

Left to right
An armorial blue and white dish, 1690–1700, diameter 8⅜in (21.3cm), $10,450 (£5,904)
An armorial charger, *circa* 1735, diameter 17⅝in (44.8cm), $29,700 (£16,780)
An armorial tea caddy, *circa* 1700, with a later pewter cover, height 4⅝in (11.7cm), $7,700 (£4,350)
An armorial enamelled copper goblet, *circa* 1735, height 6⅞in (17.3cm), $15,400 (£8,701)
An armorial blue and white pilgrim flask, 1610–20, height 12in (30.5cm), $110,000 (£62,147)

The above Chinese export porcelain, from the collection of Mrs Rafi Y. Mottahedeh, was sold in New York on 25th January 1989.

A *famille-rose* tureen, with cover and stand, modelled in mid-eighteenth-century French Rococo
silver style, Qianlong, 16¼in (41.3cm)
Monte Carlo FF777,000 (£74,000:$129,500). 5.III.89

An Imperial *famille-rose* chrysanthemum vase, mark and period of Yongzheng, height 13½in (34.3cm)
New York $1,650,000 (£1,050,955). 31.V.89
From the collection of Frederick J. and Antoinette H. Van Slyke

A *famille-rose* peach dish, mark and period of Yongzheng, diameter $19\frac{7}{8}$ in (50.5 cm)
New York $1,430,000 (£910,828). 31.V.89
From the collection of Frederick J. and Antoinette H. Van Slyke

Chinese art in Hong Kong

Sotheby's long ago realized the importance of the Far Eastern market, and in 1973 Sotheby's Hong Kong Ltd was formed to hold auctions (originally in association with Lane Crawford) of Chinese ceramics on an annual basis. Sixteen years later it is now expected that Sotheby's Hong Kong turnover for 1989 will be in the region of HK$500,000,000 (some £42,000,000 or US$64,000,000 at the time of going to press). The sales now take place twice a year, in May and November, and include not only Chinese ceramics, but also jade carvings, jadeite jewellery, works of art and contemporary Chinese paintings.

Much of the Far East has now 'opened up' but the centre of the Chinese art market still remains in Hong Kong. It is to Hong Kong that collectors and dealers from Japan, Taiwan, Singapore as well as America and Europe come to buy the best of the pieces that are described as being of 'Chinese' taste, many of which were made to Imperial order. It is from local Hong Kong collectors and dealers that the greatest demand has emanated and so it is Hong Kong which provides the best location for this type of sale.

Over the years, our auction rooms have included the best that Chinese ceramics have to offer, and the 1980s have seen the dispersal of some spectacular collections, including the Edward T. Chow Collection, the Frederick Knight Collection, the J.T. Tai Foundation Collection, the T.Y. Chao Family and Foundation Collections, the Paul and Helen Bernat Collection and most recently the collection of the British Rail Pension Fund.

The excellence of the pieces on offer coupled with the strength of the competition between local and foreign buyers, particularly since the Taiwanese have been able to participate actively after the removal of exchange controls, has lead to a dramatic rise in prices with all records broken over the last two years. The sale of the collection of the British Rail Pension Fund in May 1989 was included in a three-day series of sales totalling an unprecedented HK$300,000,000 (£25,000,000:$38,500,000). During this series the strength of the market was emphasised by the fact that the highest price ever paid for a Chinese ceramic was surpassed not once but twice; firstly by the underglaze-red Hongwu basin (see p. 284) and again by the *guanyao* brushwasher shown opposite.

A *guanyao* brushwasher, Southern Song Dynasty, with nineteenth-century fitted and inscribed wood stand, 8in (20.3cm)
Hong Kong HK$22,000,000 (£1,722,788: $2,831,403). 16.V.89

This previously unpublished vessel has been variously described as a brushwasher, a medicine mortar and a warmer, though its more probable use was for mixing the ink and shaping the tip of the brush. It is believed to be of a relatively early date, perhaps late twelfth century. Only one other *guanyao* brushwasher of this hexafoil shape appears to be recorded, from the former Imperial Chinese Collection and now in Taiwan. Two related brushwashers of five-lobed prunus flower form are known, one in the Percival David Foundation, the other in the Museum of Chinese History, Peking. The wood stand is inscribed: 'Made in the imperial kilns a long time ago for the inner chambers; at that time it was forbidden to use it in the outer rooms. From that time to this seven or eight hundred years have passed. The morning star has bequeathed it. I admire its perfection, it is as beautiful as jade. Where can one find such flawlessness?' The inscription is followed by the signature of the prominent nineteenth-century calligrapher, statesman, archaeologist and art collector, Wu Dacheng. The seal *wuchen Hanlin* seems to refer to the wuchen year (1868), during which Wu is known to have been made a bachelor of the Hanlin Academy, strongly suggesting that the brushwasher was in fact in the Wu collection.

Fig. 1
An imperial yellow-ground landscape bowl, mark and period of Qianlong, diameter 5⅞in (15cm)
Hong Kong HK$7,920,000 (£561,702:$1,014,085). 15.XI.88
From the Paul and Helen Bernat Collection

Qing imperial porcelain from the Bernat Collection

Shelley Drake

The sale of Chinese ceramics from the Bernat Collection, held in Hong Kong on 15th November 1988, commemorated one of the most outstanding collectors of Qing imperial porcelain in the West. For more than forty years, Paul Bernat searched tirelessly for the finest examples of eighteenth-century Chinese imperial porcelain, visiting dealers in London, Paris, New York, Tokyo and Hong Kong.

In terms of instinct for quality and enthusiasm for Qing imperial ceramics, Bernat ranks with the famous collectors, A.E. Hippisley, Henry Knight and Sir Percival David. With the exception of these few, connoisseurs in the West have overlooked Qing imperial porcelain. Recently, however, the strong economic position of collectors in the Far East has influenced the demand for Qing ceramics. The staggering prices fetched at the Bernat auction – surpassing previous records by two and threefold – demonstrate this and offer dramatic testament to Paul Bernat's farsightedness.

Born in Hungary in 1902, Paul Bernat emigrated to America with his family. After graduating from Harvard in 1923, he helped his father Emile, a textile weaver and restorer associated with the Boston Museum of Fine Arts, to develop the family company. Paul and his brother Eugene shared a passion for Chinese ceramics and began collecting seriously in the 1940s under the guidance of Kojiro Tomita, Curator of Asiatic Art at the Boston Museum. Tomita, perhaps sensing the competition between the two brothers, steered them in separate directions – encouraging Eugene to concentrate on Ming dynasty and earlier ceramics; and Paul, on Qing dynasty imperial monochromes and enamelled wares. Contemporary connoisseurs favoured earlier ceramics which made Paul's assignment difficult to sustain. Although at times he grew discouraged, the scorn he felt he received from his contemporaries finally invigorated him, strengthening his resolve to elevate the appreciation of Qing ceramics.

Chinese imperial ceramics can be distinguished from those produced for export or for the general Chinese market by the advanced potting technique and the quality of the painted decoration. During the height of Qing ceramic production through the Kangxi (1662–1722), Yongzheng (1723–35) and Qianlong (1736–95) periods, the imperial kilns at Jingdezhen practised a highly sophisticated system of assembly-line production. According to Père d'Entrecolles, a Jesuit missionary who visited the kilns in 1712, the production system was extremely specialized: one piece of porcelain, after firing, would have passed through the hands of sixty workers. Particularly under the direction of Tang Ying, assistant supervisor and later supervisor of the Jingdezhen factory from 1728–56, the imperial kilns achieved a level of technical virtuosity never attained before or since.

Fig. 3
An imperial coral-ground
bowl, mark and period of
Yongzheng, diameter $5\frac{7}{8}$in
(14.9cm)
Hong Kong
HK$1,760,000
(£124,823:$225,352).
15.XI.88
From the Paul and Helen
Bernat Collection

The finest pieces produced at Jingdezhen were sent to the imperial porcelain workshop inside the Forbidden City. There, the best would be painted by court artists of the Imperial Painting Academy especially for the Emperor or Empress's personal use. An exquisite example of such refined work is an imperial yellow-ground bowl of the Qianlong period (Fig.1), painted with four separate landscape scenes in rose-coloured enamel. Considered the highlight of the auction, the bowl sold for an astonishing HK$7,920,000 (£561,702:$1,014,085). Similar bowls have not been traced in the West, nor are there comparable examples in major museums in the Far East. Stylistically, the decoration is similar to landscape painting of the Qianlong era, by such leading court painters as Dong Bangda (1699–1769), Dong Gao (1740–1818), Tang Dai (1673–1752), and Qian Weicheng (1720–72). The brilliant yellow border that defines each miniature landscape scene suggests the elaborate window frame of a palace interior, a *trompe-l'oeil* effect which engages us in each setting as if we were surveying scenery from within a building. The interior of the bowl contains a charming footnote: a lyrically-composed stem of pink and white roses painted so naturally that the flowers appear to be real.

An imperial Yongzheng coral-ground bowl, painted in a *famille-rose* palette of green, blue, yellow and pink (Fig. 3) provides an exquisite example of the period.

The frieze of flowers and grasses rising from the foot-rim includes pink and off-white dianthus with delicately veined and serrated petals.

One of the chief differences between Qing ware and earlier ceramics is an interest in dynamic, rich colour. Westerners tend to overlook the fact that Qing emperors were not Chinese, but Manchurian, originally a nomadic people from the steppelands north-east of China. The Manchurians brought to Chinese ceramics a renewed emphasis on colour for colour's sake, not seen since the three-coloured earthenware of the Tang dynasty. An exquisite example of this treatment of colour can be seen on the imperial yellow-ground bowl of the Kangxi period (Fig. 4) which features four large lotus blossoms in vibrant shades of blue, aubergine, yellow, green and pink.

The sale also featured works of art from the Bernat Collection, including a very fine Peking enamel snuff bottle of the Qianlong period with painted decoration of a Western shepherd girl (Fig. 2). Bidding for this rare miniature was fierce, setting the record for the price of a snuff bottle at HK$715,000 (£50,709: $91,549). European subject matter in Chinese painting is quite rare and is found almost exclusively during the Qianlong period when Castiglione and other Western painters were accepted at the imperial court. A taste for exoticism pervaded the Qianlong era, not unlike the fashion for chinoiserie in the West.

Paul Bernat will be remembered not only for his impeccable connoisseurship, but also for his enthusiasm for collecting Chinese ceramics, which inspired countless others to follow. At the Boston Museum of Fine Arts, Paul and Helen Bernat have been rewarded for their generosity and years of service to the Museum by a gallery named in their honour. The Bernat Gallery houses Chinese imperial works of art, including many pieces of Qing imperial porcelain donated to the Museum from the original Bernat Collection.

Fig. 4
An imperial yellow-ground bowl, mark and period of Kangxi,
diameter 5in (12.6cm)
Hong Kong
HK$3,740,000 (£265,248: $478,873). 15.XI.88
From the Paul and Helen Bernat Collection

Chinese art from the collection of the British Rail Pension Fund

Julian Thompson

The first part of the collection of Chinese ceramics and works of art formed by the British Rail Pension Fund, sold in May 1989 in Hong Kong, comprised porcelain from the Yuan, Ming and Qing dynasties, as well as a small group of jades. The majority of the porcelain was made for the Imperial Court and the principal buyers in the field are Chinese collectors, though a small number of Japanese contend for the most important pieces. The predominance of Far Eastern buyers made the location of the sale most appropriate, whereas the second part of their collection, comprising Song and earlier ceramics, also ancient bronzes, to be sold in London in December 1989, will attract more buyers from Europe and America.

The collection, started in December 1974, and almost complete by 1981, was formed with the following guidelines. It was agreed first that a representative collection of Chinese art of different dynasties should be formed, concentrating on ceramics and early bronzes but omitting paintings which, due to uncertainty of attribution were regarded as too speculative. The reasons for this broad approach were two-fold. First, different categories of Chinese art had already shown much

Fig. 3
An imperial pink-ground
bowl, mark and period of
Kangxi,
diameter 5⅛in (13cm)
Hong Kong HK$8,800,000
(£689,115:$1,132,561).
16.V.89
From the collection of the
British Rail Pension Fund

variation in market performance and a spread of future risk was ensured. For the same reasons a wide variety of art collecting areas had been chosen when the whole art purchasing policy of the Pension Fund was formulated, of which the Chinese sector represented about 10%. Secondly it was decided to build a collection which could eventually be presented to the market in one or more auctions of a balanced kind, of sufficiently high quality to ensure that a fine catalogue was justified and that the sale made an impact on the market without stretching its ability to absorb too much material in any one specialised area.

An individual piece was selected for purchase only if it was the best of its type likely to become available, both in quality and condition. Only great rarities, which could greatly add to the interest of the collection as a whole, were accepted with significant damage. Objects of poor quality, however rare, were avoided. Though the majority of purchases were made at auction, some of the finest earlier objects were bought privately. On many occasions the Fund was outbid at auction, though five years was long enough to form a quite comprehensive collection, even within these admittedly ambitious guidelines. After the purchasing programme was complete the collection was reassessed and it was decided to sell certain pieces of relatively minor types which had been superseded by subsequent more significant and closely related acquisitions. On the other hand a few gaps remained – an example of the porcelain of the classic fifteenth-century period of Chenghua was still lacking and among the Song wares there was no example of *guanyao*, or indeed carved Dingyao.

In the Hong Kong sale, amongst the finest early Ming pieces was the underglaze-red decorated basin (Fig. 1), dating from the reign of Hongwu at the end of the fourteenth century, painted with formal flower patterns typical of the reign. The colour, adopted when the supply of good middle Eastern cobalt-blue became temporarily unavailable, was difficult to fire and whereas the pigment on the basin had fired to a soft, pinkish colour the red of the very rare contemporary ewer in the collection was crisper and darker. Slightly later, from the reign of Yongle, *circa* 1400, came the second basin (Fig. 2), decorated in a fine, rich tone of blue, in the interior with a branch of fruiting peach and lingzhi fungus, and on the outside with peony scrolls.

Among the imperial Qing porcelains two pieces stood out. The *famille-verte* bowl dating from the early eighteenth century and bearing the Kangxi reign mark is one of only three known examples of the pattern and came originally from the collection of Barbara Hutton. The pink-ground bowl (Fig. 3) of an experimental type enamelled in Peking, to special imperial order, dates from the end of the same reign, *circa* 1720. Two of the group of jade carvings (shown in Figs 4 and 5) are both eighteenth-century pieces and are in remarkably pure white stone.

From an investment point of view the Hong Kong sale had a good result showing an average rate of return on investment of 15.5% per annum, calculated in sterling. After allowing for UK inflation the return was 7.1%. As it turned out the Qing porcelain performed better than average, reflecting the pressure on the market from the many Hong Kong and Taiwanese collectors, also strong bidding in the highest price range from Japanese buyers. The jades, which for many years had been lagging behind showed a good return, due to keen interest from Taiwanese buyers who have only recently entered the market for fine white jade. Looking at the performance by price bracket, the seventeen pieces, each with an individual cost of £25,000 or more, gave a marginally higher than average return. It must be left to the sale of the second part of the British Rail collection in December to determine the performance of other sectors of earlier Chinese art over the same period.

Left
Fig. 4
A carved white jade screen and stand, Qianlong, height 10¼in (26cm) Hong Kong HK$2,640,000 (£206,735:$339,768). 16.V.89
From the collection of the British Rail Pension Fund

Right
Fig. 5
A carved white jade vase with cover, Qianlong, height 11in (27.9cm) Hong Kong HK$2,310,000 (£180,893:$297,297). 16.V.89
From the collection of the British Rail Pension Fund

A jadeite bangle, diameter 2⅛in (5.5cm)
Hong Kong HK$7,590,000 (£603,339:$976,834). 17.V.89

A carved jadeite bangle, diameter 2in (5.2cm)
Hong Kong HK$7,040,000 (£499,291:$901,408). 16.XI.88
Formerly in the collection of Barbara Hutton

A rock crystal inside-painted portrait
snuff bottle by Ma Shaoxuan, signed with
the artist's seal and dated tenth winter
month, 1907
London £28,050 ($51,051). 24.IV.89
From the collection of Eric Young

A snuff bottle by Baishi, signed with the
seals *Bai* and *Shi* and dated *1836*
New York $55,000 (£30,055). 22.XI.88

A black and white Suzhou jade snuff
bottle, 1750-1820
New York $52,250 (£28,552). 22.XI.88
From the collection of Cortwright
Wetherill

A pair of huanghuali horseshoe-back armchairs, seventeenth century
New York $93,500 (£54,360). 19.IV.89

Daoji (Shitao)
ALBUM OF FLOWERS
Two of a set of ten leaves, ink on paper, one with touches of colour, each signed and inscribed with a
poem, with twelve artist's seals, each leaf 12⅞in by 9¼in (32.7cm by 23.5cm)
New York $517,000 (£329,299). 31.V.89

Opposite, below
Zhao Mengfu
QIAN ZI WEN (THOUSAND CHARACTER POEM)
Ink on paper, signed and dated *Yanyou* sixth year, eleventh
month, twenty-third day (3rd January 1320), with six artist's
seals, and a great number of collectors' seals,
9⅛in by 395in (23.2cm by 1003.3cm)
New York $539,000 (£343,312). 31.V.89

Above
Wu Guanzhong
RUINS OF GAOCHANG (TURFAN)
Ink and colour on paper, with two artist's seals,
40in by 41¾in (101.6cm by 105cm)
Hong Kong HK$1,870,000 (£149,004: $240,360). 18.V.89

Tribal art

A Luba divinatory bowl, 12in (30.5cm)
London £19,800 ($33,066). 3.VII.89

A Yoruba equestrian figure, Ilobu, Western Nigeria,
height 34¾in (88.3cm)
New York $85,250 (£51,355). 8.V.89

A Fang male reliquary guardian figure, probably of the
Nzaman-Betsi style, Gabon, height 19⅜in (49.2cm)
New York $660,000 (£397,590). 8.V.89
From the collection of the British Rail Pension Fund

Above
A Kota/Obamba wood and metalwork reliquary figure,
height 15¼in (38.7cm)
London £20,900 ($34,903). 3.VII.89

Left
A Kongo oath-taking and healing figure,
height 19in (48.3cm)
New York $154,000 (£85,083). 15.XI.88

Opposite
A Benin royal bronze plaque, late sixteenth century,
20⅞in by 12¼in (53.2cm by 31cm)
London £176,000 ($293,920). 3.VII.89

A Seminole beaded cloth shoulder bag, length with attachments 30½in (77.5cm)
New York $44,000 (£23,913). 29.XI.88

Opposite
A Mezcala stone figure, Type M14, Late Pre-classic, *circa* third–first century BC, height 7½in (19cm)
New York $115,500 (£70,427). 16.V.89
From the collection of Renee and Chaim Gross

While Mezcala figures adhere to a consistency of specific form and type, this figure exhibits
an unusually dynamic combination of traits of both abstract and naturalistic styles.

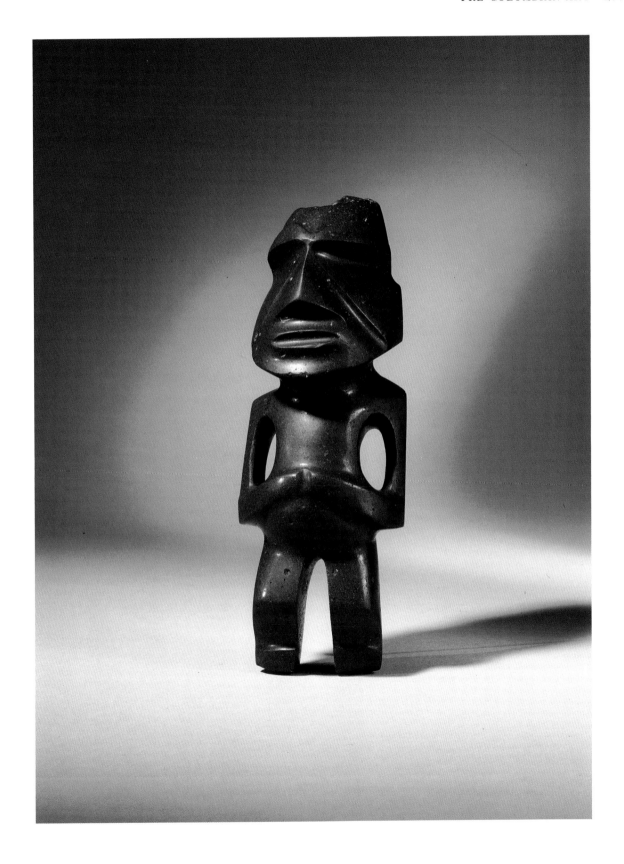

Antiquities
and Asian art

An Anatolian marble female figure, 'Kilia type',
Chalcolithic or Early Bronze Age, *circa* fourth–third
millennium BC, height 7½in (19.1cm)
London £220,000 ($380,600). 10.VII.89
From the collection of the late Madame Marion
Schuster

A Mesopotamian copper alloy foundation figurine of Gudea of Lagash, with Sumerian inscription, *circa* 2100 BC, height 6¾in (17.2cm)
London £198,000 ($342,540). 10.VII.89
From the collection of the late Madame Marion Schuster

A head of an Early Cycladic marble figure

Pat Getz-Preziosi

Among the few thousand whole and fragmentary examples of Early Bronze Age figurative sculpture now known from the Cyclades, only a handful, relatively speaking, can be considered masterworks. Of these, few, if any, had been consigned to auction prior to 1988. It is no small wonder, then, that this little known head should have caused a sensation when it broke all auction records for a work of its time and place.

Meticulously carved in the luminous white marble for which the Cyclades were justly renowned in antiquity, the superbly preserved head is of particular interest for a number of reasons. Not least of these are the beauty and economy of its taut, clean lines and controlled curves, the refinement of its proportions, and the details added in colour on the carefully smoothed surface. Although not as vivid as they once were, these purplish-red details are more fully preserved on this work than on most other extant examples still showing strong traces of actual colour. The forehead fringe (scarf, diadem, or decoration), the tattoo of dots on the cheeks and the chin, and the bold stripe down the nose are not unique to this head. Nevertheless, they are painted with such precision and delicacy that, even though we have grown accustomed to the blank faces of most Cycladic figures which have lost their original painting, on this work the colour adds to its aesthetic appeal, blending subtly with the marble form. For the Aegean islander of some 4500 years ago the painted patterns were marks of beauty and perhaps of status as well, and they probably also had strong symbolic connotations.

In 1987, the head was cleaned and some deposits of calcium carbonate (sure evidence of long burial in damp ground) were judiciously removed just before the piece was included in the exhibition 'Early Cycladic Art in North American Collections,' organized by the Virginia Museum of Fine Arts. At that point it was determined that all the surviving traces of pigment had been exposed. Originally, however, the eyes, brows and a hair mass on the back of the head were painted a bright (but fugitive) blue, which is now only indistinctly visible in places in the form of dark stains.

The head, with only a bit of the neck preserved (on the sides and back), represents about one fifth of the original sculpture: a reclining female figure with folded arms. This classic image of the Cycladic goddess of life and death was repeated again and again by island marble carvers for a period of some five centuries, from about 2700 to about 2200 BC. While iconographically it remained unchanged, the image did develop stylistically, becoming increasingly simplified and streamlined over time. Differences in scale are also observable: the earliest and the latest figures tend to be small – usually no more than 30cm in length – while those made between about 2600 and 2400 BC were frequently two or three times as long. For a brief period,

A Cycladic marble head of a goddess. Early Bronze Age II, early Spedos, *circa* 2600–2500 BC, height 8¾in (22cm) New York $2,090,000 (£1,123,656). 2.XII.88

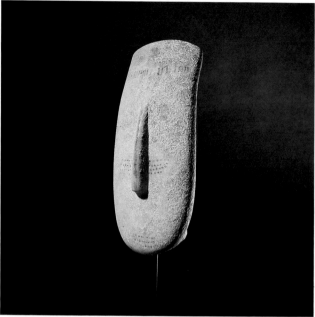

Above
Two details of the head
showing the preserved
areas of the neck, on the
sides and back, and the
narrow, elongated profile.

perhaps lasting no more than one or two generations, some sculptors carved still larger works that approach life size. Whether such works were made unusually large for a special purpose or whether the artists who made them were simply unusually energetic is unclear. In any case, it is to this small, exclusive group – the earliest large sculptures in stone in the Aegean – that the head belongs.

When complete, the work would have measured about 110cm in length. Judging from the extreme narrowness and elongation of the head, the figure must have been very slender throughout. Its widest point, at the shoulders, was probably less than one fifth of the overall length, in contrast to the proportionally much broader shoulders of figures of average size. The 1:5 ratio seems to have been preferred for uncommonly large works; it may have had a practical purpose quite distinct from any pleasing aesthetic effect. The reduced bulk would have made the figure easier for the sculptor to hold during carving, and less of a burden for bearers in a funeral or religious procession.

There can be no doubt that the figure to which the head belonged was carved by one of the finest of the prehistoric Cycladic sculptors. How this image was used once it left his hands is far less certain. How it broke and why the head became separated from the rest is even more of a mystery. To date, the largest figures found under controlled conditions, whether in a sepulchral or in what is thought to be a sanctuary setting, measure less than 60cm; furthermore, no fragments of outsized works have been found during systematic investigations.

It is the fate of orphans from antiquity – works for which all information regarding the circumstances and place of their recovery has been lost – that they are of interest chiefly for their physical charms, their unusual features, their rarity. In these respects this remarkable piece is no exception. Masklike in appearance (due in part to the loss of the neck at the front), its face remains inscrutable.

A Cycladic marble figure of a goddess, Early Bronze Age II, late Spedos, *circa* 2500–2400 BC,
height 8in (20.3cm)
New York $148,500 (£94,586). 23.VI.89
From the collection of Herb and Nancy Baker

A Greek terracotta head of Herakles, *circa* late fourth century BC, height 5⅛in (13cm)
New York $33,000 (£21,019). 23.VI.89

An Egyptian limestone
family group tomb statue
of Ka-Nefer, the Overseer
of Craftsmen and Priest
of Ptah, Saqqara, Old
Kingdom, Fifth–Sixth
Dynasty, *circa* 2475–2300 BC,
height 14in (35.5cm)
London £462,000
($799,260). 10.VII.89

A Graeco-Roman marble
telemon of a satyr,
circa first century BC,
height 30in (76.2cm)
New York $132,000
(£84,076). 23.VI.89

A Roman Imperial marble portrait head of a man, in or near the reign of Gallienus, AD 253–268,
height 11⅞in (30.2cm)
New York $132,000 (£70,968). 2.XII.88
From the collection of Martin Stansfeld

A private collection of Khmer and Thai sculpture

Brendan Lynch

'Let it be said immediately that Angkor, as it stands, ranks as chief wonder of the world today . . .'
Sir Osbert Sitwell,
Escape with Me, 1939

Fig. 1
A Khmer sandstone bust of the five-headed Siva, Pre Rup, third quarter tenth century, height 31½in (80cm) London £319,000 ($606,100). 14.XI.88

From its discovery by the French naturalist Henri Mouhot in 1860, the great temple-complex at Angkor, north-west of Phnom Penh in present-day Cambodia, has occupied a particular place in the European imagination. Mouhot himself felt '. . . transported from [the] barbarism [of Cambodia in 1860] to civilisation, from profound darkness to light' on seeing the jungle-encrusted ruins of Angkor Wat, extravagantly declaring them '. . . more grandiose than anything built in the heyday of Greek or Roman art' in *Le Tour du Monde*, a subsequent account of his travels. Six years after Mouhot's discovery, a French mission conducted the first survey of the ruins at Angkor, the results of which were published by Francis Garnier in his famous *Voyage d'Exploration en Indochine* in 1873. Further expeditions followed and were continued and intensified with the foundation of the Ecole Française d'Extrême-Orient in 1898. Through the combined efforts of generations of scholars – Coedès, Parmentier, de Coral-Rémusat, Foucher, Finot, Stern, Marchal, Groslier, Dupont and Boisselier amongst them – this institution was ultimately responsible for the clearance, excavation, documentation and restoration of many of the thousands of

Right
Detail showing the head in profile.

Fig. 2
A Khmer sandstone figure
of a four-armed male
deity, probably Vishnu,
Phnom Kulen, first
half ninth century,
height 48½in (123cm)
London £209,000
($397,100). 14.XI.88

monuments built by the Khmer kings between the seventh and the thirteenth centuries. Moreover, they established a firm chronology which resulted in the accurate dating of the main buildings in the Angkor region, thus unshrouding some of the mystery associated with the temples referred to by Mouhot and his contemporaries. They further revealed the cult of the 'god-king', established by King Jayavarman II on his return from exile in Java, through which the Khmer dynasty came to wield enormous power and claim divine kingship through the Hindu god Siva. However, the romantic idea that these unique temples were lost in time was not completely quelled by these discoveries and the temples at Angkor continued to exert what in 1943 George Coedès called '. . . a vital quality that still attracts all who see them.'

A French presence was established in Indo-China with the annexation of Saigon in 1859, followed by the establishment of a protectorate over Cambodia and Annam (now Vietnam) in 1874 and over Laos in 1893. Following the Geneva conference of 1954, these latter three countries became independent states, thus ending almost a century of French presence in Indo-China and over fifty years of archaeological research and conservation by the Ecole Française d'Extrême-Orient. Despite the establishment of museums containing Khmer art at Phnom Penh, Hanoi and Saigon (now Ho Chi Minh City), a large number of the most important Khmer sculptures had been sent to the Musée Guimet, Paris, and these today form the most important collection of Khmer sculpture extant. With few exceptions, private collections do not appear to have been formed and thus, the appearance of a collection of some twenty Khmer and Thai stone and bronze sculptures, spanning the seventh to the fifteenth centuries, at Sotheby's on 14th November 1988 created world-wide interest amongst museums, private collectors and dealers.

The collection, which formed the nucleus of a sale of one hundred and eight lots of Khmer, Thai, Indian and Himalayan works of art, was formed during the last eight to ten years by a private collector resident in Europe. The majority of the sculptures had been purchased from London dealers in the period 1978–80. The most important piece in the collection was a monumental Khmer grey sandstone bust of the five-headed Siva (Fig. 1), in the style of the Pre Rup temple at Angkor and therefore dating from the third quarter of the tenth century. Built by King Rajendravarman (r. 944–68) in honour of his parents, the temple was finished in 961. It compares in plan with the mountain-temple of East Mebon, which Rajendravarman had built between 947–52 in honour of his ancestors, both having five main towers. In erecting the statues of the god-kings and the temples which housed them, Rajendravarman was propagating the funerary cult established by his ancestors in the previous century. The apparent images of Vishnu, Siva and other gods were often in fact portraits of the antecedents of the particular king building the temple in their honour. The attachment of such importance to ancestor-worship may have been derived from Java, where princely forbears were worshipped under the guise of Brahman and Buddhist deities. Siva, the great 'Creator and Destroyer' is, with Brahma and Vishnu, one of the triad of principal gods of Hinduism. He has been worshipped in the Indian sub-continent from the earliest times and though previously considered a later form of the Vedic god Rudra, he may now be considered a pre-Indo-Aryan god. No other five-headed stone Siva image comparable in terms of quality of execution and of relatively early date, is known to have survived. The sculpture itself is of finely grained polished grey sandstone, each of its five faces carved with linear bow-shaped moustache, chiselled beard and three slender eyes with incised borders, the third eye carved vertically at the centre of the forehead as is usual for multi-headed Siva images.

The return of a Cambodian prince from exile in Java at the end of the eighth century marked the twilight of Javanese rule in Cambodia. Having achieved military domination, the man who subsequently became King Jayavarman II of Kambuja (Cambodia, now Kampuchia) introduced a new religious cult through which he became worshipped as a god-king (*devaraja*). Jayavarman (d. 850) claimed kingship had been bestowed upon him by the Hindu god Siva and the cult was initiated when in 802 a Brahman priest established a *linga* – the Savaite phallic emblem of spiritual power – on a mountain near Kulen, some eighteen miles north-east of Angkor. The concept of the *linga* enshrined in the 'temple-mountain' became the enduring spiritual ideal which inspired Khmer architecture and propagated its kings. The ninth century therefore saw a renaissance in Khmer art, dividing the earlier Indian-influenced 'Pre-Angkor' sculptures of Jayavarman's ancestors from the new more indigenous 'Angkor' style which was partly inspired by Javanese religious ideology and marked the beginning of the Angkor period. Fine sculptures from this period rarely come on the market and in consequence there was much interest in the large sandstone standing figure of Vishnu in the style of the Phnom Kulen temple, dating from the

Fig. 3
A Khmer sandstone figure of a male deity, Banteai Srei, second half tenth century, height 19⅛in (48.5cm) London £159,500 ($303,050). 14.XI.88

first half of the ninth century (Fig. 2). The figure is lacking its feet and the lower half of each of the four arms; its hands would originally have held the four attributes of the God, *viz.* the sacred wheel, conch-shell, club and lotus flower. The image conveys a monumental hieratic presence which epitomizes Khmer sculpture at its best. It was acquired by a private European collector.

The temple of Banteai Srei, meaning 'Citadel of the Women' was erected during the reign of King Jayavarman V (968–1001) and is considered one of the finest at Angkor. It consists of three small towers on a high terrace and incorporates pavilions, shrines and libraries, the main shrine being devoted to Siva.

Often described as gem-like because of its small size and its exquisite decorative carving, the most outstanding feature of the temple at Banteai Srei is the carving of vast tympana illustrating Hindu myths, one of which is now at the Musée Guimet, Paris. It is also known for its salutary male and female figures standing in niches surrounded by vigorous scrolls incorporating animal and vegetal motifs. Banteai Srei sculpture carved in the round is therefore uncommon and this profound, spiritually alluring kneeling figure (Fig. 3), with the cylindrical chignon of swagged plaits peculiar to the Banteai Srei style, is similar only to seated figures of monkey-, lion-, and bird-headed deities *in situ* at the temple.

During the later Angkor period, the Khmer kings converted to Buddhism, which had long co-existed with Hinduism in Indo-China. The Khmer empire reached its zenith under Jayavarman VII in the late twelfth and early thirteenth century but having expanded west into present-day Thailand, was from the thirteenth century subject to raids by the Thais, which ultimately resulted in the fall of the Khmer empire in the fourteenth century.

The Mons were an Indo-Burmese people who came under the hegemony of the Dvaravati kingdom of southern Thailand between the sixth and the tenth century. The Mon-Dvaravati kingdom became the centre of dispersal of Hinayana Buddhism in South-East Asia and though few of its buildings survive, its stone figures of Buddha are amongst the most remarkable monumental sculptures produced in Thailand or Burma. Under the Mon-Dvaravati rulers, craftsmen succeeded in evolving a hybrid style which though overridingly Gupta in appearance, nevertheless took influences from the Khmers, to whom they were related in language, race and culture. One of the most classic examples of this style is an over-lifesize Buddha head (Fig. 4), with scrolling hair-curls, pierced ear-lobes and deeply meditative expression, which was finally bought by a private overseas collector against various underbidders in the room. Other examples are in the British Museum, the National Museum, Bangkok and the John D. Rockefeller III Collection at the Asia Society, New York.

In the introduction to his book *The Culture of South-East Asia* (1954), the late Dr Reginald Le May, a tireless exponent of South-East Asian art who formed one of the most comprehensive collections of Thai art between the wars, attempted to define the barriers between the connoisseurship of eastern and western art, praising '. . . the spiritual appeal in Eastern art, to which something universal and deep within one responds . . ., lacking in all Greek art except the very earliest. In the Eastern artist (whether Chinese, Indian or Egyptian) there is an innate feeling for economy of line . . .', whereas the Western artist, characterised by 'his intense individualism, wishes the spectator to see the form . . . down to the very last detail . . .'.

Fig. 4
A Thai schist head of Buddha, Mon-Dvaravati, *circa* seventh century, height 19¾in (50cm) London £209,000 ($397,100). 14.XI.88

A Thai wood figure of
the walking Buddha,
Sukothai, fourteenth–
fifteenth century,
height 69¼in (176cm)
London £71,500
($135,850). 14.XI.88

A Gandharan grey schist figure of Buddha Sakyamuni, *circa* third century AD, height 38⅜in (97.5cm)
New York $49,500 (£27,654). 2.XI.88
From the Heeramaneck Collection

Works of art

Recent research has cast important new light upon the reliquary opposite, which had not
been seen since the sale of Frédéric Spitzer's collection in 1893. An earlier chapter of its
history was revealed when drawings were published last year of a collection that was in
Hildesheim, Lower Saxony during the first half of the nineteenth century. One showed
clearly the lobed head of the present object, but without a foot.

It was then argued that Spitzer had elaborated upon the piece, using as a model the
famous Reliquary of Henry II, in the Louvre (see above). The old photograph in the Spitzer
catalogue also seemed to support this case. By chance, the object itself emerged shortly
afterwards and inspection confirmed the theory.

Spitzer's choice of model was highly appropriate, for the Henry II Reliquary and the
reliquary pendant, as it originally was, are from the same school of Lower Saxon enamelling
in the second half of the twelfth century. The provenance of both, in Hildesheim in the years
after the secularisation of the monasteries in the region (1803), suggests that the pieces had
not moved far from their place of manufacture.

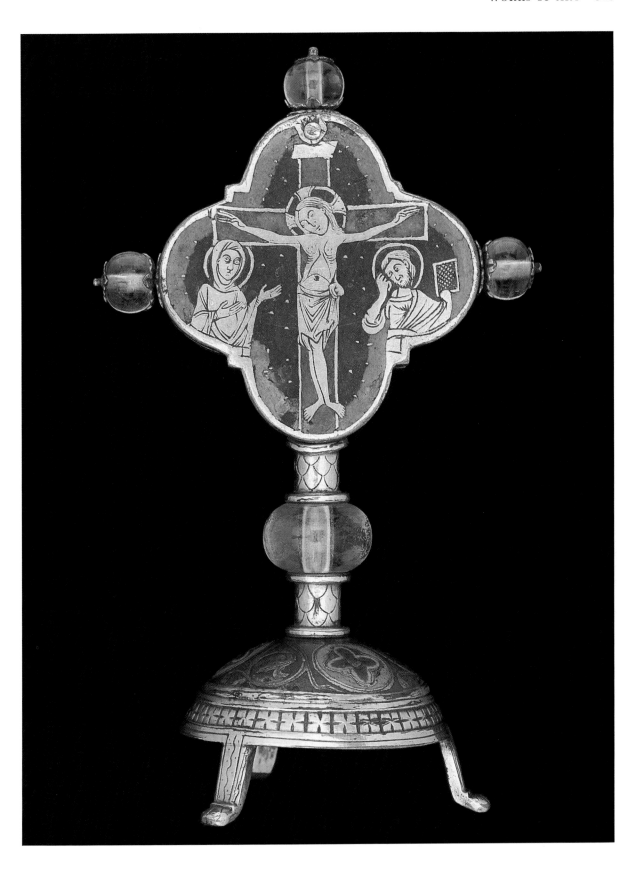

Fig. 1
A Mosan champlevé
enamel plaque showing the
Sacrifice of Cain and Abel,
mid twelfth century,
$3\frac{7}{8}$in by 4in
(10cm by 10.1cm)
London £572,000
($989,560). 6.VII.89

Right
Fig. 2
The head of Cain, a detail from an x-ray
plate of the plaque.

Cain and Abel:
an unknown Romanesque enamel

Tim Ayers

The most remarkable lot in the July sale of European works of art in London was an enamelled plaque showing the Sacrifice of Cain and Abel, dating from the middle years of the twelfth century (Fig. 1). Brought into the reception at Bond Street the February before, this major work of medieval art was previously completely unrecorded. The importance of the object lies partly in the exceptional quality of its craftsmanship and partly in its relationship to other enamels, some of which can be associated with churchmen at the centre of European political life in the mid twelfth century.

The scene depicts the two sons of Adam, sacrificing the fruits of their different pastoral and arable ways of life. Abel lifts up the firstling of his flock, which is blessed by the Hand of God, while Cain turns away at the rejection of his sheaf of corn, 'the fruit of the ground'. The first of all murders follows, Cain's jealous reaction to the rejection of his offering by God. The slightly inclined head of Cain is particularly finely drawn, turning away with a baleful look in a powerful evocation of the text in Genesis 'Cain was very angry, and his face fell' (Fig. 2). Although the gold background is slightly abraded, the richness of the colours is particularly striking. To appreciate the skill employed in their juxtaposition demands some explanation of technique.

Enamelling was not new to western Europe in the twelfth century. The cloisonné method had long been fashionable, influenced by the exquisite work of Byzantine craftsmen in the East. This involved fixing metal wires or *cloisons* onto a base plate, all generally in precious metal, and then laying powdered-glass colours into the closed areas so formed and firing them. The present object, however, is made by a different method known as *champlevé*, whereby recesses for the glasses are cut out of a copper plate. Particularly difficult was the juxtaposition of several colours in a single recessed field, as the glasses might have different melting points or run into each other. Here, the cloak and tunic of both Cain and Abel display three colours masterfully combined to give effects of shading.

Champlevé enamelling had been carried out in the West since Antiquity, but was brought to a new peak of perfection and popularity towards the middle of the twelfth century by craftsmen working in the Meuse valley in Belgium, notably for Wibald, Abbot of Stavelot and Chancellor of the Holy Roman Empire (d.1158). The most spectacular of his known commissions was the St Remaclus retable for Stavelot itself, now destroyed but from which comes the 'Operatio' roundel, part of the Von Hirsch Collection sold at Sotheby's in 1978. The beauty of these enamels, called Mosan after the River Meuse, clearly overcame doubts about the use of base metals on even the grandest devotional objects. Significantly, the inscription on a Mosan plaque depicting Henry, Bishop of Winchester (d.1171), *ars auro gemmisque prior*, 'craftsmanship before gold and gems' (Fig. 3), paraphrases Ovid's tag *materiam superabat opus*, in praise of craftsmanship over materials.

The present Mosan plaque belongs to the same group as eleven others of similar dimensions, all in major museums. The majority are from a series of scenes from the Life of Christ and a parallel series of Old Testament scenes prefiguring them. Elaborate paralleling of Old and New Testament scenes was a feature of twelfth-century Mosan iconography. As an illustration, a plaque of the Crucifixion from the series, in the Metropolitan Museum of Art (Fig. 4), is prefigured by another of Moses and the Brazen Serpent in the Victoria & Albert (Fig. 5); because St John's Gospel explains of the Crucifixion: 'This Son of Man must be lifted up as the serpent was lifted up by Moses in the wilderness.'

An intriguing aspect of the present subject is that it, too, prefigures the Crucifixion in some Mosan enamel compositions, particularly on the arms of Mosan crosses. Cain and Abel were regarded as Old Testament parallels for Synagogue and Ecclesia, the Jewish and the Christian church, which sometimes appear personified in Crucifixion scenes. It is possible, therefore, that the original layout of the plaques incorporated more than one prefiguring scene for the Crucifixion. If so, the rediscovered plaque provides a tantalizing clue to the form and layout of the object that they decorated.

There has been much discussion about the nature of this original object. At least two authorities have suggested that it was one of the most important lost works of art of the twelfth century, the vast cross commissioned by Abbot Suger to stand before the choir at St-Denis, the great French royal abbey outside Paris. Suger was a friend and advisor to Kings Louis VI and VII of France, an international statesman and a connoisseur with cosmopolitan taste. In his *De Administratione*, he describes the cross and the summoning of Mosan craftsmen to decorate the base with a typological series of scenes from the Old and New Testaments, and it is described again in a seventeenth-century inventory which incorporates earlier material. It is not known for certain when the cross was destroyed, but it may have been in the sixteenth-century Wars of Religion.

As another line of approach, recent research has emphasized close stylistic and technical affinities between the twelve plaques and two semi-circular enamelled plaques in the British Museum; one of which has already been mentioned, showing

Fig. 3
A Mosan champlevé enamel plaque depicting Bishop Henry of Winchester, before 1171, diameter 7in (17.9cm) (Reproduced courtesy of the Trustees of the British Museum, London).

Right
Fig. 4
A Mosan champlevé enamel plaque showing the Crucifixion, mid twelfth century, 4in by 4in (10.2 by 10.2cm) (Reproduced courtesy of the Metropolitan Museum of Art, New York).

Far right
Fig. 5
A Mosan champlevé enamel plaque showing Moses and the Brazen Serpent, mid twelfth century, 4in by 4in (10.2cm by 10.2cm) (Reproduced courtesy of the Trustees of the Victoria and Albert Museum, London).

the prostrate figure of Henry of Blois, Bishop of Winchester and brother of King Stephen of England (1135–54) (Fig. 3). The palette is apparently identical, including a characteristic semi-translucent red-brown enamel. The drawing is in a very similar hand to that on a square plaque in our series showing the Healing of Naaman, also in the British Museum.

Educated as a monk at Cluny, the nobly born Henry of Blois was always destined for high office and as abbot of Glastonbury (1126–71), bishop of Winchester (1129–71) and papal legate to England during the Anarchy of his brother's reign, he wielded great power. On the international stage, he was a frequent visitor to the papal curia and expensive aristocratic habits made 'the wizard of Winchester' a butt of criticism for the Cistercian St Bernard. A collector of antiquities in Rome, Henry was also a major patron of the arts in England, of building and sculpture at Glastonbury and in Winchester, for example; and of manuscript illumination, as the probable patron of the great Winchester Bible.

The provenances of the plaques themselves are inconclusive, although some support for an earlier English source is provided by the fact that eight have an English history as far back as can be traced. None of the twelve has yet been tracked beyond the mid-nineteenth century. The presence of so many in England, and of the rest on the Paris art market during the mid and later nineteenth century, might also suggest that the plaques were dispersed not long previously. If so, another possible source might be one of the churches on the Continent whose treasures were dispersed during the French Revolution, and its aftermath, just a half century before.

Whatever their provenance, the series is intimately related in many ways to the Mosan works of art commissioned by Suger, Henry and Wibald. All three were lavish patrons, in a close circle of ecclesiastical grandees contributing to the course of both secular and ecclesiastical politics. Their support goes a long way towards explaining the popularity of champlevé enamel across Europe in the third quarter of the twelfth century. Of this work, the rediscovered plaque is a superb example.

A Lombardic marble relief of the Justice of Trajan, *circa* 1500,
21¾in by 31in by 11in (55.2cm by 78.7cm by 28cm)
New York $57,750 (£37,258). 22.VI.89
From the collection of Walter P. Chrysler, Jr

Right
A Florentine terracotta
statue of St Jerome in the
Desert, sixteenth century,
height 30in (76.2cm)
London £99,000
($180,180). 20.IV.89

A thermoluminescence
test indicates a firing
between 1429 and 1619.
The piece-moulded
manufacture is a
masterpiece of the
greatest complexity.

Opposite, left
A Franconian limewood
relief of the death of the
Virgin, *circa* 1500,
42in by 38½in
(106.7cm by 97.8cm)
London £31,900
($62,205). 8.XII.88

Far left
A French polychrome
limestone group of the
Virgin and Child, Ile de
France, second quarter
fourteenth century,
height 56½in (143.5cm)
London £71,500
($139,425). 8.XII.88

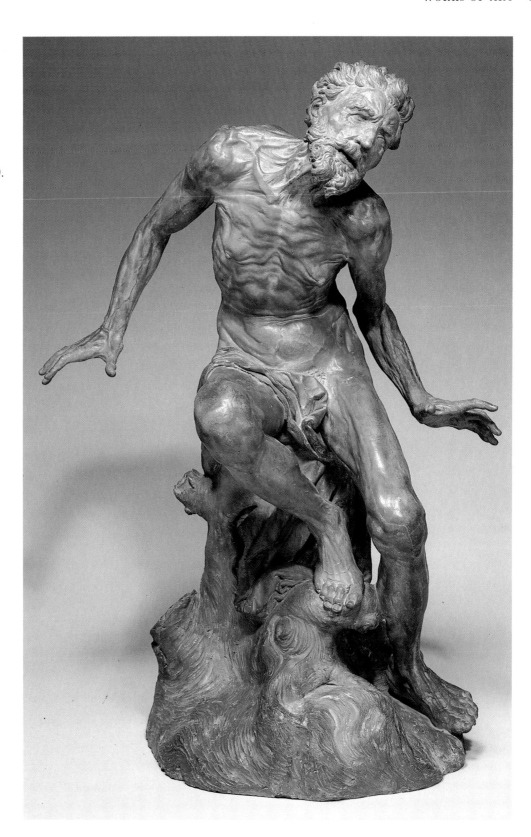

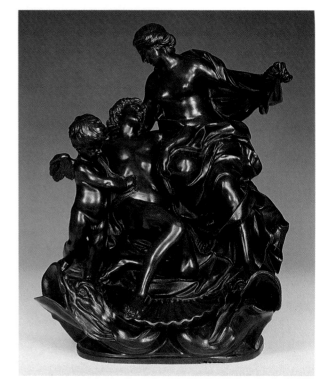

Opposite, left
A bronze statuette of Venus combing her hair, early seventeenth century, perhaps Florentine, height 9in (22.9cm)
London £104,500 ($190,190). 20.IV.89

The figure is inspired by the large bronze figure *La Fiorenza* at the Villa Petraia, in Florence. This was part of a fountain designed by Tribolo, with the water running down the maiden's hair signifying the city of Florence itself flourishing at the confluence of the rivers Arno and Mugnone. Giambologna completed the project and was painted by Hans von Aachen with the casting model before 1571.

Above
A Florentine bronze group of one of the Labours of Hercules attributed to Ferdinando Tacca, seventeenth century, from the collection of Louis XIV, height 23in (58.5cm)
Monte Carlo FF9,768,000 (£930,286:$1,628,000). 17.VI.89

This group is recorded in the French royal collection in 1713 and was at Château de Meudon for much of the eighteenth century. It was probably acquired with seven other listed groups showing scenes from the life of Hercules, late in the reign of Louis XIV.

Right
A Roman bronze group of the death of Adonis by Alessandro Algardi, second quarter seventeenth century, height 18⅞in (48cm)
Monte Carlo FF3,885,000 (£370,000:$647,500). 17.VI.89

The group has been given to Algardi by Jennifer Montagu and dated *circa* 1630.

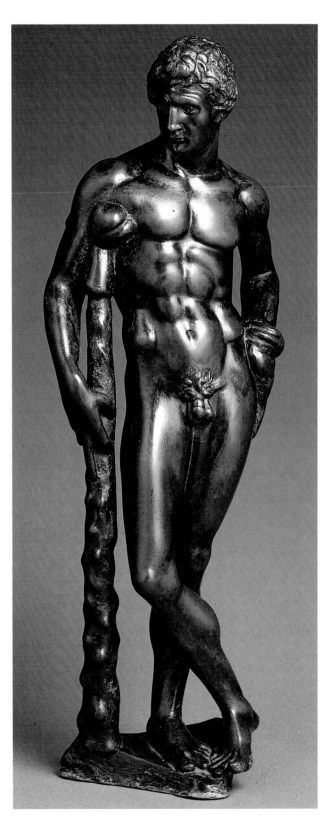

Right
A North Italian bronze statuette of Hercules resting, late fifteenth century, height 13in (33cm)
London £253,000 ($460,460). 20.IV.89

A German or Netherlandish bronze group of Neptune and a
Hippocamp with silver eyes, late sixteenth–early seventeenth
century, height 10¼in (26cm)
London £99,000 ($193,050). 8.XII.88
Formerly in the collection of Dr Alexander von Frey

Few parallels have been found in bronze for this group,
which in its exquisite handling recalls, rather, goldsmiths'
work. It has been associated traditionally with a drawing
of a *Triton and Nereid* sometimes attributed to Adrien de
Vries, in Munich. The bronze might be a product of the
collaboration of such Northern artists as de Vries,
Spranger or Paulus van Vianen at the court of Rudolph
II in Prague.

A set of twelve Limoges *grisaille* enamel dessert plates depicting the Labours of the Month by Jean de Court (the Master IC), late sixteenth century, diameters 7⅞in (20cm) London £198,000 ($386,100). 8.XII.88

Opposite, right
A Roman silver figure of a flagellator after a model by Alessandro Algardi, second quarter seventeenth century, height 9⅛in (23.2cm) New York $115,500 (£74,516). 22.VI.89

This is the left hand figure of a flagellation group, which occurs in two variations. This figure belongs to the variant attributed to Algardi; the other is associated with François Duquesnoy.

Fig. 1
St Laurence before the Roman prefect

Fig. 2
St Laurence presenting the poor to the prefect

Fig. 3
St Laurence blessing the poor in church

Fig. 4
The martyrdom of St Laurence

Rediscovered stained glass roundels

Florian Eitle

Two coloured lithographs from the archives of the church of St Laurence at Ahrweiler, near Bonn, West Germany, *circa* 1840, illustrating the roundels depicting (*above*) *St Laurence before the Roman prefect* (Fig. 1), *St Laurence blessing the poor in church* (Fig. 3), and *St Laurence in prayer;* and (*below*) *St Laurence ordained, St Laurence presenting the poor to the prefect* (Fig. 2) and *The martyrdom of St Laurence* (Fig. 4).

These extremely rare stained glass roundels (Figs 1 to 4), in brilliant glowing colours, are from the choir of the church of St Laurence at Ahrweiler, near Bonn in West Germany. Their whereabouts had been a mystery for many years until they reappeared for sale in New York during the autumn of 1988 and were identified by a resident of Ahrweiler.

The church of St Laurence, founded in 1248 by Konrad von Are-Hochstaden von Burg Art Altenahr, originally had five stained glass windows. On 30th December 1723, the glass maker Jakob Kalkar of Linz was commissioned to replace three of the windows and repair the other two. The roundels were removed in 1809 when Christian Geerling of Cologne, a glass painter and restorer, acquired them. In 1826 Geerling published a collection of lithographs of stained glass windows, including those from the church of St Laurence. These lithographs show five of the six roundels offered at auction, arranged vertically in two groups of three, framed in a foliate design and within lunettes. The roundels were mentioned again in 1856 by the glass painter Grass who wrote in a letter that they had been sold in 1848. After that the roundels disappeared and were presumed lost.

Of the six roundels sold at auction, five are believed to have originated from the choir of the church of St Laurence in the thirteenth century and the sixth is thought to have been added to the group sometime after the roundels were removed from the church. All six depict scenes from the life of St Laurence, martyred in Rome in AD 258. The first, a late-thirteenth-century restoration, illustrated in the lithograph, shows him being ordained a deacon by Pope Sixtus II. The second depicts him before the Roman prefect (Fig. 1). After his arrest the Pope ordered Laurence to distribute the church's treasures to the poor; Laurence did so, but the Roman prefect demanded instead that all should be surrendered to him. Indicating the poor and sick around him (shown on the third roundel: Fig. 2), Laurence is said to have replied, 'Here are the treasures of the church'. On the fourth (Fig. 3), Laurence blesses the poor within a church and on the fifth (Fig. 4) he is punished by martyrdom on the gridiron. The sixth roundel on the lithograph showed St Laurence in prayer flanked by angels; the nineteenth-century replacement is of a different subject, apparently Laurence before the prefect again.

Opposite
A group of four stained glass roundels depicting scenes from the life of St Laurence, from the choir of the church of St Laurence at Ahrweiler, near Bonn, West Germany, second quarter thirteenth century, diameters 24⅛in (61.3cm)
New York $137,500 (£75,137). 22.XI.88

Fig.1
A marble bust of Christ the Redeemer, by Giovanni Caccini, 1594–98, height 28½in (72.4cm)
London £858,000 ($1,673,100). 8.XII.88
From the collection of Sir John Leslie, Bt

Giovanni Caccini and the rediscovered bust of Christ

Herbert Keutner

The achievements of the sculptor Giovanni Caccini in the visual arts have been less widely recognised than those of his elder brother Giulio in the field of music. Giulio Caccini and Jacopo Peri, as members of the *Camerata* of the Conte de' Bardi in Florence, established opera as a new musical form in the late sixteenth century.[1] Giovanni was also an innovator, however, initiating a new epoch in Tuscan sculpture. For this, he deserves more attention than he has hitherto received.[2]

The year and place of birth of the two brothers remain uncertain. Giulio (died 1615) is thought to have been born between 1545 and 1550, while Milancsi simply states, without giving any documentary evidence, that Giovanni (died 1613) was born on 24th October 1556.[3] Although the name Caccini has a Florentine ring to it, Rome or Tivoli have usually been considered their place of origin. They sometimes signed themselves *romano* and both received their early training in Rome (albeit under Florentine masters), Giulio from the singing master Scipione della Palla and Giovanni from the sculptor and architect Giovan Antonio Dosio. However, the Florentine chronicler Raffaello Borghini, a friend of the brothers, wrote of the young Giovanni in 1584:

I want to say that Giovanni di Michelangelo Caccini gives great hope of success in sculpture, brother of Giulio, who is such an excellent singer, known as Giulio Romano, although he is actually Florentine.[4]

A recently discovered document of 1578 mentioning 'Giovanni Caccini of Montopoli' does little to elucidate the problem, as this could either be Montopoli in Sabina on Roman territory or the Florentine Montopoli in the Arno Valley.[5] Whatever their origins, it was Florence which later claimed the Caccinis as her sons, nourishing their talent and paying homage to their work.

While Giulio had settled in the city by 1565–66, Giovanni and his master Dosio only arrived *circa* 1575. Dosio (1533–1609) had lived in Rome since the late 1540s,[6] acquiring his knowledge of sculpture and architecture from Raffaello da Montelupo (1505–1566/67). Raffaello instilled in him an interest in antique sculpture and restoration, which Dosio in his turn passed on to his favourite pupil Giovanni.

The presence of the young Caccini in Florence by August 1578 is known from the document referred to above.[7] This important archival note reveals that he was based in the workshop of Giovanni Bologna in the convent of Santa Maria Novella and that he was engaged upon the restoration of three antique busts.[8] The description of the first of them, 'an ancient head of Charlemagne' is of particular interest. This can only be the antique head of Homer in SS Apostoli, Florence, once thought to depict Charlemagne, legendary founder of the church (Fig. 2).[9] It was placed in the choir, together with another bust by Caccini of Archbishop Antonio Altoviti, who was considered the second founder.[10]

This, Caccini's first known work, leads us on to say something about his seldom discussed activity as a renovator of antique sculpture.[11] Restoration was often considered of secondary importance by sculptors, but Caccini was eager to put into practice the antiquarian knowledge he had accumulated under the guidance of Dosio in Rome. The resulting works initially for private patrons eventually received wider acclaim and for decades Caccini was preferred above others by the Grand Ducal Court for such undertakings.[12] On several occasions he would be given a simple torso to be reconstructed as a complete figure. Examples of this are the group of Dionysus with the satyr Ampelus and the figure of Apollo leaning on his lyre (Fig. 4); sculptures which we no longer consider restorations but admire as Caccini's own work, born of his profound antiquarian knowledge.[13]

The recently discovered document of 1578 indicates that Giovanni Caccini was working in the *bottega* of Giovanni Bologna – 'sta in bottegha di Gio. Bolog.a' ('He is in the workshop of Gio. Bolog.a'). This confirms the traditional view that he belonged to the close circle of his pupils and followers.[14] However, the sentence suggests that he was not a collaborator; rather, it should be interpreted as meaning that the new arrival had simply been allowed to set up in the master's studio. Nevertheless, Caccini would certainly have received Giovanni Bologna's advice and assimilated some of his artistic ideas.

An instructive example of his response to the work of Giovanni Bologna may be found in a statue of Temperance, commissioned *circa* 1578–79 by Mons. Giovanni Battista Milanese, Bishop of Marsi (Fig. 3).[15] The overall composition and the

Opposite, left
Fig.3
A marble statue of Temperance by Giovanni Caccini, 1578–84, height 72in (183cm) (Reproduced courtesy of the Metropolitan Museum of Art, New York).

Fig.2
A marble bust of Charlemagne, modelled by Giovanni Caccini from an antique bust of Homer, 1578–80, height 24⅜in (62cm) (Reproduced courtesy of SS Apostoli, Florence).

arrangement of the folds falling from the high waist follow Giovanni Bologna's model for a bronze figure of the same subject destined for the chapel of Luca Grimaldi in Genoa.[16] Caccini modified significant details, however, impressing on the work a personal understanding of art and beauty, which owed more to his classical training in Rome than to the Florentine mannerism of Giovanni Bologna. The statue he created is an open composition, and both its pose and meaning are immediately accessible. It has all the distinctive qualities of Caccini's own style and future work.

Some years later, in Florence, Caccini collaborated with the architect Bernardo Buontalenti (1523–1608) on a project to renew the façade of Santa Trinità. In 1594–95 the sculptor carved the large relief of the Trinity above the main door and in 1595–97, a statue of S. Alessio for a niche to the left (Fig. 5).[17] As with the Temperance and Apollo figures, he depicted the pilgrim saint in *contrapposto*, calm and balanced. But unlike the allegorical figure of Temperance, the attributes and distinguishing features of Apollo (the lyre and gryphon) and S. Alessio (the pilgrim's costume and emblems) are presented in a bold and straightforward fashion.

These works also bear witness to Caccini's exceptional technical mastery. A certain imbalance and harshness in the fall of Temperance's drapery is no longer to be found in the mantle of Apollo or the garments of S. Alessio: we can make out clearly in the marble the soft leather of the boots, the felt of the hat, the light material of the short tunic and the heavier stuff of the mantle. While there is a monotony of form and expression in the face of Temperance, the features of Apollo and S. Alessio are modelled with great sensitivity, the first imbued with a mood of compassion and calm, and the second with an air of pious devotion.

Caccini's recently discovered bust of Christ was made for another project of the 1590s in collaboration with Buontalenti (Fig. 1).[18] The architect was commissioned to design two tabernacles for monuments to the Benedetti and Anselmi families, one on either side of the nave in the Dominican church of Santa Maria Novella. These were relatively simple compositions,[19] with bases including the family arms and inscriptions, rectangular marble frames and arched pediments. Each housed a painting: *The martyrdom of St Peter Martyr* by Ludovico Cigoli and *The vision of St Hyacinth* by Jacopo da Empoli, signed and dated 1594; and each was crowned with a marble bust by Caccini, one of the Redeemer and the other of the Virgin.[20] The date of Empoli's painting suggests that the two projects were begun in 1593–94; while an inscription on the Benedetti tabernacle indicates that they were only completed in 1598.[21] It can therefore be assumed that Caccini's bust of Christ dates from between 1594 and 1598.

The tabernacles were dismantled during an extensive remodelling of the church in 1858–60.[22] The architectural elements were then transferred by monks to the interior of the monastery where they can still to be found today. The subsequent history of the Virgin is still unknown, but the bust of the Redeemer was acquired from the monastery in 1876 as a work of Pietro Francavilla. It was bought by John Leslie of Castle Leslie, Glaslough, County Monaghan in Ireland. He took it back to his country seat and it was from there that the bust emerged for sale last year.

Caccini was at the height of his creative powers in the 1590s and his fame had spread well beyond Florence. In this decade he sculpted saints for the Duomo in Orvieto and the Certosa in Naples; prepared reliefs and statuettes in bronze for the principal doors of the Duomo in Pisa; and in Florence, the figures of Francesco I and Charles V for the Palazzo Vecchio, as well as allegorical figures of Summer and Autumn for the garden of the Acciaioli (transferred in 1608 to the Ponte Trinità).[23] From 1598–99, at the behest of the Michelozzi family, he erected an immense altar in Santo Spirito, in the form of a canopy decorated with statues of saints and candle-bearing angels, completing these last between 1600 and 1604 (Fig.6).[24]

This period, then, saw the creation of the bust of Christ the Redeemer, conforming

Fig.5
A marble figure of S. Alessio, by Giovanni Caccini,
1595–97, height 90½in (230cm)
(Reproduced courtesy of Santa Trinità, Florence).

Fig.6
A marble statue of an angel, by Giovanni Caccini, 1600–1604,
height approximately 90½in (230cm)
(Michelozzi altar; reproduced courtesy of Santo Spirito, Florence).

to a traditional prototype, wearing an undergarment with a U-form neckline typical of his other depictions of saints, and with a mantle placed loosely about His shoulders. In contrast to the head of the Santo Spirito angel, which followed his own aesthetic conceptions, he gave the head of Christ an ideal beauty. Even more clearly than in the S. Alessio, affected as it is by exposure to the elements, the surface of the bust of the Redeemer and of the angel reveal his, by now, exceptional ability to use his sculptor's tools; to model, so to speak, the marble. He invests the faces of the two figures with tranquillity and thoughtful absorption; in the elaborate sensitivity of the eyebrows and eyes, the eyelids lowered; or in the shape of the mouth with lips lightly closed. He succeeds in giving an imperceptible pulsing life to the cheeks and neck by the delicate treatment of the skin. Certainly Caccini, as a sculptor, should not be put on the same level as the younger genius Gian Lorenzo Bernini, but he is not inferior to him in his virtuosity in the sculpting of marble. He demonstrates his *bravura* without ostentation, depicting serenity and quiet composure.

We will finish our account with a word on the position of Caccini in the history of Tuscan sculpture. When the young man set up in Florence after his Roman apprenticeship, in 1575–76, the field was dominated by Giovanni Bologna and his circle. While working under his aegis at Santa Maria Novella, Caccini was striking out, as we have seen, in his own direction. In contrast to Giovanni Bologna's conception of art as an autonomous world with its own rules, Caccini held, recalling the early Renaissance, that experience of reality, nature and the art of antiquity were the sure foundations of artistic activity. He saw the satisfactory practice of his profession not in isolating a work of art from the real world, but in grounding it firmly in everyday life; depicting figures not in unusual compositions, such as Giovanni Bologna's *Mercury* or the *Rape of the Sabines*, but rather in simple and serene poses.

Similar attempts to break away from the old practices and rules were also being made by painters, particularly the pupils of Santi di Tito, and above all Ludovico Cigoli. Although some critics have noted the different character of the works of Caccini and Giovanni Bologna,[25] this has not been emphasized and is more often overlooked. The difference needs to be reaffirmed; furthermore, it can be argued that Caccini's position in sculpture is analogous to that of Cigoli in painting, as reformer and precursor of the Tuscan baroque.

From the end of the 1590s, the aspiring sculptors of the younger generation no longer felt drawn to Giovanni Bologna, but rather to Caccini, and sought apprenticeship in his workshop in Via della Scala. The pupils and successors of Bologna, heirs to his workshop, his foundry and his models, supplied the European courts with bronzes, above all small bronzes, copies and variants of the master's compositions, until the middle of the seventeenth century and beyond; but they had no influence worth noting on the development of marble sculpture in Florence. It was Caccini and his pupils Gherardo Silvani, Agostino Bugiardini, Chiarissimo Fancelli and Orazio Mochi, with their younger assistants Domenico and Giovan Battista Pieratti or Antonio Novelli, who were to determine the image and development of sculpture in the early baroque – a measured baroque corresponding to the characteristic conservatism of the Tuscans.

Notes

[1] For a summary of the life of Giulio Caccini, see G. Casellato, 'Giulio Caccini', in the *Dizionario biografico degli Italiani*, XVI, 1973, 25–33.

[2] For the life and work of Giovanni Caccini, see A. Venturi, *Storia dell'arte italiana. La scultura del Cinquecento*, X, 3, Milan, 1937, 792–816; A. Morini, *Giovanni Caccini, Scultore e Architetto fiorentino*, thesis, Florence, 1940; J.K. Schmidt, *Studien zum statuarischen Werk des G.B. Caccini*, dissertation (Munich), Cologne, 1971; M. Bacci, 'Giovan Battista Caccini', in *Dizionario biografico degli Italiani*, XVI, 1973, 23–25; C. Caneva, 'Giovanni Battista Caccini', in *Seicento fiorentino. Arte a Firenze da Ferdinando I a Cosimo III*, exhib. cat., Florence, 1986, I: 44–46 and II: 429–30.

[3] C. Pini and G. Milanesi, *La scrittura degli artisti italiani dei sec. XIV–XVII*, 3 vols., Rome, 1869–76, III, 241.

[4] R. Borghini, *Il Riposo*, Florence, 1584, 647–48.

[5] This document may, however, be the key to a future solution to the problem: the precise date of birth given by Gaetano Milanesi, the distinguished authority on the Tuscan archives, suggests that Montopoli sull'Arno is the more likely.

[6] For Dosio, see C.J. Valone, *Giovanni Antonio Dosio and his patrons*, Ann Arbor, Michigan, 1975 (with bibliography).

[7] In September 1578 he is documented again as carrying out a stucco figure of 'Earth' for the festival of St Luke at the Accademia del Disegno, and in the following October his first payment is mentioned as a member of the Accademia, see C.J. Valone, op.cit., 191 and 249, Nos. 65–66.

[8] See State Archives, Florence, Guardaroba, 98 (Memoriale di manifattori E, 1576–80), c.226 v: 'MDLXXVIII, Adi II d'agosto. A. Giovanni Caccini da Montopoli ha l'appie statue di marmo a rasetarsi, sta in bottegha di Gio. Bolog.ª a Sta. M. Nov.ª'. Una testa antica di marmo di Carlo magno, con suo busto N.º 1–. Uno busto di marmo antico, senza testa et peduccio N.º 1–. Una testa di uno Vitelio di marmo per rifargli il piede, porto detto adi 21 di marzo 1580. N.º 1–.'

[9] Examples of heads of Homer were known in the sixteenth century, but not identified as the poet. For a drawing of such a head by Andrea del Sarto, see M. Winner, *Zeichner sehen die Antike*, exhib. cat., Berlin, 1967, 108–10. The identification of our head as that of Charlemagne would seem an isolated instance.

[10] For the preparation of the choir as the final burial place of Antonio Altoviti and for the positioning of the two busts, see J.K. Schmidt, op.cit., 12–13 and 141–42; and C.J. Valone, op.cit., 204–208. The choir was altered between 1578 and 1583 by Dosio. Both busts have traditionally been regarded as original works by Caccini. F. Bocchi, *Le bellezze della città di Firenze*, Florence, 1591, 61 makes no distinction, and all subseqent writers have followed him. Only J.K. Schmidt, op.cit., 142, noted that 'the sculptor for his prototype of the bust of Charlemagne used an antique head of Homer.' However, besides a superficial recarving of the whole head of Homer, Caccini only added the nose and opened the blind eyes by incising the pupils.

[11] For Caccini as a restorer, see A. Grünwald, 'Uber einige unechte Werke Michelangelos', in *Münchner Jahrbuch d. bild. Kunst*, V, 1910, 64–70; and more recently G. Mansuelli, *La Galleria degli Uffizi, Le sculture*, I, Rome, 1958, index.

[12] The State Archives in Florence note documents relating to his restoration work until at least 1600.

[13] Indeed the archaeologist, Mansuelli, op.cit., 47, No. 23, judges Caccini's work on the torso 'an erudite reconstruction'.

[14] See A. Morini, op.cit., 7 and M. Bacci, op.cit., 24.

[15] The statue, acquired in 1967 by the Metropolitan Museum, New York (Inv. 67.208) is mentioned for the first time by R. Borghini, op.cit., 648. For a discussion of the figure, see O. Raggio, 'The Metropolitan Marbles', in *Art News*, LXVII, 1968, No. 4, 45–47 and J.K. Schmidt, op.cit., 20–28 and 141.

For the placing of the commission in 1578–79 I refer to J.K. Schmidt, op.cit., 141, who without furnishing evidence, indicated January 1579 as the date of death of Milanese, explaining the delay in completion of the figure by the unexpected demise of the patron. This dating is still to be confirmed, as according to A. D'Addario, the Monsignore's death did not occur until 1584, *Aspetti della controriforma a Firenze*, Rome, 1972, 251.

[16] The contract of 24th July 1579 for the decoration of the Grimaldi Chapel would not have been drawn up without prior correspondence between the patron and Giovanni Bologna, who had probably known each other since 1577. The artist could, therefore, already have executed designs and models for the project before July 1579: see M. Bury, 'The Grimaldi Chapel of Giambologna in San Francesco di Castelletto, Genoa', in *Mitt. d. Kunsth. Institutes Florenz*, XXVI, 1982, 86–87.

[17] For the statue of S. Alessio see J.K. Schmidt, op.cit., 59–64 and 158–59 and C. Caneva, op.cit., II, 430.

[18] The bust was first published in the catalogue of *European Works of Art and Sculpture*, Sotheby's, London, 8th–9th December 1988, lot 99.

[19] An idea of the simple form of the epitaph, with the bust above, can be gleaned from an eighteenth-century view of the interior of the church.

[20] Divergent descriptions of the tabernacle can be found in F. Bocchi – G. Cinelli, *Le Bellezze della Città di Firenze*, Florence, 1677, 258 and 394; G. Richa, *Notizie istoriche delle chiese fiorentine*, 10 vols., Florence, 1754–62, III (1757), 79; F. Fantozzi, *Guida della città e contorni di Firenze*, Florence, 1844, 507 and 515; G. François, *Nuova Guida della Città di Firenze*, 1850, 503; and M. Bucci, 'Martirio di S. Pietro Martire', in *Mostra del Cigoli e del suo ambiente*, catalogue, San Miniato, 1959, 57–59, No. 14; and most recently in J.K. Schmidt, op.cit., 177 (among the lost works).

[21] *Deo, ac Divo Petro Martiri Catholicae Fidei propugnatori acerrimo. Johannes, Johannes baptista atque Angelus Benedicti fratres, filii Marci, ob praecipuum in eum studium ac pietatem erexerunt . . . annuente 1598.* Cited by N. Sermartelli, *Libro delle Cappelle e Sepolture della Chiesa di Santa Maria Novella*, convent archive, Ms. of 1617, c.95. I would like to thank Father Grossi O.P., who has made the manuscript available to me.

[22] For the dismantling of the tabernacle, see W. and E. Paatz, *Die Kirchen von Florenz*, 6 vols., Frankfurt, 1940–54, III, 737 and S. Orlandi O.P., *S. Maria Novella e i suoi Chiostri monumentali*, 3rd edn, Florence, 1966, 8–9.

[23] For an account of these, see J.K. Schmidt, op.cit., passim and C. Caneva, op.cit., 44–46.

[24] The height of the four angels is approximately 230cm. For the history of the canopy and for the extent of the collaboration of his pupils, see J.K. Schmidt, op.cit., 95–114, 165–68 and C. Caneva, op.cit., 45.

[25] The first observations in this direction are to be found in M. Weinberger, 'Bronze Statuettes by Giovanni Caccini', in *The Burlington Magazine*, LVIII, 1931, 231–35; whilst J.K. Schmidt, op.cit., passim states this view emphatically.

Opposite
A marble bust of Jacques-Rolland Moreau by Jean-Louis Lemoyne, signed, inscribed and dated *I.R. MOREAV. 1712*, height 36⅝in (93cm) Monte Carlo FF4,662,000 (£444,000:$777,000). 4.III.89

The bust dates from the last years of Louis XIV, when J.-L. Lemoyne was at the height of his powers.

An ivory relief of Cephalus and Procris by Joachim Henne, late seventeenth century, 4½in by 4¾in (11.4cm by 12cm) London £22,000 ($42,900). 8.XII.88

By coincidence, two major ivory carvings by Joachim Henne (*circa* 1663 – after 1707) were offered in the December 1988 sale. Henne worked as a portraitist and carver in relief for the courts of Northern Europe, in Schleswig-Holstein, Denmark and Berlin – in ivory, wood and wax and as a medallist. Both of the ivories on offer dated from his Danish stay. The one illustrated here is reputed to be from an old Danish collection, while the second shows King Christian V himself wearing the Danish Order of the Elephant.

Opposite, above
Johann Ludwig Bleuler
THE RED SQUARE, MOSCOW
Watercolour and gouache,
signed, 10⅜in by 16½in
(26.5cm by 42cm)
London £19,800 ($35,838).
7.IV.88

The Vladimir Mother of God, Moscow, *circa* 1500, 12⅜in by 10¼in (31.5cm by 26cm)
London £11,550 ($21,945). 14.XI.88

Opposite, below
A commemorative album of the coronation of Emperor Alexander II Nikolaevich in 1856, 95 pages,
with wood-engraved illustrations mounted on india paper, eighteen full-page, hand-coloured,
chromolithographic plates printed by Lemercier, each plate with caption in French and Russian,
original green Morocco binding designed by the architect Monegetti, 27½in by 36in (70cm by 91.5cm)
London £37,400 ($67,694). 7.IV.89
Formerly in the library of H.I.H. The Grand Duke Alexander Alexandrovich, later Emperor
Alexander III

Above, left to right
A Fabergé carved agate model of an owl, marked with initials of workmaster Henrik Wigström, St Petersburg, *circa* 1900, height 1⅝in (4cm)
$14,300 (£9,470)
A Fabergé carved agate model of an owl, marked with initials of workmaster Henrik Wigström, St Petersburg, *circa* 1900, height 2¾in (7cm)
$59,400 (£39,338)
A Fabergé carved agate model of an owl, marked with initials of workmaster Henrik Wigström, St Petersburg, *circa* 1900, height 2in (5cm)
$33,000 (£21,854)

All three owls, from the collection of Rose and Harry Rudick, were sold in New York on 14th June 1989.

Above
A Fabergé gold and blue enamel cigarette case, workmaster Henrik Wigström, 1908–17, height 3⅞in (9.8cm)
Geneva SF57,200 (£20,212: $33,846). 11.V.89
From the collection of Mrs George Keppel

Left
A Fabergé lapis-lazuli, gold, silver and enamel desk clock, marked with initials of workmaster Henrik Wigström, St Petersburg, *circa* 1900, height 2⅝in (6.7cm)
New York $82,500 (£45,330). 15.XII.88

A gold and enamel snuff box by Jean Moynat, the lid painted with a still life attributed to Philippe
Parpette, Paris, 1758, width 2¼in (5.7cm)
Geneva SF176,000 (£62,191:$104,142). 11.V.89

A *quatre-couleurs* gold and enamel snuff box by Jean Frémin, Paris, 1767, width 3¼in (8.2cm)
Geneva SF101,200 (£35,760:$59,882). 11.V.89

German School
JOSEF JACOB GRAF WEISS VON
KÖNIGSACKER (BIANCHI DI
CAMPOREGIO)
Circa 1735, 2½in (6.6cm)
Geneva SF9,350
(£3,542:$6,448). 17.XI.88

Gregory Musikisky,
attributed to
EMPEROR PETER THE
GREAT
Circa 1720, 1⅝in (4.1cm)
Geneva SF17,600
(£6,667:$12,138).
17.XI.88

Edward Nash
MOODA MAJI OF COORG
Engraved on the reverse *The
Coorga Rajah's/ daughter Mooda/
Majee./ 1807*, 2¾in (7.1cm)
London £6,380 ($11,803).
24.X.88

Jean-Laurent Mosnier
CHARLOTTE ALBERTINE
JOSEPHE MARIE DE BUISSERET,
VICOMTESSE DE PODENAS
Signed and dated *1779*,
2⅛in (5.3cm)
Geneva SF15,400
(£5,833:$10,621). 17.XI.88

Peter Cross
COLONEL FINCH
Signed with monogram and titled on the
reverse, *circa* 1690, 3¼in (8.3cm)
London £8,800 ($14,872). 4.VII.89

Christian Friedrich Zincke
CAROLINE OF BRANDENBURG
ANSBACH, WIFE OF GEORGE II OF
ENGLAND
Signed with monogram below
the Prince of Wales' crown,
circa 1727, 1½in (4cm)
London £3,520 ($6,512).
24.X.88

Jean-Baptiste Isabey
A GENTLEMAN
Signed, *circa* 1805, 2½in (6.5cm)
London £7,150 ($13,299). 9.II.89

A green-ground etui, Bilston,
circa 1765, painted with a
portrait of *The Unknown Lady*
after van der Mijn,
height 3⅞in (10cm)
London £4,180 ($7,775).
9.II.89

An Imperial presentation two-colour gold
and enamel *boîte à portrait* by Augustin-André
Héguin, inscribed *Donné par l'Empereur/ au Mr
Lannes/ Portrait du Mr de la Mme et de leur fils*
and *Marguerit Joaillier de la Couronne de leurs
Maj^{és} Imp^{les} et Roy^{les}*, the miniatures on the lid
and base signed by Louis-François Aubry,
Paris, 1798–1809, width 3⅜in (8.5cm)
Geneva SF50,600 (£17,880:$29,941). 11.V.89

A hawk's head bonbonnière, Birmingham,
circa 1765, length 2⅜in (6cm)
London £6,820 ($11,526). 4.VII.89

A double-lidded, leopard's head bonbonnière,
Birmingham, *circa* 1765, 3in (7.5cm)
London £11,550 ($19,520). 4.VII.89

Clocks and watches

Right
A Charles II ebony veneered quarter repeating longcase timepiece, inscribed *John Wise Londini Fecit, circa* 1685, height 5ft 7½in (171.5cm)
London £39,600 ($76,428). 13.XII.88

Below
A Bréguet 'Pendule Sympathique' No.257 and its watch No.4745, *circa* 1820, height with watch 18⅛in (46cm)
Monte Carlo FF3,219,000 (£306,571:$536,500). 18.VI.89

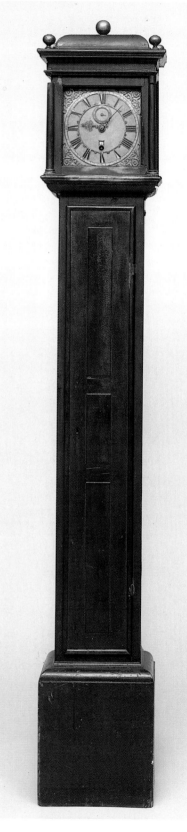

Right
A German perpetual calendar and globe library pedestal clock, inscribed
J.C.Schuster Mechanikus in Ansbach 1823, height 31⅛in (79cm)
London £50,600 ($93,104). 13.X.88

Below, left
A silver and Limoges perpetual calendar mantel timepiece, the Limoges
panel on the reverse inscribed *CP* for Claudius Popelin, *circa* 1900,
height 13½in (34.5cm)
London £16,500 ($30,360). 13.X.88

Right
A German gilt-metal elephant automaton clock, Augsburg, early
seventeenth century, the clock movement later, height without later base
10¾in (27.5cm)
New York $101,200 (£56,854). 18.II.89

A gold and enamel centre
seconds musical automaton
watch by Piguet & Meylan,
circa 1820,
diameter 1¾in (4.4cm)
London £20,900 ($38,247).
21.III.89

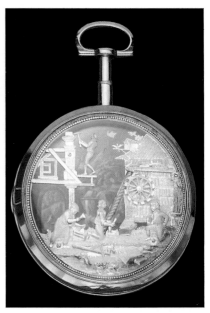

A gold hunting cased minute repeating chronograph with
perpetual calendar and moonphases, inscribed *The World's
Columbian Exposition, Hors Concours, Chicago, USA, 1892–1893*,
by Patek Philippe & Co., Geneva, *circa* 1890,
diameter 2⅛in (5.5cm)
New York $88,000 (£50,286). 25.X.88

A gold and enamel automaton watch
by Piguet, Geneva, *circa* 1810,
diameter 2¼in (5.7cm)
New York $28,600 (£18,571). 16.VI.89
From the Thielmann Collection

A gold double-dialled centre
seconds cylinder quarter
repeating calendar watch,
inscribed *Grondal Fils, Aspa*,
circa 1770, diameter 1⅞in (5cm)
London £11,000 ($21,230).
13.XII.88

A gold and enamel singing bird watch, probably
by Piguet & Meylan, *circa* 1800,
diameter 2¼in (5.8cm)
Geneva SF143,000 (£50,530:$84,615). 9.V.89

A gold solar/sidereal watch inscribed *Daniels London*,
1982–84, diameter 2½in (6.2cm)
Geneva SF220,000 (£83,333:$151,724). 17.XI.88

A cylinder calendar and astronomical watch inscribed
Jn. Ellicott London, circa 1740, the walnut watch stand
later, diameter 2in (5.3cm)
London £24,200 ($44,528). 13.X.88

Left
A gold-cased minute repeating, perpetual calendar,
chronograph watch with stop-watch by Leroy à Paris,
1876, the case inscribed *J. Nodiot Fecit 1896*,
diameter 2½in (6.2cm)
Geneva SF572,000 (£202,120:$338,462). 9.V.89
From the collection of the late Antonio Ramos Pinto

An 18 carat gold Rolex
perpetual moonphase and
calendar wristwatch, *circa*
1955, diameter 1½in (3.8cm)
London £8,800 ($16,192).
13.X.88

An 18 carat gold wristwatch
by Patek Philippe & Co.,
Geneva, 1926,
length 1⅝in (4.2cm)
London £14,850 ($27,324).
13.X.88

An 18 carat two-colour gold
Rolex Prince, inscribed *Rolex
Extra Prima*, *circa* 1936,
length 1⅝in (4.2cm)
London £6,270 ($12,101).
13.XII.88

A stainless steel Rolex Oyster
perpetual moonphase and
calendar wristwatch, *circa*
1950, diameter 1¼in (3.3cm)
London £9,350 ($17,111).
21.III.89

Left
A rock crystal, gold and silver sun and moon desk clock by Cartier, Paris, *circa* 1920,
diameter 3⅞in (10cm)
Geneva SF52,800 (£20,000:$36,414). 17.XI.88
From the collection of the Sam and Rie Bloomfield Foundation

Below, left
An 18 carat gold octagonal mystery watch by Cartier, 1930, width 1⅝in (4.1cm)
New York $110,000 (£71,429). 17.VI.89

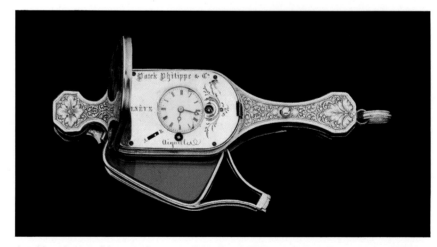

A gold and enamel *lorgnette* form watch by Patek Philippe & Co., Geneva, *circa* 1860,
length 3¼in (8.3cm)
New York $16,500 (£10,714). 17.VI.89

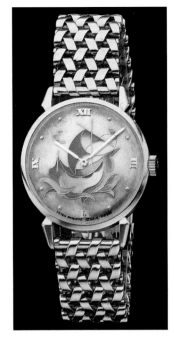

An 18 carat gold perpetual calendar chronograph wristwatch with tachometer, registers and moonphases by Patek Philippe & Co., Geneva, *circa* 1945, diameter 1⅜in (3.4cm) Geneva SF165,000 (£62,500:$113,793). 17.XI.88

An 18 carat gold wristwatch, the dial with the cloisonné enamel arms of Paris, by Patek Philippe & Co., Paris, *circa* 1950, diameter 1⅜in (3.5cm) Geneva SF110,000 (£38,869:$65,089). 9.V.89

A gold minute repeating wristwatch by Patek Philippe & Co., *circa* 1958, diameter 1¼in (3.3cm) New York $176,000 (£98,876). 17.II.89

An 18 carat gold calendar wristwatch with moonphases at twelve o'clock, made for the Italian market by Patek Philippe & Co., Geneva, *circa* 1936, diameter 1⅛in (3cm) New York $242,000 (£138,286). 25.X.88

A platinum and gold *grande modele* tank wristwatch by Cartier, European Watch & Clock Co., Inc., *circa* 1925, length 1⅞in (4.7cm) New York $90,750 (£58,929). 16.VI.89

A gold chronograph calendar and moonphases wristwatch with tachometer and register by Audemars Piguet, Geneva, *circa* 1943, diameter 1⅜in (3.6cm) New York $148,500 (£96,429). 17.VI.89

A gold and cloisonné enamel world time watch by Patek Philippe & Co., Geneva, *circa* 1947, diameter 1¼in (3.1cm) New York $275,000 (£178,571). 17.VI.89

An 18 carat gold wristwatch by Audemars Piguet for Cartier, *circa* 1973, length 2¼in (5.6cm) New York $37,400 (£20,108). 4.XII.88 From the Andy Warhol Collection

A crystal, onyx and diamond 'Portico' mystery clock by Cartier, 1924, height 15in (38.1cm)
New York $660,000 (£377,143). 18.X.88

Portico Mystery Clocks by Cartier

'Marvels of the clockmaker's art, unreal and seemingly woven from moonbeams' was the critic's appraisal of Cartier's 'Portico' Mystery Clocks when they were first displayed in 1925.

These elegant timepieces, on which jewelled hands glide across a crystal face with no apparent connection to the clock's movement, were a French invention of the 1870s. Just after the turn of the century, Louis Cartier began to collaborate with master horologist Maurice Coüet and their designs soon became 'musts' for millionaires and crowned heads from J.P.Morgan to Queen Mary. The six 'Portico' Mystery Clocks, created between 1923 and 1925, were their culminating achievement, and it is a testament to their perfection that all six survive today. Clock No. 1 is in the Cartier Museum Collection and Nos 2, 4, 5, and 6 are in private hands. Clock No. 3 was sold to an American private collector in October 1988 for the record price of $660,000 (£377,143).

Executed in a dramatic design of black onyx and rock crystal, with gold and diamond detailing, each clock took up to a year to complete, with the hands requiring the most intricate skills of the jeweller. As Sylvie Raulet has observed:

The hands of the most gorgeous clocks – the 'mystery clocks' – were wrought and chased into miniature works of art; with Cartier they became diamond-covered snakes or a fire-breathing dragon uncoiling in the centre of the dial, its head marking the hours, its tail the minutes.

The technical brilliance was Maurice Coüet's. Early in his association with Cartier, he mastered the illusion created by mounting each hand on a transparent disk attached by a shaft to the movement in the base. With the 'Portico' series, the 'mystery' was carried on to new heights as the crystal itself was suspended on a gold chain. In fact the links conceal a single axle that connects both disks to the movement above.

In design, these clocks combine the Art Deco and Oriental elements that pervaded Cartier pieces throughout the 1920s. Of all the 'Portico' clocks, the Oriental influence is strongest in No. 3. Ferocious Chinese lions stand guard at the base of the columns and above the dial is a frieze carved with Chinese fretwork with a stylized *Shou*, the symbol of long life, at the centre. The Cartier firm worked as a collective and it is thus impossible to attribute the design to any individual. It is known, however, that Charles Jacqueau, the most brilliant of the designers and the most accomplished Art Deco stylist, was particularly fascinated by the Orient. Certainly he must have been at least influential in the creation of these clocks, which are destined, according to Diana Scarisbrick, for the 'highest place in the artistic achievements of our century'.

Jewellery

An invisibly-set ruby and diamond leaf brooch by Van Cleef & Arpels, Paris
New York $236,000 (£134,857). 18.X.88

Opposite
A ruby and diamond pendant-brooch/necklace by Van Cleef & Arpels, New York, dated *1964*,
New York $286,000 (£182,166). 6.VI.89
From the Estate of Sylvia N. Lasdon

Far left
A pair of diamond pendent
earrings by Harry Winston
Geneva SF6,380,000
(£2,407,547: $4,310,811).
16.XI.88

Left
A pair of invisibly-set ruby
and diamond earclips with
detachable pendants by
Van Cleef & Arpels
New York $165,000
(£105,096). 6.VI.89
From the Estate of Sylvia
N. Lasdon

A diamond butterfly brooch, set with six antique diamonds weighing approximately 20 carats,
mid nineteenth century
New York $220,000 (£117,647). 5.XII.88

A ruby and diamond necklace by Oscar Heyman & Bros, Inc.
$759,000 (£446,471)
A ruby and diamond bracelet by Oscar Heyman & Bros, Inc.
$440,000 (£258,824)
The President Vargas diamond No.4 weighing 28.03 carats, mounted as a ring by Harry Winston
$781,000 (£459,412)

These three items from the Estate of Lydia Morrison were sold in New York on 13th April 1989.

The star of Sierra Leone diamond No.2 weighing 32.52 carats, mounted as a ring by Harry Winston
New York $3,520,000 (£2,011,429). 18.X.88

Opposite
A cultured pearl and diamond necklace/bracelet combination
$1,045,000 (£618,343)
A pair of cultured pearl and diamond earclips
$176,000 (£104,142)

These two pieces were sold in New York on 13th April 1989.

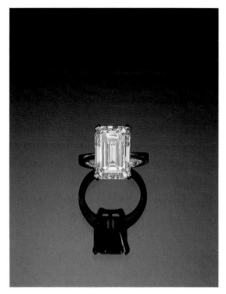

Left to right
A fancy light blue diamond weighing
5.74 carats, mounted as a ring
SF1,265,000 (£446,996:$748,521)
A fancy dark blue diamond weighing
4.12 carats, mounted as a ring
SF1,760,000 (£621,908:$1,041,420)

These two items were sold in Geneva on
10th May 1989.

A fancy pink diamond weighing
9.09 carats, mounted as a ring
Geneva SF3,740,000
(£1,321,555:$2,213,018). 10.V.89

A fancy blue diamond weighing 4.17 carats
New York $594,000 (£351,479). 13.IV.89

A ruby and diamond ring, weight of ruby
10.01 carats
Geneva SF2,530,000
(£893,993:$1,497,041). 10.V.89

A diamond weighing 29.30 carats,
mounted as a ring by Tiffany & Co.
New York $1,705,000 (£911,765). 6.XII.88

A cabochon emerald and diamond ring,
weight of emerald 11.39 carats
New York $253,000 (£144,571). 18.X.88
From the Estate of E.L. King, Jr

Left to right
An Art Deco emerald, sapphire and diamond lapel watch by Mauboussin, *circa* 1930
SF39,600 (£14,143:$24,750)
An Art Deco enamel, emerald and diamond sautoir with detachable pendant by Mauboussin,
circa 1930
SF275,000 (£98,214:$171,875)

These two pieces were sold in St Moritz on 16th February 1989.

An emerald and diamond
cruciform pendant and
necklace, *circa* 1840
New York $110,000
(£65,089). 12.IV.89

Opposite
A gold, enamel and
gem-set Renaissance-
Revival demi-parure,
comprising a necklace
supporting detachable
brooch/pendant and a
bracelet, *circa* 1855
London £22,000
($43,340). 5.XII.88

A diamond bracelet by Van Cleef & Arpels, New York
$181,500 (£115,605)
A pair of diamond feather brooches by Van Cleef & Arpels
$55,000 (£35,032)

These items from the Estate of Sylvia N. Lasdon
were sold in New York on 6th June 1989.

Opposite, left to right
A diamond brooch/pendant, last quarter nineteenth century
£3,520 ($5,843)
A diamond brooch, last quarter nineteenth century
£1,980 ($3,287)
A pearl, enamel and diamond necklace by Carlo and Arthur
Giuliano, *circa* 1900
£24,200 ($40,172)
A diamond brooch/pendant, *circa* 1880
£3,080 ($5,113)

These four items were sold in London on 22nd June 1989.

A marquise diamond weighing 22.54 carats,
mounted as a ring by Gérard
Geneva SF1,760,000 (£621,908: $1,041,420).
10.V.89

An Egyptian-Revival Art Deco diamond and gem-set brooch with a central yellow sapphire by Van
Cleef & Arpels, Paris, 1924
Geneva SF198,000 (£69,965: $117,160). 10.V.89

A pair of gem-set earclips by Bulgari
Geneva SF110,000 (£38,869: $65,089). 10.V.89

Opposite
A ruby and diamond ring, weight of ruby 15.97 carats
New York $3,630,000 (£2,074,286). 18.X.88

A pair of ruby and diamond pendent earrings of *girandole* design,
late eighteenth century
St Moritz SF37,400 (£13,357; $23,375). 18.II.89

Silver

A German parcel-gilt model of the horse 'Zöldfikár', maker's mark of Abraham Drentwett I, Augsburg,
circa 1654, height of horse 13½in (34.5cm)
Geneva SF550,000 (£194,346: $325,444). 8.V.89

This horse originally formed part of an equestrian statue with an accompanying basin,
made to commemorate the death in battle against the Turks of László Esterházy at
Nagyvezekény, in 1652. He is the rider on a later model of the horse, sold on
the same day for SF165,000 (£58,304: $97,633).

Fig. 1
Das Gehör, by Adriaen Brouwer (Bayerisches Staatsgemäldesammlungen, Munich).

Below
Fig. 2
A detail showing the reverse side of the flask.

A German silver-gilt flask, maker's mark of Johann Christoph Treffler,
Augsburg, 1685, height 7¼in (18.5cm)
Geneva SF198,000(£70,714:$104,211). 14.XI.88
From the collection of the British Rail Pension Fund

This scene is taken from *Das Gehör*, a painting by the Flemish
artist Adriaen Brouwer (1605–38), now in the Bayerisches
Staatsgemäldesammlungen, Munich (Fig.1; reproduced with their kind
permission). The original picture depicts a scene indoors and includes two
additional figures while the woman is laughing rather than drinking from a
flask. The scene on the other side (Fig.2), with two men and a woman
drinking, is based on a composition in reverse by Adriaen van Ostade.
This flask was sold previously at Sotheby's on 16th October 1975 for
£8,800 ($17,600) and is illustrated in *Art at Auction 1975–76*, p.283.

A Queen Anne covered jug, engraved with contemporary royal armorials, maker's mark of Thomas
Bolton, Dublin, 1702, height 12in (30.4cm)
London £55,000 ($106,150). 17.XI.88

A set of three William III casters, maker's mark of Thomas Bolton, Dublin, 1699,
heights 8¾in (22.2cm) and 7¼in (18.5cm)
New York $104,500 (£61,471). 6.IV.89

A James II
chinoiserie
porringer, inscribed
*The Gift of
Edward Hutton*,
maker's mark *I.I.*
above fleur de lys,
London, 1688,
height 4¾in (12cm)
London
£20,900 ($37,829).
27.IV.89

A Charles II
sideboard dish,
maker's mark *C.K.*
above pellets,
London, 1675,
diameter
19⅝in (50cm)
London
£66,000 ($119,460).
27.IV.89

A pair of George II silver-gilt tea caddies, maker's mark of James Shruder, London, *circa* 1745,
height 4¾in (12cm)
New York $82,500 (£48,529). 6.IV.89

The decoration on these caddies is undoubtedly taken from engravings after the French
rococo artist Jacques de Lajoue (1686–1761). The side cartouches are taken directly from
Lajoue's second *Livre de Cartouches* (1734), engraved by Huquier.

One of a pair of George IV soup tureens with covers, liners and stands, maker's mark of Paul Storr, London, 1822, overall height 16¾in (42.5cm)
New York $924,000 (£522,034). 28.X.88

Opposite
A pair of George IV four-light candelabra centrepieces, maker's mark of Paul Storr, London, 1822, heights 28⅝in (72.7cm)
New York $467,500 (£264,124). 28.X.88

Ceramics and glass

An Urbino Istoriato dish depicting the Rape of Proserpine, painted by Nicola da Urbino, *circa* 1530,
diameter 12in (30.5cm)
London £99,000 ($183,150). 18.X.88
Formerly in the Damiron Collection

A Chelsea octagonal teacup and yellow-ground saucer with fable decoration, painted by Jefferyes Hamett O'Neale, *circa* 1752, height of cup 2⅛in (5.5cm)
New York $11,000 (£6,250). 26.X.88

Below
A documentary Nuremburg parcel-gilt-mounted tankard, painted by Georg Friedrich Grebner, signed and dated *1730 d. 23. Juny*, height 9⅞in (25.2cm)
London £38,500 ($71,995). 21.II.89

A Whieldon-type figure of a pug, mid eighteenth century,
height 5in (12.7cm)
London £16,500 ($30,855). 21.II.89

A pair of Sèvres vases and covers, 1767, height 32in (81.3cm)
Geneva SF143,000 (£54,167: $97,944). 15.XI.88

A Vincennes *bleu céleste seau à liqueur du Roy*, 1754, height 6in (15.2cm) New York $57,750 (£35,648). 20.V.89

A Vezzi teapot and cover, 1723–27, 5⅞in (15cm) London £39,600 ($73,260). 18.X.88

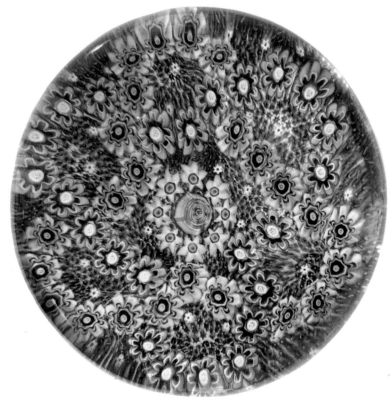

Above, left to right
A South German mounted 'Rubinglas' jug, seventeenth–eighteenth century, 8⅞in (22.5cm), £7,700 ($14,245)
Two of six South German 'Rubinglas' engraved cups and two of five saucers, early eighteenth century, £4,620 ($8,547)
One of four South German mounted 'Rubinglas' bottles, early eighteenth century, 4⅜in to 5½in (11cm to 14cm), £3,850 ($7,123)
One of a set of five South German 'Rubinglas' bottles, seventeenth–eighteenth century, height 3⅞in (10cm), £3,520 ($6,512)
A South German mounted 'Rubinglas' candlestick, seventeenth–eighteenth century, height 6½in (16.5cm), £2,640 ($4,884)
A South German mounted 'Rubinglas' teapot, seventeenth–eighteenth century, height 4½in (11.5cm), £4,620 ($8,547)

The above items were sold in London on 17th October 1988.

Left
A Clichy millefiori moss-ground paperweight, diameter 2½in (6.5cm) New York $20,900 (£11,297). 30.XI.88

A cameo glass plaque of *The Dancers*, attributed to George Woodall, *circa* 1880, diameter 12½in (32cm)
London £12,100 ($20,691). 18.VII.89

Furniture

A Louis XIV clock by André-Charles Boulle, movement signed *Thuret à Paris, circa* 1715–20, height 31½in (80cm)
Monte Carlo FF3,996,000 (£380,571: $666,000). 17.VI.89

A Louis XIV bureau plat attributed to André-Charles Boulle, *circa* 1715–20, length 75½in (192cm)
Monte Carlo FF7,770,000 (£740,000:$1,295,000). 4.III.89

This bureau, formerly in the collection of the duchesse de Talleyrand, is one of a famous
series of writing tables produced in the workshop of André-Charles Boulle between 1710 and
1720. They are all identical except for the corner bronzes. These are generally of heads of
satyrs or heads of women. On this desk they were formed as women wearing Chinese hats in
the shape of cockle-shells. There is only one other bureau of this type known, although the
Chinese-style corner mount is used in at least three later tables of the 1730s.

Two bronzes, however, are found on almost all the bureaux of this series: these ornament
the drawers on either side, and represent Democritus and Heraclitus, or 'the philosopher
who laughs and the philosopher who cries'.

A Louis XV ormolu-mounted satinwood parquetry commode attributed to Charles Cressent,
mid eighteenth century, width 60in (152.4cm)
New York $385,000 (£218,750). 14.X.88

A study of various inventories of the contents of Cressent's workshop and of catalogues of the
sales of his belongings (1749 and 1765), show that he repeatedly used mounts of a design
identical to those on this commode. Moreover an inspection of the carcass, essentially made
of large panels of pine, a recurring feature on most commodes generally accepted as being
the work of Cressent, corroborates the attribution to this maker.

Opposite, above
A Louis XV bureau plat by Bernard II Vanrisamburgh, stamped *BVRB, circa* 1745–49,
length 76¾in (195cm)
Monte Carlo FF6,882,000 (£655,429:$1,147,000). 17.VI.89

Below
A pair of Louis XVI ormolu-mounted mahogany consoles attributed to Adam Weisweiler,
last quarter eighteenth century, height 36¼in (92cm)
New York $352,000 (£200,000). 14.X.88

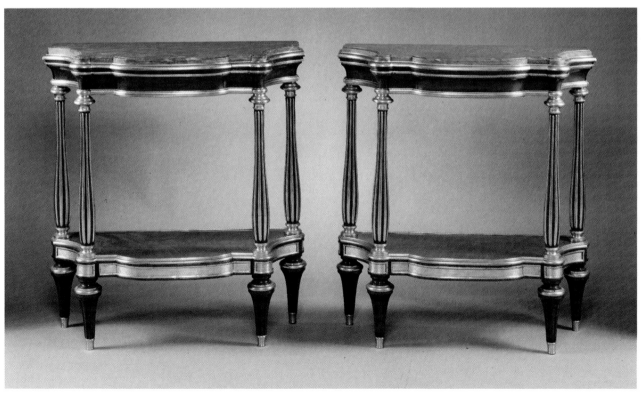

French furniture

Susan Morris

In the seventeenth and eighteenth centuries France made furniture of a luxury and inventiveness which has never been surpassed. This was partly because of a strict guild system, which made each man absolute *maître* of his craft; also because of royal patronage, which produced an insatiable demand for the highest quality of goods.

With brief falls from favour, French furniture has been avidly collected ever since. The sale in London on 24th and 25th November 1988 brought together a dazzling array of pieces ranging in date from the reign of Louis XIV to the early nineteenth century. Several had been collected by the British Rail Pension Fund as part of its programme of investing in art, carefully chosen as outstanding examples of their type.

Among the most spectacular items in the sale was a glass table-top made for Louis XIV (Fig.1). It appears as No. 276 in an inventory listing furniture in the French royal collection before 1681; in 1752 it was sold to M. Boucher, possibly the painter François Boucher, who collected *meubles curieux* such as this. The glass is patterned

with abstract designs, flowers and figures representing the Judgement of Paris, divided by strapwork borders of *repoussé* brass. The glass is worked both in *millefiori* technique (glass rods arranged in a flower-like pattern) and lampwork, in which glass rods softened by a lamp are twisted into shape. Layer upon layer of glass was built up on a copper base to achieve intricate designs, like the shepherd Paris sitting under a tree with his sheep grazing around him.

Furniture made for Louis XIV is very rare, but this table-top is unique, as much an experimental *tour de force* stretching the medium to the limit, as a functional object. It is clearly inspired by sixteenth-century Venetian glassmaking, but reveals sophisticated new techniques that only gained wide use in the nineteenth century. The table was probably made by Bernard Perrot (Bernardo Perrotto), an Italian from Monteferrat who set up a glassworks at Orléans, an important centre for emigrant glassmakers. Perrot is credited with several inventions, including the specialized casting of glass to make larger sheets possible; the highly skilled mix of *millefiori* and lampwork is no doubt also his innovation.

France had a tradition of attracting immigrant artists and craftsmen (such as the Italians who worked at Fontainebleau) whose foreign skills were absorbed into a French idiom. Some of the most famous eighteenth-century cabinetmakers – Oeben, Riesener, Weisweiler – have names which proclaim their non-French origin. Jean-Pierre Latz, who produced the superb bureau plat (Fig.2), emigrated from Cologne to Paris in 1719 and worked there until his death in 1754. In 1740 he was given a *brevet d'ébéniste privilégie du Roi*, which allowed him to work without being a member of the corporation of *maîtres ébénistes*, a guild which was opposed to foreign craftsmen.

Above
Fig.2
A Louis XV marquetry bureau plat, attributed to Jean-Pierre Latz, mid eighteenth century, width 5ft 5in (165cm)
London £407,000 ($785,510). 24.XI.88
From the collection of the British Rail Pension Fund

Opposite
Fig.3
An early Louis XVI marquetry *secrétaire à abattant*, attributed to Pierre-Antoine Foullet, *circa* 1776, height 4ft 10⅝in (149cm)
London £473,000 ($912,890). 24.XI.88
From the collection of the British Rail Pension Fund

The simple, flat topped desk known as a bureau plat was a type that endured throughout the eighteenth century. The desk by Latz is beautifully proportioned, its floral marquetry enhanced by the elegant rococo curves of the gilt-bronze mounts. These Latz made himself, contravening the strict demarcations of the French craft guilds, and earning him an arraignment from the corporation of *fondeurs-ciseleurs* (metal casters and chasers) in 1749.

Latz's involvement with more than one furniture making process is an exception; most pieces of eighteenth-century French furniture are brilliant collaborations between two or three craftsmen. The harmony that could be achieved is demonstrated by a *secrétaire à abattant* (fall front bureau; Fig.3) dating from *circa* 1776, when the Neoclassical style favoured by the court of Louis XVI was firmly established. It is almost identical to another now in the Wallace Collection, which has marquetry signed *foulet:* either Antoine Foullet (received Master in 1749), or his son Pierre-Antoine (received Master in 1765).

By the second half of the eighteenth century, *ébénistes* had over one hundred native and imported woods available for the pictorial marquetry which became fashionable after 1750. On the *secrétaire* Foullet created an elaborate scene of classical ruins and smaller cartouches of gardening and hunting, reflecting the aristocratic owner's lifestyle. The Neoclassical theme of the marquetry is echoed by the magnificent gilt-bronze mounts – the cascade of military trophies on the apron, the severe classical figures on the corners. The *secrétaire* has lost the asymmetric curves of the Rococo, gaining a sobriety but losing none of the richness which is the hallmark of French craftsmen in this century.

During his vast building programme, Louis XIV patronized furniture makers of all kinds. Little furniture created for him survives, partly because of later redecorations, partly because much of Louis' furniture was solid silver, melted down to pay for his endless wars. As the economy recovered under his successors, so did royal patronage and extravagance. Marie-Antoinette has a justifiable reputation for profligacy with money: expenditure on furniture between 1780 and 1790 was more than twice that of the previous decade. Furniture ordered for Marie-Antoinette is rare on the market and eagerly sought after when it comes to auction. A console table made by Jean-Henri Riesener for Marie-Antoinette's *cabinet-intérieur* at Versailles (Fig.4) brought £1.65 million ($3.18 million), making it the most expensive piece of French furniture ever to be sold at auction.

The *cabinet-intérieur* was a favourite refuge of Marie-Antoinette, a room for relaxing away from the chill formality of the Versailles state rooms. The Queen began to redecorate it in 1770, replacing the heavy taste of Maria Leczinska with white and gold *boiseries*, which are still there today. The chimney piece is of the brown marble known as *griotte d'Italie*; the console table, which stood beneath a pier glass opposite, has a top of the same marble. Riesener's table is delicate and simple, its austere lines relieved by gilt-bronze mounts in the form of exquisite garlands of flowers. The furnishings of the *cabinet-intérieur* were changed winter and summer, and this console table is recorded as part of the winter furnishings, replaced in summer by another in carved and gilded wood. In 1785 the table was moved to the newly acquired château of St Cloud, and probably sold from the royal collection during the Revolution, though it is not mentioned in the Versailles sales.

Fig.4
A Louis XVI console table, made by Jean-Henri Riesener for Marie-Antoinette, probably after designs by Jacques Gondoin, 1781, width 3ft 7¾in (111cm)
London £1,650,000 ($3,184,500). 24.XI.88
From the collection of the British Rail Pension Fund

Such was the fame of French furniture makers that they attracted patrons among foreign royalty as well. The charming Weisweiler cabinet (Fig.5) decorated with Sèvres plaques was bought in 1784 by the future Tsar Paul I and his wife Maria Feodorovna, during an incognito visit to Paris as the Comte and Comtesse du Nord. They did not buy directly from Weisweiler but from the leading *marchand mercier* Daguerre, one of the powerful retailers who orchestrated taste in the reign of Louis XVI. Daguerre's predecessor Poirier was among the first to commission furniture mounted with Sèvres porcelain plaques, and Daguerre retained his monopoly over the supply of Sèvres for furniture. According to Maria Feodorovna's companion, the Baronne d'Oberkirch, when they arrived Daguerre's showroom was packed with people admiring a buffet 'of astonishing workmanship'. The Weisweiler cabinet, with its classical gilt-bronze mounts, lozenge parquetry and naturalistic flowers (painted on Sèvres by Bouillat *père*), epitomizes the luxury of the last years of Louis XVI's reign.

The Revolution swept away aristocratic patronage and the rigid guild system, but failed to destroy France's furniture making skills. The sale included a pair of Empire giltwood chairs, stamped *Jacob D.R. Meslee* and made for the Comtesse d'Osmond of Normandy and Brittany (Fig.6). The firm of Jacob, responsible for some of the most elegant Neoclassical and Empire furniture, is here working in Gothic style, incorporating the Comtesse's coat of arms into intricate medieval finials.

Something of their extravagance is apparent in an important gilt-bronze, *tôle peinte* (painted metal) and glass chandelier (Fig.7), made by Claude Galle, who worked both for Louis XVI and Napoleon. It has a star-spangled blue globe encircled by a band with signs of the zodiac, and griffons alternating with candle brackets. When Louis XVIII was restored to the throne, Galle offered the Garde Meuble de la Couronne a chandelier which fits this description, which he had made for the 'Exposition des Produits de l'Industrie Française' in 1819. Galle's chandelier shows that post-Revolutionary furniture makers had lost none of their inventiveness: from the globe (reminiscent of Montgolfier's balloon) is suspended a glass bowl, to be filled with goldfish 'whose movements will delight the eye'.

Fig.5
A Louis XVI Sèvres porcelain-mounted secrétaire cabinet, stamped *A. Weisweiler, circa* 1784, height 4ft 2¼in (127.5cm)
London £990,000 ($1,910,700). 24.XI.88
From the collection of the British Rail Pension Fund

Fig.6
A pair of giltwood chairs in the Gothic style, stamped *Jacob D.R. Meslee*, inscribed with motto *nihil obstat*, early nineteenth century
London £90,200 ($174,086). 25.XI.88

Opposite
Fig.7
A Restauration gilt-bronze, *tôle-peinte* and glass chandelier, with eighteen scroll branches encircling a blue globe and hanging glass fish-bowl, by Claude Galle, *circa* 1819, height 3ft 7¼in (110cm)
London £275,000 ($530,750). 24.XI.88
From the collection of the British Rail Pension Fund

A Venetian painted commode, mid eighteenth century, width 51⅛in (130cm)
London £66,000 ($128,700). 9.XII.88

A German Rococo walnut
bureau cabinet attributed to
Johann Philipp Raab, Mainz,
circa 1765,
height 8ft 8in (264cm)
London £187,000 ($317,900).
26.V.89

Raab was one of a group of
cabinet makers working in
Mainz during the 1760s who
developed a distinctive form
of bureau cabinet. A
characteristic feature of his
work is his use of detached,
moulded scrolls at the angles
of his pieces.

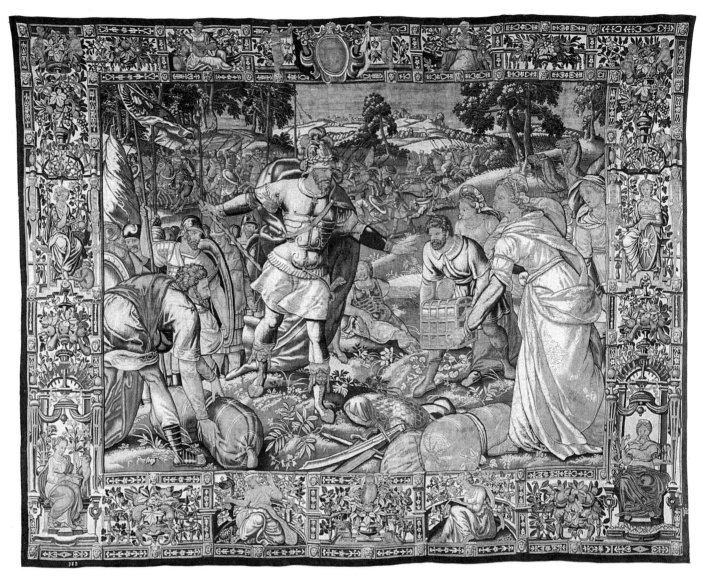

A Brussels historical tapestry by Joos van Herzeele from the *Story of Scipio*, with Brussels town mark and weaver's monogram, mid sixteenth century, 10ft 4in by 13ft 1½in (315cm by 400cm)
London £24,200 ($47,190). 9.XII.88

A Polish biblical tapestry, by the workshop of Biala Potloska, after a design by Pieter Coecke van Aelst,
representing the shipwreck of St Paul on the island of Malta and the Miracle of the Snake,
early eighteenth century, 11ft 8in by 11ft 11in (355.5cm by 363cm)
New York $66,000 (£36,066). 23.XI.88

The design for this tapestry can be found in a mid-sixteenth-century weaving by Pieter
Coecke van Aelst, preserved in the Bayerisches Nationalmuseum, Munich. The Biala
Potloska workshop was founded by Princess Ann Radziwill. The coat of arms is that of the
Zaluski family.

A George II mahogany commode in the manner of Thomas Chippendale, *circa* 1755,
width 57in (145cm)
London £550,000 ($951,500). 7.VII.89

This commode belongs to a group based upon Plate XLIII of Thomas Chippendale's first
edition of *The Gentleman and Cabinet-Maker's Director* (1754). It seems inevitable that
Chippendale's name be associated with this group of furniture, though there are no
documented Chippendale pieces in the full-blown Rococo style of the *Director*, arguably the
most important of all English pattern books. Chippendale's large country house commissions
date from the 1760s when the Neoclassical style had largely supplanted the briefly-lived
English Rococo. It seems likely that Chippendale must have made pieces similar to his
published designs, even if they were altered in execution. It is interesting to note that all the
commodes share considerable divergence from the original engraved source. Various
idiosyncratic features such as the rope-twist cock-beading, the unusual rocaille handles, even
the serpentine outline, are not found in the published design. The most salient points of
correspondence between the commodes and the design are the elaborate 'C' scrolls at the
angles which form the legs, and the cabochon carving at the angles which give all the
commodes their special character.

A George III ormolu-mounted rosewood commode attributed to Pierre Langlois, *circa* 1765,
width 67in (170.2cm)
New York $880,000 (£497,175). 29.X.88

This commode belongs not to the English tradition of carved and gilded wood but to the
late-seventeenth-century French Baroque manner, recalling the work of André-Charles
Boulle. The bold voluted outline and formal symmetry of the commode was a departure even
for Langlois, whose earlier work had evoked the more lyrical designs of the French *ébénistes* of
the second quarter of the eighteenth century. By 1763, however, the year he delivered the set
of four commodes now at Buckingham Palace, Langlois' style had changed dramatically.
This piece, together with the Buckingham Palace pieces and several others, form what is now
considered as one of the most revolutionary groups of English early Neoclassical furniture
known. Langlois' oeuvre during the short period of three years was of no apparent influence
on his London contemporaries nor was it prodigious, despite evidence that he did supply
lesser quality pieces; even if one embraces all of the Langlois-style pieces from his shop, there
are still few. His clients may have been drawn to him as a purveyor of a more exotic, 'French'
aesthetic and if this is true then we may assume that by definition his works are not part of
the mainstream of London style. Finally, with the exception of John Channon, Langlois'
exceptional use of gilt-bronze mounts as a primary decorative motif ties him strongly to the
Neoclassical tradition, and in 1765, the innovations of Continental and especially, French
designers, architects and cabinet-makers.

An English needlepoint carpet, signed *Pontremoli*, *circa* 1925, approximately 38ft 5in by 14ft 8in
(1171cm by 447cm)
New York $209,000 (£118,079). 29.X.88

One of a pair of George III giltwood side tables, *circa* 1760, width 63in (160cm)
New York $528,000 (£298,305). 29.X.88

One of a pair of brass chandeliers, late seventeenth century, height 50in (127cm)
London £93,500 ($167,365). 5.V.89

Opposite
A japanned bureau cabinet, early eighteenth century, height 6ft 11in (211cm)
London £231,000 ($413,490). 5.V.89

The nationality of early-eighteenth-century japanned bureau cabinets of this type has been
the source of some debate. They are normally ascribed either to Dresden or London. The
problem is complicated by the patterns of trade during this period and the itinerant nature of
many craftsmen. This piece is a case in point; the *bombé* outline of the lower half is of Flemish
inspiration, but occurs regularly on documented English pieces throughout the first half of
the eighteenth century.

A pair of George III mahogany library armchairs, *circa* 1760
New York $495,000 (£289,474). 21.IV.89

These chairs are from the well-known set of seat furniture ordered by the 4th Earl of
Shaftesbury for St Giles's House, Dorset during the refurbishing and building schemes he
initiated in the early 1740s. Henry Flitcroft was chosen to survey, design and oversee the
project. Research over the years has produced much speculation but little substantial
information regarding the authorship of the pieces, acquired during the twenty-year
expansion and redecoration project. Links have been suggested with Thomas Chippendale,
William Hallett, Benjamin Goodison, William Vile and John Cobb. An entry in the
Shaftesbury papers dated 2nd February 1745 which reads 'Paid as pr.Bill to Mr Hallett for
carved chairs £167,' is the most solid indication in the files but obviously falls short as
reliable grounds for attribution. There is a strong tie to Chippendale on stylistic grounds,
and furthermore the suite has been linked with a pair of chairs from Raynham Hall, Norfolk.

One of a set of eight early George III mahogany dining chairs, *circa* 1755
New York $418,000 (£236,158). 29.X.88

Nineteenth-century decorative arts

A red tortoiseshell-veneered and gilt-bronze writing desk, 1847–50, the central drawer with a lock stamped *Chubb's Patent St. Paul's C^h Y^d* and numbered *175026*, width 6ft 5⅛in (196cm)
London £107,800 ($180,026). 9.VI.89

This desk is in the style of the early eighteenth century in France although no model for it has been identified. There may also be an influence from the English Regency period with its strong chinoiserie mounts reminiscent of those on pieces at the Brighton Pavilion.

Opposite
One of a pair of Louis-Philippe *premier* and *contre-partie* 'Boulle' marriage coffers, *circa* 1840, height 47¼in (120cm)
London £52,800 ($96,096). 17.III.89

The form of these coffers is adapted from a pair now in the Wallace Collection, which may have been made for the French Royal family at the turn of the seventeenth century by André-Charles Boulle. The coffers are certainly in the manner of Boulle, and each is surmounted with the crown of France, resting on a tasselled cushion in brass. Pieces by André-Charles Boulle, and those in his style, are at present increasing in popularity on the market. A pair of Napoleon III gilt-bronze mounted brown tortoiseshell 'Boulle' commodes, modelled on the celebrated pair in the Wallace Collection, were sold on 9th June 1989, also in London for £79,200 ($132,264).

A Louis XV style gilt-bronze-mounted tulipwood marquetry kingwood side cabinet, inscribed
F. Linke, circa 1890, height 6ft 7in (201cm)
New York $275,000 (£158,960). 12.X.88

A close connection has recently been revealed between the work of François Linke (fl. 1882
–1935) and the lesser known furniture maker Julius Zwiener of Berlin, six pieces of whose
work commissioned by Freiderich Wilhelm II of Prussia, came up for auction in New York
on June 29th 1989. Both worked in Paris in the 1890s, in the popular Louis XV style.
The work of the two firms is very close, both in its bold, massive, sculptural outlines and in
the details: the small bronze birds which appear on a dressing table by Zwiener appear on a
screen by Linke, in his trade catalogue. Linke and Zwiener both employed the sculptor Leon
Messangé, although it is not known which sculptor was used for this piece. An identical
cabinet is illustrated in Christopher Payne's *Nineteenth Century European Furniture*, p. 166.

A Louis-Philippe Rococo-Revival Royal mantel clock by
Thomire, probably made for the Dauphin of France, Paris,
circa 1830–40, height 3ft (91.5cm)
London £25,300 ($46,046) 17.III.89

Between the two seahorses and directly under the Neptune
figure is the armorial device of the Dauphin. Louis XIX,
duc d'Angoulôme was Dauphin from 1824 to 1836 and
died in exile in 1844. It is unusual to find a Rococo-Revival
piece by the Thomire family. Though the most celebrated
bronziers in Paris at this time, they are not commonly
associated with this style.

A Napoleon III gilt-bronze and marble dressing table, *circa* 1870,
height 6ft 8in (203.2cm)
New York $40,700 (£26,258). 29.VI.89

An Italian micro-mosaic and giltwood low table, the central panel depicting Romulus and Remus, surrounded by eight large views of Rome, mid nineteenth century, diameter 38in (96.5cm)
New York $66,000 (£38,372). 3.III.89

Opposite
One of a pair of Bohemian Egyptian-Revival tulipwood and ebony-veneered side cabinets, *circa* 1870, height 7ft 2¼in (219cm)
London £88,000 ($160,160). 17.III.89

Twentieth-century decorative arts

Left and above
An oak, glass and leaded glass writing
cabinet designed by Charles Rennie
Mackintosh for Hous'hill, Nitshill,
Glasgow, 1904, height 45½in (115.5cm)
London £82,500 ($153,450). 21.X.88

This desk by the Glasgow architect Charles Rennie Mackintosh
(1868–1928) was designed for his most important patron, Miss
Cranston. Constructed in oak, it is of strictly rectilinear design,
softened by such characteristic Mackintosh details as the subtle
curves of the recessed compartments, and the central panel of
leaded glass with its highly formalized flower.

Mackintosh worked for Miss Cranston over a period of several
years, designing the interiors and furnishings of her Glasgow
tearooms. In 1903–1904 he was commissioned to redecorate her
home, Hous'hill. The house was eventually destroyed by fire
and many of the remaining furnishings dispersed at auction in
Glasgow in 1933. Few pieces survive.

Mackintosh's furniture was always designed for specific
interior schemes, and most pieces are unique or were made in
small series. The desk was designed for the so-called Blue
Bedroom of Hous'hill, and appears in a contemporary
photograph of the room (illustrated left). Several of the pieces
of furniture from the Blue Bedroom have been rediscovered and
sold at Sotheby's between 1973 and 1976, and the reappearance
of this desk adds another element to the rediscovery of this
superb scheme.

Composition in Light, a leaded glass window designed by Frank Lloyd Wright for the Avery
Coonley Playhouse, Riverdale, Illinois, *circa* 1912, height 60½in (153.7cm)
New York $286,000 (£185,714). 16.VI.89

The decorative elements which Wright incorporated in this and the other windows
from the Coonley Playhouse (illustrated above) were purportedly inspired by the
balloons, flags and confetti of a parade. The whimsy conveyed by the design and
the use of vibrant, luminous colours was a departure from the 'Prairie' motifs, yet
was ideally suited for the playhouse, which functioned as a school run by
Mrs Avery Coonley.

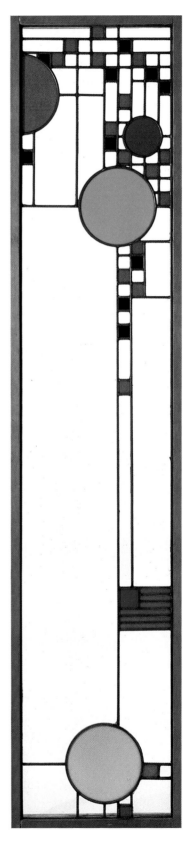

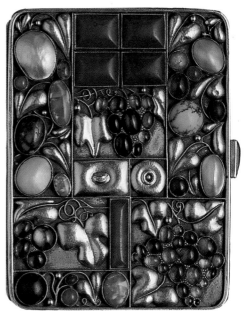

A Wiener Werkstätte gold, opal, mother of pearl, lapis, turquoise and semi-precious stone cigarette box designed by Josef Hoffman, stamped *WW*, 1912, 3⅛in by 2½in (8cm by 6.3cm) Monte Carlo FF366,300 (£34,886: $61,050). 4.XII.88

A Liberty & Co. 'Cymric' silver, enamel and onyx cup, maker's mark of Archibald Knox, stamped *Cymric*, Birmingham, 1903, height 8⅞in (22.5cm) London £22,000 ($40,040). 3.III.89

Opposite, above
A wood and iron desk by Pierre Chareau, *circa* 1926–27, length 63¾in (162cm) Monte Carlo FF688,200 (£65,543: $114,700). 4.XII.88

Below
A Macassar ebony and silvered bronze mobile bar on skis by Emile-Jacques Ruhlmann, *circa* 1930, length 36⅞in (93.5cm) Monte Carlo FF1,720,500 (£163,857: $286,750). 4.XII.88

A Tiffany favrile reactive paperweight glass exhibition vase, *circa* 1904,
height 7½in (19cm)
New York $101,750 (£55,601). 18.XI.88

Opposite
A Gallé mould-blown cameo glass white elephant vase, *circa* 1920, signed,
height 15in (38.1cm)
New York $170,500 (£93,169). 17.XI.88

A Tiffany favrile glass
and bronze wisteria lamp,
shade and base stamped,
1899–1920,
height 27½in (69.9cm)
New York $231,000
(£150,000). 16.VI.89
From the collection of
Walter P. Chrysler, Jr

Opposite
A Morris & Co.
Hammersmith carpet
designed by William
Morris with John Henry
Dearle, woven at Merton
Abbey, late 1880s,
149½in by 110¼in
(380cm by 280cm)
London £82,500
($136,125). 23.VI.89

Fig.1
Philip Johnson's New York
Townhouse, East 52nd
Street, designed in
1949–50 for Mrs John D.
Rockefeller 3rd,
reconstructed from an
1860s carriage house
New York $3,520,000
(£2,107,784). 6.V.89

Masters of twentieth-century design

Philippe Garner

The cool, minimalist space of Philip Johnson's Manhattan townhouse (Fig. 1) was for a brief decade the home of an exceptional collection of furniture by Pierre Legrain and Eileen Gray. Both the house and its contents were sold together in New York on 6th May. The core of the collection was originally assembled by the celebrated connoisseur Jacques Doucet. Around 1912, Doucet's collecting took a dramatic new direction. Having sold his splendid eighteenth-century furniture he began collecting Oriental, tribal and avant-garde artworks. Over the next few years he enlisted the collaboration of Pierre Legrain (Fig.2), Eileen Gray (Fig.3) and others to produce furniture and decorations with the strong contemporary forms and minimal decorative detail that would display these works to best advantage. This modern setting was realized in the late 1920s at his Studio St James in Neuilly, where such quintessential works as Picasso's *Demoiselles D'Avignon* and Rousseau's *Charmeuse de Serpents* were displayed with others by Braque, de Chirico, Ernst, Matisse, and Picabia. The present collection included some original drawings for Legrain's work for Doucet as well as for many of his other pieces, together with contemporary photographs showing how the furniture was arranged by Legrain.

Left
Fig. 4
An ebony and palisander circular low table by Pierre Legrain, *circa* 1920, height 20⅜in (51.8cm)
New York $220,000 (£131,737). 6.V.89

Below
Fig. 5
The salon in Doucet's Studio St James, showing the low table.

The African-style drum table (Fig.4) is shown here in the salon of Doucet's Studio St James (Fig.5); it had formed part of the display installed by the architect Pierre Chareau, shown to critical acclaim at the Salon des Artistes Décorateurs in 1924. In complementary African style is the ebony and gold lacquer banquette of around 1920 (Fig.6; and drawing Fig.7), shown at the Salon the previous year.

Doucet's influence pervades the pieces made for him; Legrain expressed himself very differently in his work for other clients. One of the most important of these was Mme Jeanne Tachard, to whom Doucet introduced Legrain. The present collection included Legrain's furniture and designs for her villa at La Celle-Saint-Cloud, in which a contemporary critic recognized Legrain's ability to break with the past in his search for a vernacular of design, drawing a parallel with the Cubists' search for a new formal language in painting. Legrain's inventive modern spirit is evident in the white-gold and black seats and low table (Fig.8), a Cubistic armchair and a lacquered sofa designed for Mme Tachard, and in a snake-skin covered table of the same period (Fig.9).

Opposite, left and right
Fig. 8
Two white-gold leaf and ebonized wood stools by Pierre Legrain, *circa* 1920, heights 16½in (42cm), each stool $115,500 (£69,162)

Centre
A lacquered white-gold leaf and ebonized wood low table by Pierre Legrain, *circa* 1920, height 21⅜in (54.3cm), $104,500 (£62,575)

These pieces were sold in New York on 6th May 1989.

Fig. 7
Design for Fig. 6, by Pierre Legrain, pencil with white, black
and gold gouache on paper, 18¾in by 16½in (47.6cm by 41.9cm)
New York $6,050 (£3,623). 6.V.89

Fig. 6
A limed African oak, ebony and gold lacquer banquette by
Pierre Legrain, *circa* 1920, height 40⅛in (102cm)
New York $275,000 (£164,671). 6.V.89

Fig. 9
A snakeskin and nickel-
plated low table by Pierre
Legrain, *circa* 1925,
length 7ft 2in (218.4cm)
New York $264,000
(£158,084). 6.V.89

Doucet was first attracted to the remarkable lacquer work of Eileen Gray exhibited at the Salon of the Société des Artistes Décorateurs in 1913 and his subsequent commissions were an important step in her career. She trained with the Japanese lacquer artist Sugawara and went on to collaborate with the architect Jean Badovici. The well-known 'Transat' chair (Fig.10) was designed for the house they created together: 'E.1027', a name derived from the numerics of Gray and Badovici's initials. The marvellous lacquer screen (also Fig.10) is one of a series of block screens which derive from her design for an entrance hall lined with lacquer blocks created for Mme Mathieu Levy.

The Philip Johnson townhouse was commissioned in 1949–50 by Mrs John D. Rockefeller 3rd and dates from immediately after Johnson's famous Glass House project. The house, described by Andy Warhol as 'the original New York loft', had a brief spell as a guesthouse for the Museum of Modern Art, after which it returned to private ownership. Standing as a symbol for what are arguably the key architectural ideas of the century, it demands to be considered as a work of art in its own right and in this capacity it has proved a first, as the only house ever auctioned at Sotheby's.

Fig.10
A black lacquer, chromed-
steel and leather 'Transat'
armchair by Eileen Gray,
circa 1925–26,
height 29½in (74.9cm),
$231,000 (£138,323)
A black lacquer folding
block screen by Eileen
Gray, *circa* 1922–25,
height 7ft½in (214.6cm),
$374,000 (£223,952)

Both pieces were sold in
New York on 6th May
1989.

American decorative arts

L. Johnston
FARM SCENE WITH BARN, BARNYARD WITH ANIMALS AND WHITE FARMHOUSE
Oil on pine planks, inscribed with artist's name in stencilled lettering, in a grain painted frame,
nineteenth century, 44in by 53in (111.8cm by 134.6cm)
New York $88,000 (£50,000). 27.I.89

The four panels on which this farm scene was painted may have been used as a shop sign or
possibly as a fireboard. Sign and ornamental painters often identified their work by stencilling
emblems or their names inconspicuously on their work. The prominent display of the
stencilled eagle emblem and the name suggests the possession of this panel by the artist.

American School
THE DERBY FAMILY IN AN EARLY FEDERAL INTERIOR: A GROUP PORTRAIT
Watercolour, pen and ink on paper, in the original frame, *circa* 1800, 15¾in by 21¼in (40cm by 54cm)
New York $52,250 (£29,688). 22.X.88
From the collection of the Derby family

A Neoclassical carved, gilded, ebonized and brass-mounted marble-top pier table, stamped *Charles Honoré Lannuier, New York*, and *Jacob*, *circa* 1815, width 48in (121.9cm)
New York $594,000 (£337,500). 22.X.88

According to family tradition, this table was owned by Madame Eugénie de la Bouceardie, who opened a gaming house in Paris with Madame de Stäel in the first half of the nineteenth century.

Opposite
A Chippendale carved cherrywood tall-case clock, signed by Benjamin Willard, Grafton, Massachusetts, *circa* 1770, height 7ft 9in (236.2cm)
New York $77,000 (£49,359). 21.VI.89

Left to right
A silver teapot, maker's mark of John Brevoort, engraved with contemporary initials *CH*, New York,
circa 1740, height 7½in (19cm),
$165,000 (£93,750)
A silver tankard, maker's mark of Simeon Soumaine, engraved with contemporary arms and initials
ITM, New York, *circa* 1730, height 8in (20.3cm),
$148,500 (£84,375)
A silver coffee pot and stand, maker's mark of Charles le Roux, engraved with contemporary arms,
New York, *circa* 1730, height 9¾in (24.8cm),
$308,000 (£175,000)

These three items were sold in New York on 27th January 1989.

A silver-gilt, enamel and pearl-set three piece coffee set with tray and sugar tongs, the tray engraved
with the initial *M*, by Tiffany & Co., New York, *circa* 1900, height of coffee pot 9⅝in (24.4cm)
New York $115,500 (£65,625). 27.I.89

Musical instruments

Below
An Italian violoncello by David Tecchler, Rome, 1706,
length of back 29¾in (75.5cm)
London £60,500 ($108,900). 30.III.89

A gold and tortoiseshell-mounted
violin bow by François Tourte,
Paris, *circa* 1820
London £79,200 ($152,856).
23.XI.88

This bow and the violins
opposite, from the collection
of the Sam and Rie Bloomfield
Foundation, were sold in
London on 23rd November
1988. Sam Bloomfield was
born in New Jersey and
educated in both Germany
and Switzerland. An
enthusiastic violinist, he was
well known to leading players,
in particular the late Jascha
Heifetz. The collection
contained a selection of superb
quality, historically important
pieces, including this Tourte
Bow and the Guarneri. The
violin by the famous Tyrolean
luthier Jacob Stainer is
unusual in remaining in its
unaltered 'Baroque' state. The
violin to the far right, by Jean-
Baptiste Vuillaume, was made
as part of a special order for
the duc Caraman de Chimay
and bears his coat of arms.

Left to right
A violin by Jacob Stainer, Absam, 1668, length of back 14in (35.6cm), £71,500 ($137,995)
A violin by Joseph Guarneri del Gesù, Cremona, 1743, length of back 13⅞in (35.4cm), £572,000 ($1,103,960)
A violin by Jean-Baptiste Vuillaume, Paris, 1865, length of back 14⅛in (35.9cm), £46,200 ($89,166)

The above violins from the collection of the Sam and Rie Bloomfield Foundation were sold in London
on 23rd November 1988.

Arms, armour and sporting guns

A cased pair of flintlock saw-handled duelling pistols, inscribed *H.W. MORTIMER & SONS,*
LONDON, GUN-MAKERS TO HIS MAJESTY, with accessories, *circa* 1809, size of case
18¾in by 8⅝in (47.5cm by 22cm)
London £13,200 ($25,740). 8.XII.88

A Lloyd's Patriotic Fund Trafalgar sword, blade blued and gilt overall, inscribed in gold *FROM THE*
PATRIOTIC FUND AT LLOYD'S TO PHILIP CHA^S. DURHAM ESQ^R CAP^{TN} OF
H.M.S. DEFIANCE FOR HIS MERITORIOUS SERVICES IN CONTRIBUTING TO THE SIGNAL
VICTORY OBTAINED OVER THE COMBINED FLEETS OF FRANCE & SPAIN OFF CAPE
TRAFALGAR ON THE 21ST OCT^R 1805, length 36½in (92.7cm)
London £23,100 ($45,045). 8.XII.88

A pre-production model 7.63mm self-loading pistol, serial No.189, engraved *SYSTEM MAUSER*, 5½in
stepped barrel, 1896
London £28,600 ($55,770). 8.XII.88

One of a pair of lightweight 12-bore 'twelve-twenty' action self-opening sidelock ejector guns by
Stephen Grant & Sons, 1938
London £41,800 ($76,076). 19.IV.89

Coins and medals

Roman, Claudius (AD 41–54), gold aureus, struck to commemorate the occupation of Britain in AD 43
London £6,380 ($11,420). 5.X.88

Islamic, 'Abd al-Malik b. Marwan, gold dinar, dated AH 77, the first issue of a purely Muslim coin
London £165,000 ($293,700). 29.IX.88

Roman, Vespasian (AD 69–79), gold aureus, struck to commemorate the subjugation of the Jews in AD 70
London £18,700 ($33,473). 5.X.88

Below
Charles II, gold Naval Reward medal, issued following the Battle of Lowestoft in 1665
London £23,100 ($42,042). 9.III.89

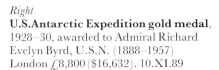

Above

Battle of Britain D.S.O., D.F.C. and bar group of medals, awarded to Group Captain Peter Townsend, R.A.F. C.O. of No. 85 Squadron
London £22,000 ($41,580). 10.XI.88

Left

U.S.A., pattern half-dime, 1859, the so-called 'stateless' issue
New York $15,400 (£8,953). 21.III.89
From the collection of Harry Warshaw

Right

U.S. Antarctic Expedition gold medal, 1928–30, awarded to Admiral Richard Evelyn Byrd, U.S.N. (1888–1957)
London £8,800 ($16,632). 10.XI.89

Postage stamps

British Columbia – Vancouver Island, 1865 5*c.* rose, imperforate, unused with original gum
London £15,950 ($28,232). 12.V.89

Great Britain, 1860 1½*d.* rosy mauve, Plate I, prepared for use but not issued, marginal block of eight on Dr Perkins blued paper, including the error of lettering *OP-PC* for *CP-PC*
London £11,550 ($21,252). 13.X.88
From the collection of Christopher Beresford

Bechuanaland, 1891 cover, from Jack Brown, addressed to his father in England, bearing the British South Africa Company/Post Office/Fort Tuli datestamp
London £2,200 ($4,246). 24.XI.88

Rhodesia, 1913–22 Head Die III, Perf.15,
2*d.* black and brownish grey, unused corner
block of four
London £12,100 ($21,780). 9.IX.88.
From the collection of Robert M. Gibbs

France, 1869 5*f.* lilac-grey,
unused, with *5* and *f* in blue
London £2,200 ($3,916).
11.V.89

Great Britain, 1841 2*d.* blue, Plate 3, corner
block of eight showing the Plate number, full
original gum
London £19,800 ($35,244). 11.V.89

Rhodesia, 1913–22 Head Die III, Perf. 14,
2*s.* black and yellow-brown, unused corner
block of four
London £2,750 ($4,950). 9.IX.88
From the collection of Robert M. Gibbs

Rhodesia, 1913 10*d.* Colour
trial, scored through, mounted
on card
London £990 ($1,772). 8.IX.88
From the collection of
Robert M. Gibbs

Rhodesia, 1913–22 Head Die III,
Perf.14, 5*s.* blue and pale sage-green,
unused block of four
London £2,860 ($5,062). 12.V.89

Collectors' sales

An usherette's dress from the première of
the film *A Hard Day's Night*, signed
and dedicated by all four members of
The Beatles, Brian Epstein and Cynthia
Lennon, 1964, length 38½in (98cm)
London £2,310 ($4,135). 12.IX.88

The dress was signed while the usherette
was wearing it at the charity premiere.

Left
A rooster by Dentzel,
circa 1895
New York $148,500
(£84,857). 25.II.89
From the collection of the
Magic Shop

Opposite
The piano and bench from the Paris flashback scene at the Belle Aurore Café
from the film *Casablanca*, Warner Bros, 1942–43, height 42in (106.7cm),
$154,000 (£84,615)
The original witch's hat from the film *The Wizard of Oz*, MGM, 1939,
worn by Margaret Hamilton as the Wicked Witch of the West,
height 14in (35.6cm), $33,000 (£18,132)
Clark Gable's personal leather bound script from the film *Gone With the
Wind*, 27th November 1937, $77,000 (£42,308)

These three items were sold in New York on 16th December 1988.

Opposite
A French musical automaton of a pumpkin
eater by Gustave Vichy, *circa* 1870,
height 20½in (52cm)
London £22,000 ($39,160). 20.IX.88

Left
An American painted tinplate clockwork
horse-drawn 'Broadway & 5th Avenue'
omnibus by George W. Brown, *circa* 1874,
length 13in (33cm)
New York $36,300 (£19,945). 16.XII.88

Below
A German spirit fired fire-engine by Märklin,
circa 1902, length 20in (51cm)
London £15,620 ($27,804). 20.IX.88

Above
A Charles II stumpwork picture, *circa* 1660
11⅞in by 9⅜in (30cm by 24cm)
London £5,500 ($10,340). 16.II.89

Above, left
A Charles II oak baby house
on stand, *circa* 1675,
width 55½in (141cm)
London £25,300 ($45,034).
20.IX.88

A German tinplate clockwork
battleship 'Maine' by Märklin,
circa 1904, length 20⅞in (53cm)
London £39,600 ($74,448).
16.II.89

Above
A German bisque character doll by Kämmer and Reinhardt, *circa* 1909, impressed *105 K star R 55*, height 21⅝in (55cm)
London £90,200 ($169,576). 16.II.89

Above, left
A French 'Circle and Dot' bisque doll by Bru, the head impressed with a circle and dot and *BRU jne.11, circa* 1875, height 29⅛in (74cm)
London £17,600 ($29,568). 25.V.89

Left
A French Paris-doll by Danel et Cie, stamped *PARIS-BEBE TETE DEPOSEE* and incised *16*, height 35in (89cm)
London £13,200 ($22,176). 25.V.89

Left to right, from top
Fig. 1
Roger Rabbit and Baby Herman, a Walt Disney six cel progression from *Who framed Roger Rabbit*, 1988,
each cel 9½in by 14in (24.1cm by 35.6cm)
New York $14,850 (£9,519). 28.VI.89

Who framed Roger Rabbit?

Ronald Varney

Who framed Roger Rabbit, winner of four Academy awards for its technical wizardry
and the undisputed box office champion for 1988, has been hailed as a milestone in
the history of animation. The premise of the film is novel enough: in the fantasy world
of Hollywood, humans and ink and paint cartoon creatures (or Toons) work side by
side, their lives hilariously intertwined. Cartoon characters have in the past appeared
in many live-action films. Porky Pig had a walk-on part in the 1940 Warner Brothers
production *You Ought to be in Pictures;* Gene Kelly danced with Jerry the Mouse in
the 1945 MGM musical *Anchors Aweigh*; and Dick Van Dyke entered a chalk-painted
world of singing barnyard animals and dancing penguins in the 1964 Disney classic
Mary Poppins. But these efforts were primitive compared to what goes on in *Roger
Rabbit*. As *Film Comment* describes it: 'This is definitive animation'.

That Walt Disney Studio was both willing and eager to give the green light to this
ambitious undertaking says a lot about its regard for co-producer Steven Spielberg and
his Amblin Entertainment. But it also says a lot about Disney's own sense of history
and tradition. Since its earliest days, the studio has been fascinated by the challenge of
integrating live actors and cartoon characters in a motion picture, making them part
of the same three-dimensional world.

In 1923 Walt Disney was a struggling young animator in Hollywood, just starting
his own company. He shared a small apartment with his brother Roy, occasionally
was forced to borrow money from anxious friends and relatives back home in Missouri,
and often dined on beans. His first venture was a series of innovative low-budget films
entitled *Alice Comedies*. In them, a little girl cavorts with real-life neighbourhood play-
mates while, in her dreams, she slips magically into the world of cartoon characters
to share their adventures. *Alice* was Walt Disney's first film attempt to combine live
action with animation, and he left nothing to chance. He drew the animation,
operated the camera, directed the actors, even constructed the sets. These films were
instrumental in helping Disney launch his studio and, sixty-five years later, might be
described as *Roger Rabbit*'s first cousins.

An international army of over 700 cast and crew worked for three years on the
project. Essentially, two separate films were shot and then pieced together. One was
the live-action film, a period piece set in Los Angeles in 1947, directed by Robert
Zemeckis (*Back to the Future, Romancing the Stone*). In the live-action film human actors,
with the aid of elaborate mechanical props, nimbly and convincingly played their
roles opposite invisible cartoon co-stars who would be drawn later.

Since these invisible co-stars, when drawn in, would be inhabiting the real world
of studio boss R.K. Maroon, private eye Eddie Valiant and real estate tycoon Marvin

Fig. 2
*Jessica's first
appearance*, a Walt
Disney cel from *Who
framed Roger Rabbit*,
1988, 11⅜in by 17¼in
(28.9cm by 43.8cm)
New York $13,200
(£8,462). 28.VI.89

Acme, elaborate special effects were required to heighten the illusion. All the props that were moved or carried by the cartoon characters – such as the trays carried by the penguin waiters at the Ink & Paint Club or the pistols brandished by Judge Doom's weasels – had to be physically moved on the set with mechanical arms and wires. These would later be drawn over by the animation, but they were crucial to making Roger Rabbit and his cohorts a natural part of Eddie Valiant's world. As the film's special effects supervisor, Michael Lantieri, explained in *Cinefex* (The Journal of Cinematic Illusions), no detail could be overlooked. 'If one of the animated characters had to step into a mud puddle, it was up to us to create a small splash. If they walked through some bushes, we had to move bushes. If they made footprints in the dirt, we had to create those footprints.'

Next came the animation film, which took about fourteen months to complete and was supervised by Academy award-winning animator Richard Williams, who worked on several of the Pink Panther films. Working frame by frame with high-quality photostat enlargements of the edited live-action film, teams of artists first made pencil sketches superimposing the cartoon characters onto the live-action background. The movements and expressions of the cartoon figures had to be painstakingly integrated into the action to create a vivid sense of three-dimensional realism. These sketches were then hand-painted onto sheets of acetate and photographed one at a time.

The Disney Archives proved indispensable to the animators in researching the original animated characters and finding the right look for the animated sequences, such as the Toontown finale. In that sequence, for example, the three hummingbirds who chirp hello to Eddie Valiant were based on characters from Disney's *Song of the South*.

The final job of marrying live action with thousands of animation cels was performed at George Lucas's Industrial Light and Magic (ILM) in northern California. One of the thousand visual effects ingeniously added to the film made Jessica's gown shimmer and sparkle with heart-stopping brilliance. ILM's finishing touches to *Roger Rabbit* made it one of the most technologically complex films of all time.

More than 550 hand-painted animation cels depicting many memorable scenes from the movie were sold in New York in June. The monumental task of examining nearly 100,000 cels created for *Roger Rabbit* and choosing the 'setups' (cartoon cels applied to film background) for the auction fell to Russ Cochran and Bruce Hamilton, two internationally respected creative and conceptual consultants with longstanding ties to Disney. Russ Cochran has described the process:

First we watched a print of the finished film, looking for the key scenes that were the most representative and visually exciting. By screening the film several times and slowing down the projection speed from the standard 24 frames per second, we were able to identify the scenes we wanted. Next, using a horizontal flat-bed editing table at Amblin, I went through the film and clipped out the frames we had chosen. Then, with the film clips as a guide, we searched through hundreds of boxes of cels to find the best from each scene. A Disney film-editor located in the live-action footage the exact frames to match the cels we had chosen. An enlargement was then made of each to make the finished print the correct size to register with the painted animation cels.

All the famous faces were there: the earnest Eddie Valiant, the villainous Judge Doom, the seductive Jessica (Fig.2) and, of course, Roger himself. Many of the cels were arranged as progressions to recreate the action of the scene – Baby Herman's escapades (Fig.1), Roger and Eddie in handcuffs, the harrowing ride in Benny the Cab, and so forth. But most memorable were the three-foot-long images of the Toons rejoicing with their famous colleagues – Bugs Bunny, Betty Boop, Porky Pig, Goofy, Donald Duck *et al* – at the victory over Judge Doom and the preservation of Toontown (Fig.3). Here, some of the best-loved characters were assembled for the first time, a historic moment in a landmark of animation art.

Fig. 3 *Detail Toons*, a Walt Disney composite cel from *Who framed Roger Rabbit*, 1988, 10⅛in by 39¾in (25.7cm by 101cm) New York $50,600 (£32,436). 28.VI.89

Veteran and vintage cars

A 1932 Alfa Romeo 8C 2300
supercharged coupé, with
coachwork by Graber
London £368,500 ($725,945).
5.XII.88

A 1928 Bentley 4½ litre
Le Mans replica four seat
tourer
London £209,000
($349,030). 3.VII.89
From the collection of the
late W.R. Cash

A 1928 Bugatti type 35C
Grand Prix two seater
London £506,000
($915,860). 20.III.89
From the collection of the
late Alan K. Haworth

A 1934 Mercedes-Benz 500K Special Roadster
Monte Carlo FF19,758,000 (£1,881,714:$3,293,000). 23.VII.89

A 1950 Frazer Nash Le Mans replica
London £209,000 ($349,030). 3.VII.89

Garden statuary

Right
A lead figure of Punch, with traces of early paint, eighteenth century, height excluding pedestal 44in (112cm)
Billingshurst £18,700 ($33,286). 27.IX.88

Opposite page
A bronze group of two eagles and a lynx by Christophe Fratin, signed, *circa* 1880, height 77⅛in (196cm)
Billingshurst £50,600 ($84,502). 31.V.89

Below
Chienne et ses petits, one of a pair of cast iron groups, the other entitled *Loup et petit chien*, by Pierre-Louis Rouillard, *circa* 1860, width 67in (170cm)
Billingshurst £61,600 ($102,872). 31.V.89

Wine

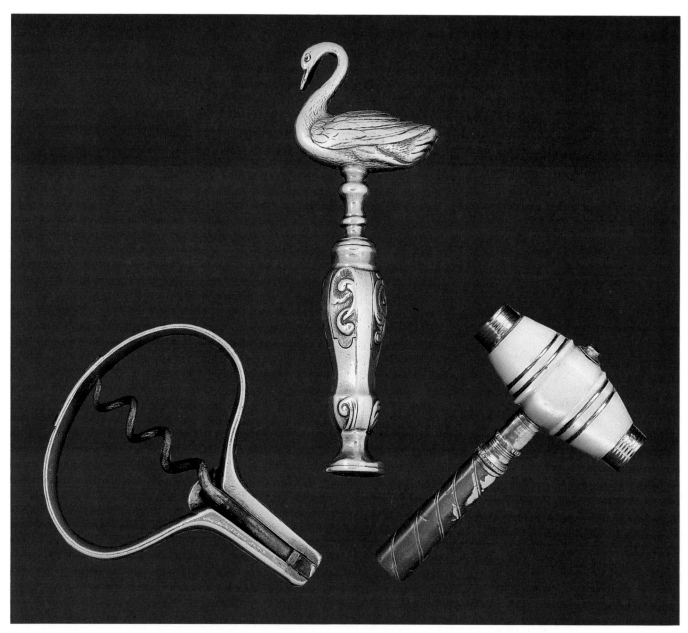

Left to right
A Dutch silver corkscrew, maker's mark of Jan Richters, Delft, 1765, £1,540 ($2,741)
An Irish silver corkscrew by Thomas Williamson, Dublin, 1717-40, £1,815 ($3,231)
A gold and mother of pearl corkscrew, fitted with glass magnifying lenses at each end, maker's mark of
Jacques Cottin, Paris, 1726-32, £4,730 ($8,419)

All three corkscrews were sold in London on 21st September 1988.

Above, left
One of three bottles of
Cognac de la Motte, Fine
Petite Champagne,
distilled 1914 OB,
£462 ($855)
One of three bottles of
Cognac de la Motte, Fine
Grande Champagne,
distilled 1919 OB,
£462 ($855)

These six bottles of Cognac
were sold in London on 8th
February 1989.

Right
One of three bottles of
Marqués de Murrieta
Reserva (White) 1925 OB,
£1,001 ($1,952)
One of three bottles of
Castillo Ygay Reserva
Especial (White) 1950 OB,
£187 ($365)
One bottle of Marqués de
Murrieta (White) 1901 OB,
£770 ($1,501)

These seven bottles of wine
were sold in London on 7th
December 1988.

There is little doubt that the wine market has recovered from the slide which began in the summer of 1985. After a slow start to the season in September 1988, perhaps caused by the difficult 'en primeur' campaign of the lack lustre 1987 Bordeaux earlier in the year, new highs have now been recorded, especially for mature wines. All good claret vintages prior to 1980 appear to be in strong demand and even the 1981, 1982 and 1983s have seen increased interest particularly towards the end of the season. Only the 1984 'Cinderella' vintage appears to be out of favour. 1985s have appeared at auction for the first time in significant quantities and although results have been erratic this is much in line with expectations.

Young vintage ports have been surprisingly slack considering the interest shown in them a couple of years ago but there has been a significant rise in price of vintages prior to 1970 and a firming up of the post 1970 vintages in July which suggests there could be further gains in the near future.

There have been a number of highlights of which the following are perhaps the most significant. In December the first major offering at auction this century of Spanish table wine was made with the exceptional range of 51 consecutive vintages (1900 to 1950) of outstanding wines from Bodegas Marqués de Murrieta, one of Spain's most important privately-owned estates, famed for its white wines as well as its reds. The tasting before the sale confirmed the quality and longevity of its wines. In December again Armagnac Castarède, the oldest established armagnac company, offered an unrivalled range of 21 vintages from 1881 to 1968 with further lots in subsequent sales which have now deservedly attracted a strong following. In the same month three five-gallon wicker covered demi-johns of Madeira 1867, originally purchased by Senator Henry Cabot Lodge, were sold for £2,035 to £2,640 each.

Principal officers and experts

The Rt.Hon. The Earl of Gowrie
Chairman, Sotheby's UK
John L. Marion
Chairman, Sotheby's North America
Julian Thompson
Chairman, Sotheby's International
Diana D. Brooks
President, Sotheby's North America
Timothy Llewellyn
Managing Director, Sotheby's UK
Simon de Pury
Managing Director, Sotheby's Europe

American decorative arts and furniture
Leslie B. Keno *New York* 606 7130
William W. Stahl, Jnr *606 7110*

American folk art
Nancy Druckman *New York, 606 7225*

American Indian art
Dr Bernard de Grunne *New York, 606 7325*

American paintings, drawings and sculpture
Peter B. Rathbone *New York, 606 7280*

Antiquities and Asian art
Richard M. Keresey *New York, 606 7328*
Felicity Nicholson (antiquities) *London, 408 5111*
Brenda Lynch (Asian) *408 5112*

Arms and armour
Michael Baldwin *London, 408 5318*
Florian Eitle *New York, 606 7250*

Books and manuscripts
Roy Davids *London, 408 5287*
David N. Redden *New York, 606 7386*
Dominique Laucournet *Paris, 33 (1) 42 66 40 60*

British paintings 1500-1850
James Miller *London, 408 5405*
Henry Wemyss (watercolours) *408 5409*

British paintings from 1850
Simon Taylor (Victorian) *London, 408 5385*
Janet Green (twentieth-century) *408 5387*

Ceramics
Peter Arney *London, 408 5134*
Letitia Roberts *New York, 606 7180*

Chinese art
Carol Conover *New York, 606 7332*
Mee Seen Loong
Arnold Chang (paintings) *606 7334*
Julian Thompson *London, 408 5371*
Colin Mackay *408 5145*
Robert Kleiner (Hong Kong sales) *408 5149*

Clocks and watches
Tina Miller (watches) *London, 408 5328*
Michael Turner (clocks) *408 5329*
Daryn Schnipper *New York, 606 7162*

Coins and medals
Tom Eden (Ancient and Islamic) *London, 408 5313*
James Morton
(English and paper money) *408 5314*
David Erskine-Hill
(medals and decorations) *408 5315*
Mish Tworkowski *New York, 606 7391*

Collectables
Dana Hawkes *New York, 606 7424*
Hilary Kay *London, 408 5205*

Contemporary art
Hugues Joffre *London, 408 5400*
Lucy Mitchell-Innes *New York, 606 7254*

European works of art
Elizabeth Wilson *London, 408 5321*
Florian Eitle *New York, 606 7250*

Furniture
Graham Child *London, 408 5347*
George Read (English) *New York, 606 7577*
Thierry Millerand (French and Continental) *606 7213*
Robert C. Woolley *606 7100*
Alexandre Pradère *Paris, 33 (1) 42 66 40 60*

Glass and paperweights
Lauren Tarshis *New York, 606 7180*
Perran Wood *London, 408 5135*

Impressionist and modern paintings
David J. Nash *New York, 606 7351*
John L. Tancock *606 7360*
Marc E. Rosen (drawings) *606 7154*
Michel Strauss *London 408 5389*
Julian Barran *Paris, 33 (1) 42 66 40 60*

Islamic art and carpets
Richard M. Keresey (works of art) *New York, 606 7328*
William F. Ruprecht (carpets) *606 7380*
Professor John Carswell *London, 408 5153*

Japanese art
Peter Bufton *New York, 606 7338*
Neil Davey *London, 408 5141*

Jewellery
David Bennett *London, 408 5306*
John D. Block *New York, 606 7392*
Nicholas Rayner *Geneva, 41 (22) 32 85 85*

Judaica
Jay Weinstein *New York, 606 7387*

Latin American paintings
Anne Horton *New York, 606 7290*

Musical instruments
Charles Rudig *New York, 606 7190*
Graham Wells *London, 408 5341*

Nineteenth-century European furniture and works of art
Christopher Payne *London, 408 5350*
Elaine Whitmire *New York, 606 7285*

Nineteenth-century European paintings and drawings
Alexander Apsis *London, 408 5384*
Nancy Harrison *New York, 606 7140*
Pascale Pavageau *Paris, 33 (1) 42 66 40 60*

Old master paintings and drawings
Timothy Llewellyn *London, 408 5373*
Julien Stock *408 5420*
Elizabeth Llewellyn (drawings) *408 5416*
George Wachter *New York, 606 7230*
Alexander Nystadt *Amsterdam, 31 (20) 27 56 56*
Nancy Ward-Neilson *Milan, 39 (2) 78 39 11*
Etienne Breton *Paris, 33 (1) 42 66 40 60*

Oriental manuscripts
Nabil Saidi *London, 408 5332*

Photographs
Philippe Garner *London, 408 5138*
Beth Gates-Warren *New York, 606 7240*

Portrait miniatures, objects of vertu, icons and Russian works of art
Martyn Saunders-Rawlins (icons) *London, 408 5325*
Julia Clarke (vertu) *408 5324*
Haydn William (miniatures) *408 5326*
Heinrich Graf von Spreti *Munich, 49 (89) 22 23 75*
Gerard Hill *New York, 606 7150*

Postage stamps
John Michael *London, 408 5223*

Pre-Columbian art
Stacy Goodman *New York, 606 7330*

Prints
Marc E. Rosen *New York, 606 7117*
Ian Mackenzie *London, 408 5210*

Silver
Kevin L. Tierney *New York, 606 7160*
Peter Waldron (English) *London, 408 5104*
Harold Charteris (Continental) *408 5106*
Dr Christoph Graf Douglas *Frankfurt, 49 (69) 74 07 87*

Sporting Guns
James Booth *London, 408 5319*

Tribal art
Dr Bernard de Grunne *New York, 606 7325*
Roberto Fainello *London, 408 5115*

Twentieth-century applied arts
Barbara E. Deisroth *New York, 606 7170*
Philippe Garner *London, 408 5138*

Vintage cars
Malcolm Barber *London, 408 5320*
Dana Hawkes *New York, 606 7424*

Western manuscripts
Dr Christopher de Hamel, FSA, *London, 408 5330*

Wine
David Molyneux Berry, MW, *London, 408 5267*
Christopher Ross, *408 5271*

Contributors

Tim Ayers has edited a variety of books for Philip Wilson Publishers, including *Art at Auction*. He ran Sotheby's *Preview* magazine for several years, and is now a cataloguer in Sotheby's European sculpture and works of art department.

Roberta Bernstein is an Associate Professor of Art History at the University at Albany, State University of New York. A specialist on Jasper Johns, she has published numerous articles as well as a book on the artist, *Jasper Johns' Paintings and Sculptures 1954–1974: 'The Changing Focus of the Eye'* (1985).

Kathleen Burnside of Hirschl & Adler Galleries, is the co-author of the forthcoming catalogue raisonné on Childe Hassam. She recently curated and wrote the exhibition catalogue of *Childe Hassam in Connecticut*, held at the Florence Griswold Museum, Old Lyme, Connecticut (1987).

Richard Cork was formerly the editor of *Studio International*, the art critic of the *Evening Standard*, and is currently the art critic of *The Listener*. From 1989–90 he will be Slade Professor of Fine Art at Oxford University. His publications include *The Social Role of Art* (1979), *Art Beyond the Gallery* (1985), and *David Bomberg* (1987). He is currently working on a book about international art and the Great War.

Shelley Drake served as Coordinator of 'Contemporary Oil Paintings from the People's Republic of China', an exhibition held at the Harkness House, New York in April, 1987. She is currently on the staff of the Department of Asiatic art at the Museum of Fine Arts, Boston.

Florian Eitle is a Vice President and Director of the European works of art department at Sotheby's New York. He received his education in Art History at the University of Munich and has had extensive training in furniture restoration and cabinet-making.

Philippe Garner joined Sotheby's in 1970. He is now a Director and is responsible for sales in applied arts from 1880. He has written extensively on the decorative arts and is the author of *Emile Gallé* (1976). He is editor of the *Phaidon Encyclopaedia of the Decorative Arts 1890–1940* (1978) and has recently revised and edited Martin Battersby's *Decorative Arts of the Twenties* and *Decorative Arts of the Thirties*.

Pat Getz-Preziosi is a prehistorian specializing in the prehistory of the Cyclades. Her most recent publications include *Sculptors of the Cyclades: Individual and Tradition in the Third Millennium BC* (1987) and *Cycladic Art in North American Collections* (primary author of exhibition catalogue, 1987). She is currently writing a book on stone vessels of Early Cycladic cultures.

Dr David James is an authority on Islamic manuscripts, with particular interests in calligraphy, illumination and miniature painting. He has recently published *Qur'ans of the Mamluks* (London, 1988). For many years Dr James was at the Chester Beatty Library, Dublin, and is currently Curator of the Nour Collection, London.

Herbert Keutner has worked variously as a lecturer, librarian, professor and director at the art historical institutes of Cologne, Berlin, Munich, Aquisgrana and Florence, producing numerous articles on sculptors ranging from Filarete to Soldani. Among his other publications are a commentary on the *Life of Cellini* and *History of Western Sculpture: Renaissance to Rococo*. He is currently working on a monograph on Giambologna.

Selby Kiffer, who specializes in printed Americana, books of natural history and travel, atlases and maps, is an Assistant Vice President in the books and manuscripts department at Sotheby's New York.

Mary-Jo Kline, an expert in manuscript Americana, is a Vice President of the books and manuscripts department at Sotheby's New York. Prior to joining Sotheby's she was editor-in-chief of the Aaron Burr papers at the New York Historical Society and supervised the publication of the two-volume *Political Correspondence and Public Papers of Aaron* (1983).

Brendan Lynch, who joined the Antiquities department at Sotheby's in 1977, is responsible for Indian, Himalayan and South-East Asian art. He has written various specialist articles ranging in subject from British and Irish collectors in India, to his contribution to *Ivory: A History and Collector's Guide* in 1987.

Rosa Maria Malet joined the Joan Miró Foundation, Barcelona in 1975 and has been in charge of cataloguing the museum's holdings. Since 1980 she has been Director and has organized many exhibitions on various aspects of Miró's work. She has published several books, including *Joan Miró* (1983), as well as numerous articles.

Charles McCorquodale specializes in European art of the sixteenth and seventeenth centuries, particularly Italian. His books include *The Baroque Painters of Italy*, *Bronzino* and *The History of Interior Decoration*. He arranged and catalogued the Royal Academy of Arts exhibition *Painting in Florence 1600–1700* and he contributes regularly to a wide range of art periodicals. He is at present writing a book on *The Scottish House: Domestic Architecture in Scotland 1500–1914*.

James Miller joined Sotheby's in 1973 to take charge of British prints then moved on to drawings and watercolours. He is currently Director of the department of British paintings and watercolours 1500–1850. He has published various articles on the subject and catalogued the picture collection at Bowood Park.

Susan Morris completed a doctorate at the Courtauld Institute of Art on the English watercolourist Thomas Girtin. She was a Mellon Fellow at Yale University where she curated an exhibition on Thomas Girtin and is currently writing for the *Antique Collector*.

Timothy Sammons is a director of Sotheby's London, heading a department that arranges private treaty sales to the nation and offers in lieu of tax (Heritage sales). Before joining Sotheby's he qualified as a solicitor. He is also an expert in Chinese art and was formerly Director of the Chinese art department at Sotheby's New York. He is a Director of Sotheby's Hong Kong.

Scott Schaefer is a Vice President and Director of Fine Arts and Museum Services in New York, as well as a Senior Expert Consultant. Prior to joining Sotheby's, he was Curator of European paintings and sculpture at the Los Angeles County Museum of Art where he organized two major exhibitions, *A day in the country: Impressionism and French Landscape*, and *Guido Reni 1575–1642*.

Michel Strauss joined Sotheby's Impressionist paintings department in 1961, after post-graduate research in Post-Impressionism at the Courtauld Institute of Art. While still at the Courtauld he was modern art critic for the *Burlington Magazine*. He became head of all Sotheby's picture departments in 1980, and joined the board of Sotheby Parke Bernet & Co. in 1982.

Simon Taylor is the author of numerous articles on Victorian painting, and has lectured on the subject all over the world. He has been a director of Sotheby's since 1984 and is currently writing a history of Victorian painting.

Julian Thompson, head of Sotheby's Chinese department in London since 1969, became Chairman of Sotheby's London in April 1982 and at the same time Chairman of Sotheby's International. He was responsible for the inauguration of Sotheby's sales of Chinese works of art in Hong Kong, which began in 1973. He has also published numerous articles on Chinese ceramics.

Dr Helen Wallis, OBE retired recently as Map Librarian of the British Library. She has written extensively on the history of cartography and has organized many exhibitions at the British Library including 'Chinese and Japanese Maps', 1974. She is President of the International Map Collectors' Society (IMCOS) and Associate Editor of *The Map Collector*, and was awarded the Gold Medal of the British Cartographic Society in 1988.

Dr Susan Wharton developed her interest in manuscripts whilst doing research for a doctorate on a late Medieval French author, and spent a year in Paris working on his manuscripts. She joined Sotheby's in 1977 to catalogue Continental manuscripts. Her critical edition of Réné d'Anjou's *Livre du cuer d'amours espris* was published in Paris in 1980.

Index

Charter of Godwine granting to Leofwine the Red the swine-pasture of Swithraedingden for the rent of forty pence and two pounds and an allowance of corn, in Anglo-Saxon, document on vellum, Christ Church, Canterbury, 1013–20, 2in by 10⅛in (5.3cm by 25.8cm)
London £126,500 ($209,990). 20.VI.89